The Right Book,
The Right Time

Related Titles of Interest

Essentials of Children's Literature, Second Edition
Carl M. Tomlinson and Carol Lynch-Brown
ISBN: 0-205-16751-9

Poetry across the Curriculum: An Action Guide for Elementary Teachers
Aaren Yeatts Perry
ISBN: 0-205-19807-4

Helping Students Learn to Write Poetry: An Idea Book for Poets of All Ages
Joyce C. Bumgardner
ISBN: 0-205-26169-8

Helping Students Learn to Write: An Idea Book for K-7 Teachers
Joyce C. Bumgardner
ISBN: 0-205-17571-6

The Right Book, The Right Time

Helping Children Cope

Martha C. Grindler
Beverly D. Stratton
Michael C. McKenna
all of Georgia Southern University

Allyn and Bacon
Boston • London • Toronto • Sydney • Tokyo • Singapore

*For one thing is certain as we grow older: The few people who have truly passed through us and us through them, until the dreams, images, memories are passed sorting out, these people become precious links to our continuity.**

We dedicate this book to our pasts: Margie C. Bagwell, Ronald M. Dlugokecki, and James McKenna and to our futures: Liz and Jim; Amy and Kim; and Katy, Patrick, and Jimmy.

*From Gail Sheehy, 1974, *Passages: Predictable crises of adult life*. NY: Dutton & Co., Inc.

Library of Congress Cataloging-in-Publication Data
Grindler, Martha C.
    The right book, the right time : helping children cope / Martha C.
Grindler, Beverly D. Stratton, Michael C. McKenna.
        p.   cm.
    Includes bibliographical references (p.   )
    ISBN 0-205-17272-5
    1. Bibliotherapy for children.   I. Stratton, Beverly D.
II. McKenna, Michael C.   III. Title.
RJ505.B5G75 1996
615.8'516'083--dc20   96-43988
                                                        CIP

Printed in the United States of America

10 9 8 7 6 5 4 3 2 1   00 99 98 97 96

Contents

Preface

This book is designed primarily as an in-service teacher resource, one that will assist classroom teachers, library media specialists, and parents in matching children who face important issues in their lives with (1) fiction featuring characters in similar circumstances and/or (2) self-help nonfiction selections.

We believe that bibliotherapy may have dramatic uses in the classroom, both in helping children through difficult situations and in assisting them to form positive beliefs about books. We hope that this book will serve as a reference for parents, teachers, counselors, school psychologists, and other specialists whenever a need to match books and children occurs.

Chapter 1

What Is Bibliotherapy?

> *You think your pain and your heartache are unprecedented*
> *in the history of the world, but then you read. It was books*
> *that taught me that the things that tormented me most*
> *were the very things that connected me with all the*
> *people who were alive, or had ever been alive.*
> —JAMES BALDWIN

Bibliotherapy has a long and rich history. Although the term "bibliotherapy" was not adopted until much later, classical philosophers such as Aristotle believed in the healing powers of literature and its ability to arouse the affective domain in readers (Zaccaria & Moses, 1968). The word *bibliotherapy* first appeared in 1930 in an article by G. O. Ireland (Ouzts, 1991). It was first used as a type of therapy with people who were emotionally ill. This usage understandably evokes an image of a physician, one who first diagnoses a problem and then prescribes an appropriate remedy.

Indeed, the concept of bibliotherapy was long regarded as a counseling technique and of no real potential in classroom settings (Ouzts & Hewett, 1993). It is probable, too, that the term itself has led many teachers to believe they lacked the clinical expertise to attempt it. The medical metaphor may be too limiting, however, in view of the range of applications now denoted by the term.

The term "bibliotherapy" has been defined by Karen Bromley as "the practice of using books to promote mental health, solve personal problems, and become aware of societal concerns" (1992, p. 59). This definition is sufficiently broad to encompass two major categories of books useful to the bibliotherapist and two major strategies for using them. Both *fiction trade books* and *nonfiction self-help books* can be used to help boys and girls either *proactively* or *reactively*. These strategies are discussed in Chapter 3.

Beyond the obvious goal of helping children work through their problems, bibliotherapy has the potential to improve attitudes toward books and reading.

Present-day models of attitude and reading (Mathewson, 1994; McKenna, 1994) predict that attitudes are affected in part by the beliefs students harbor about reading. If the utility of books can be demonstrated to them at an early age, then positive beliefs should follow and, with them, more positive attitudes toward reading.

The Need for Bibliotherapy

Three current trends in American education argue persuasively for the use of matching books and children. One is the prevalence of literature-based reading instruction with its emphasis on the need for authentic literary experiences. Another is the proliferation of quality children's books, a fact which places unprecedented pressure on a classroom teacher to remain current. Finally, the increasing diversity of the population of American schoolchildren, in terms of their cultural linguistic, socioeconomic, and familial background, presently confronts teachers with a far greater variety of student problems than in former years.

As a result, teachers must become familiar with a wide variety of children's literature that is well written, attractive, and informative so that the match between children and the basic needs of the early childhood and elementary grades is made. To match children and books in the classroom, teachers must know about their students' needs, interests, reading levels, and personal development. Teachers must also be good and active listeners. They are in a position to hear what problems children own—problems often brought on by circumstances beyond the child's control. Books can help.

A good teacher is perceptive of students' needs and is in a better position to describe which books should be presented at what time. Although the explosion of children's literature together with the growing awareness of the issues that surround its use in the classroom have placed increased burdens on teachers, these trends nevertheless provide the opportunity to sensitize children to critical issues confronting them in contemporary society.

In educating the "whole" child, teachers must not ignore the affective and emotional responses elicited by literature and encourage only cognitive and academic aspects. The social aspects of learning and literature need to be considered along with the intellectual. Bibliotherapy addresses the needs of the "whole" child.

Important Assumptions

If bibliotherapy is to be effective in its *purest* sense, three assumptions must be made:

1. a need, problem, or issue must be identified by the student and/or teacher;
2. the reader must be able to identify with or relate to the character who shares the same problem, issue, or need; i.e., this demand requires "active" reading as opposed to "passive" reading; and

3. the student must experience new insight, knowledge, or understanding after having read a selection.

This is not to say that all bibliotherapy must be intense, focused, and so direct that intervention must be deliberate at the onset. For our purposes, the notion is much broader. For example, bibliotherapy can be done *proactively*, in order to prepare students for problems they may encounter at some future date. In addition, the idea of placing appropriate books into the hands of troubled children remains an important part of this newer concept. This approach, obviously, is a *reactive* one.

What Bibliotherapy Isn't

We by no means take the view that teachers should become therapists, in the sense of providing direct counseling to troubled children. We do believe that the teacher's role as intermediary between children and books has the potential to help them think through many of the issues they face and at the same time demonstrate, in a very relevant way, how reading can be instrumental in their resolution. Bibliotherapy is *not* the answer to deep-seated psychological problems. Effective, knowledgeable teachers know to refer students with a need for intervention to the appropriate community professionals, guidance counselors, or school psychologists.

Emphasis should be on *coping* with life's problems, not on therapy given by adults who are not trained to do so. Books can help children cope more effectively with issues they confront. When children discover that others have problems similar to theirs, they are often better able to cope with their own. As C. S. Lewis was fond of quoting, "We read to know we are not alone." Children may find comfort when they discover what solutions or options characters in books exercise when confronted with real-life problems. Reading about others with similar problems and discussing how they resolve these difficulties can provide important alternatives.

Finally, simply reading a book does not ensure that bibliotherapy has taken place. Also, not all books are suited for bibliotherapy purposes. To be most effective, there must be a proper match between the book and the reader. Although some readers can and will benefit from a chance match, it is best not to rely on happenstance in the hope that books and readers will find each other. Also, some books are better suited to specific children than others. Gentle guidance by an adult who knows the child and the literature is the ideal.

Appropriate Books for Bibliotherapy

According to Charlotte Huck:

A book may be considered as suitable for bibliotherapy if it tells an interesting story and yet has the power to help a reader

1. acquire information and knowledge about the psychology and physi-
   ology of human behavior,
2. learn what it means to 'know thyself,'
3. find an interest outside himself,
4. relieve conscious problems in a controlled manner,
5. utilize an opportunity for identification and compensation, and
6. illuminate difficulties and acquire insight into his own behavior.

(Huck, 1987, p. 264)

$$Chapter \quad 2$$

How Effective Is Bibliotherapy?

*...certain books are stimulants. They do not so much
furnish us with thoughts as set us to thinking. They awaken
faculties which we have allowed to be dormant. After reading them
we actually feel differently and frequently we act differently.*
— SAMUEL CROTHERS

Using books to solve personal problems (bibliotherapy) has been advocated for a long time by teachers, counselors, and other school personnel as they have worked with children (Baruth & Phillips, 1976; Ciancolo, 1965; Hopkins, 1979; Russell & Russell, 1979; Tartagni, 1976; Watson, 1979). Bibliotherapy (sometimes called "bibliocounseling") means guided reading designed to help individuals gain an understanding of themselves as well as the environment, learning from others, and finding solutions to problems (Schrank, Engels, & Silke, 1983). The term bibliotherapy, used originally in a psychiatric context, evokes the image of a teacher as a "physician," as one who first diagnoses a problem and then prescribes an appropriate remedy. However, the research evidence related to bibliotherapy is scant.

History of Bibliotherapy

In their Phi Delta Kappa Fastback *Bibliotherapy: The Right Book at the Right Time*, Cornett and Cornett provide an excellent chronology of bibliotherapy. According to the Cornetts (1980), bibliotherapy has its roots in stories that were told around campfires. Through this oral tradition people learned to emphasize and view their own problem through a new and different perspective. These stories or traditions report that:

> Aristotle used readings to arouse healing emotions in himself and his students. The great Roman orator, Celsus, is said to have directed the mentally ill to read and to improve their capacity for making judgments. And Chinese author and philologist Lin Yutang observed that "Reading of best kinds always gives … understanding of life and oneself.
>
> *(Cornett & Cornett, 1980, p. 11)*

Inscriptions over the entrances to ancient libraries provide historic examples of the early recognition that books could be used to help fulfill human needs. Examples include the epigraph on the library founded in Alexandria about 300 B.C. which read, "Medicine for the Mind"; the motto of the library at ancient Thebes, "Healing of the Soul"; and the inscription on the medieval Abbey Library of Saint Gall in Switzerland, "Medicine Chest for the Soul" (Cornett & Cornett, 1980).

The formal use of books to help people cope with their mental and physical needs is believed to have begun in Europe.

> By the end of the eighteenth century books were being used to treat the mentally ill in France, England, and Italy. Libraries had become a part of nearly all European mental hospitals by 1900. In the United States, doctors like Benjamin Rush began to prescribe the Bible or other religious readings to their patients. Gradually, mental hospitals in the United States began to establish libraries that served as intellectual and emotional pharmacies for patients.
>
> *(Cornett & Cornett, 1980, p. 12)*

During the same period, librarians came to recognize the applications bibliotherapy could have with their patrons.

The American Library Association gave its support to the bibliotherapeutic process early in the twentieth century. Over the years courses were established in libraries and schools, conferences were held, and numerous articles, dissertations, and speeches were prepared on the topic. "Psychologists, clergymen, and educators soon recognized that bibliotherapy was a tool they too could use in their professions (Cornett & Cornett, 1980).

Research Evidence

Much of the experimental research on bibliotherapy has not been conducted in public schools but has appeared in behavior therapy journals. Bibliotherapy has been utilized as a comparison treatment in research on behavioral approaches to control weight (Borden, Hansen, Hall & Hall, 1976; Brownell, Heckerman, & Westlake, 1978; Hagen, 1974; Jeffrey & Christensen, 1972), to treat phobias (Crowder & Thornten, 1970; Girodo & Henry, 1976; Hogan & Kirchner, 1968), to modify self-concept (Altmann & Nielsen, 1974; Fordyce, 1977), and to modify prejudicial attitudes toward African Americans (Litcher & Johnson, 1969; Stanley & Stanley, 1970; Yawkey, 1973). Experimental research on bibliotherapy suggests that it may be questionable as a psychotherapeutic intervention. However, promising results have been noted in the area of attitudinal change (Stevens & Pfost, 1982).

There is evidence to suggest that individuals can be influenced by what they read and the bibliotherapy process seems to be a way to structure reading to influence individuals (Schrank, Engels, & Silke, 1983). Bibliotherapy research findings are varied, but there is solid evidence to support the contention that bibliotherapy can be a useful tool. In elementary schools, the effects of bibliotherapy have been studied and reported on fear reduction, attitude change, self-concept, and achievement factors. Each category of bibliotherapy research offers different implications.

Fear Reduction

The bibliotherapeutic model provided the basis for an investigation to reduce generalized fear in second-grade children that might otherwise inhibit normal learning and basic functioning at home and in the school environment. Examples included fear of animals, the dark, and new places. Support for such an approach comes from Meyers, 1976; Rich and Bernstein, 1975; and Webster, 1961; all of whom demonstrated successful positive attitude change related to children's fears. However, teachers working with young children may be wise to exercise caution using bibliotherapy, as it is possible that they may instill in some children the very fear they have tried to reduce.

Ongoa (1979) used bibliotherapy to lessen the normal, developmental fears of three to five year olds. In this investigation, children listened to stories concerning fears all children experience. Following each story there was time for the discussion of feelings and reactions related to the story. Sixteen books were read during eight week period. Following completion of the program, Ongoa found a significant difference in the adjusted mean posttest score of a group of young children experiencing bibliotherapy through listening.

Attitude Change

Fisher (1965), Kimoto (1974), King (1972), Schrank (1977), Tauran (1967), and Yawkey (1973) reported positive effects of guided reading related to attitude change. In the study conducted by Fisher with fifth-grade students, one story about Native Americans was read by children in six classrooms each Monday and Wednesday for three weeks. Similarly, one story about Native Americans was read *and discussed* by children in another six classrooms during the same period. Attitudes toward Native Americans changed significantly more in experimental groups than control groups. Reading in conjunction with discussion changed attitudes more than reading alone.

In a related investigation, Tauran (1967) studied the effects of children's literature on attitudes of third graders toward Eskimos. Stories were read by children during their regular reading classes, three times per week for two weeks.

When the children read literature that portrayed Eskimos in a positive light, the children's attitudes became favorable to the Eskimos. Similarly, when the children read literature that portrayed the Eskimos in a negative light, the children's attitudes toward Eskimos became negative.

(Schrank, Engels, & Silke, 1983, p. 25)

Grindler, Stratton, McKenna, and Smith (1994) conducted an action research project to investigate the utility of bibliotherapy to improve attitudes toward books and reading. In this study, bibliotherapy was used to assist a kindergarten-age victim of sexual abuse. Utilizing a partnership approach consisting of teacher educators, the classroom teacher, and a school psychologist, a proactive bibliotherapeutic unit on "body safety" was conducted in the child's kindergarten class. Following brief, individual interviews, four books related to "body safety" were read aloud to the students with follow-up discussion. Follow-up interviews were conducted by the classroom teacher. Content analysis of student interview data indicated that the children grew demonstrably in their knowledge of strategies they might employ when confronted by a sexual abuse situation and in their understanding that books could be useful in solving problems. In addition, examination of the children's follow-up interview responses revealed that fifteen of the sixteen children were able to provide at least one defensible strategy after bibliotherapy compared with eleven children in the prereading phase. The most dramatic result was the breakthrough in one child's acknowledgement of the sexual abuse he had experienced. These positive results were successfully replicated for a different class and a less controversial topic (Grindler, Stratton, & McKenna, 1995).

"Bibliotherapy is no panacea, but even when no statistically significant attitude changes were found, benefits of using the technique were still reported (Schrank, Engels, Silke, 1983 p. 25)". Although Beardsley (1980) drew no conclusions about using the technique for modifying attitudes toward handicapped peers, Schrank (1977) concluded that reading a story about a handicapped child was equally as effective in changing attitudes as seeing a filmstrip and then discussing it. Although Agness (1981) did not observe a significant change in attitudes, but reported that all of the teachers involved believed a bibliotherapy program was useful, enjoyable, and had a positive effect on the attitudes of students.

Self-Concept

While several researchers have reported finding improved self-concepts through the use of bibliotherapy (Kanaan, 1976; King, 1972; Lundstein, 1972; Robinson, 1980), other studies yielded no significant evidence that bibliotherapy made any difference in the development of self-concept (Altman & Nielsen, 1974; Dixon, 1974; Ponder, 1969; Roach, 1975; Schultheis, 1970; Shearon, 1975). Three studies, however, revealed beneficial uses of bibliotherapy for influencing the self-concept. King (1972) discovered that children who received bibliocounseling had significant gains in reading self-concepts over those who did not receive counseling. In studying the effects of bibliotherapy for improving the self-concepts of fifth grade low self-concept isolates, Kanaan (1976) found positive changes in self-concept that were attributed to bibliotherapy. A case study of a withdrawn boy called Fred and the successful bibliotherapy program developed for him was reported by Lundstein (1972).

Achievement

Most research findings suggest that bibliotherapy does not affect achievement (Dixon, 1974; Ponder, 1969; Schultheis, 1970). However, one study stands in contrast. King (1972) learned that groups receiving a ten-week bibliocounseling program scored significantly higher in reading vocabulary and comprehension in the immediate posttesting period than control groups. The reading comprehension gains held constant for six months, the vocabulary gains did not. King's results suggest that when gains in academic achievement are made, they may be an incidental benefit of the bibliotherapy process.

Key Findings

"In summary, then, there has been a sizable amount of research done concerning the uses of bibliotherapy for children's development (Shrank, Engels, Silke, 1983, p. 27)." These research findings clearly provide an empirical basis for the positive effects of bibliotherapy in the elementary school, yet much research remains to be conducted. Conclusions from the research evidence related to its use with children indicate that:

- bibliotherapy can produce positive attitude change related to the reduction of children's fear,
- listening and reading used in conjunction with discussion may change attitudes more than listening or reading alone,
- positive changes in self-concept can be attributed to bibliotherapy,
- bibliotherapy provides children with knowledge of strategies they might employ in particular situations, and
- books can be useful in helping children solve problems and in helping children realize the usefulness of books for this purpose.

How Does Bibliotherapy Work?

*Reading is to the mind, what exercise is to the body. As
by the one, health is preserved, strengthened, and
invigorated: by the other, virtue (which is the health of
the mind) is kept alive, cherished, and confirmed.*
—JOSEPH ADDISON

This chapter identifies guidelines for the use of bibliotherapy with individual students and describes instructional strategies useful with groups.

The Bibliotherapeutic Process

The process of bibliotherapy as it is now used in schools is largely credited to Caroline Shrodes, whose doctoral research on bibliotherapy in 1949 has become a classic. She identified three stages through which a reader progresses in bibliotherapy.

  1. *Identification.* The reader begins to relate to or empathize with the characters in a book (if the work is fictional). When the reader sees similarities between his life and that of the book character, a "shock of recognition" happens. This identification lays the groundwork for the next stage.

  Identification is the holistic name for the process under which the other two processes are subsumed (Russell, 1970). It begins with the connection between the reader and a character in the story. This connection may enlarge a child's perspective or reduce his feelings of being different from others.

2. *Catharsis.* At the peak of identification and empathy, the reader is able to release pent-up emotions and feelings. Catharsis takes place when the reader shares the character's feelings, motivations, or experiences and vicariously expresses them. The release is a safe and secure one because the reader is not the actual person involved in the crisis. Similarities, however, allow for a new perspective on the problem. Shrodes calls this "standing apart and being involved." This release of emotions clears the way for a more reasonable and open look at the problems and possible solutions.

3. *Insight.* Once possible solutions are identified, the reader can mentally gather data on what suggestions might be integrated into her options for solutions. Insight occurs when the reader realizes she is identifying with the characters.

Proactive and Reactive Approaches

Bibliotherapy can be both proactive and reactive. Some children can read books and learn how to handle certain life situations before they even take place. Others may read to discover that it is possible to overcome some common developmental problem they are presently experiencing.

A proactive approach begins with the identification of a problem that might be encountered by students in the future (e.g., pregnancy, drug use, parental divorce, and so on) but that may not yet have affected them personally. The teacher selects appropriate books and plans a group unit in the spirit of what Bromley (1992) has termed "the promotion of mental health." But another meaning associated with the term is a reactive approach in which the teacher identifies an existing problem facing an individual student. The teacher then suggests certain books, sometimes without mentioning the reason. This approach is low-key, private, and indirect.

Many times a teacher may find a number of children who are experiencing a similar problem. The teacher may want to introduce a selection to the entire class or the small group by reading aloud a short book or a chapter or episode from a longer book. Discussion may ensue and a creative problem-solving session may result. The group setting allows for such discussion. Solutions may be generated in a group setting that may not occur to individuals.

To some teachers, books can simply be made available to children and individuals who can choose those selections which best fit their personal interests and needs at that particular moment. This low-key approach is inoffensive but does sensitize children to possible concerns/difficulties and may change their attitudes toward a particular group of students with unique or special circumstances or abilities.

Types of Books Appropriate for Bibliotherapy

Books that can be used include both nonfiction and fiction, the former entailing self-help titles, reference materials, and other informative books designed for that target social readerships. The use of nonfiction raises the question of whether text-books and other course materials might have bibliotherapeutic value, and the answer to that question must certainly be yes. In the case of fiction, the strategy has involved selecting protagonists who face specific personal problems or obstacles and then encouraging the reader to make the intended connections and to derive coping strategies vicariously from the experience of the fictional character.

Jalengo (1983) suggests using an interest inventory to select literature with general appeal. The three criteria to be used in selecting books for bibliotherapy, according to Jalengo, include: potential for controversy, accuracy or credibility, and value of literature.

Bibliotherapy in the Classroom

Dan Ouzts and Stephanie Hewitt (1993) identify a four-phase process for using bibliotherapy in the classroom.

1. *Planning and Preparation.* This step should include setting purposes and dis-covering what one wishes to accomplish through a piece of literature. Teacher and students together can decide who will be involved in reading various selections. Sometimes the entire class may read the same book. Timing is important in that a match between a child's experience and the story protagonist's conflict is the idea.

2. *Selection.* Choosing books should be done carefully. Not all books match all children. Some books are obviously designed for individual reflection rather than group reading. Typically, common experiences, such as the death of a pet, are not as socially sensitive as, for example, books about sexual abuse or homosexuality. Teachers should be aware of controversial books and issues.

3. *Presentations.* In presenting the book, teachers can set expectations, guide the discussions, and relate to students' experiences. This is the appropriate time for reflection.

4. *Assessment.* Gauging the effectiveness of bibliotherapy may simply involve documentation of changes in attitudes when specific books have addressed a stu-dent's personal problems or the use of interest inventories that note behavior changes.

We have offered a more specific eight-step procedure for implementing these four phases of bibliotherapy in the classroom. These steps include:

1. Identify one or more students currently confronting a problem situation. Rely on observation, discussion, input from colleagues, and any other sources of infor-mation.

2. Judge whether the problem is common enough that it might affect other stu-dents at some point in the future. Keep in mind that even an uncommon problem (e.g., cerebral palsy) might warrant a group unit because of the understanding and empathy it is likely to foster among classmates.

3. Identify appropriate books. Use electronic or print resources, or consult your library media specialist. Consider such factors as age-appropriateness, length, and illustrations. Where possible, utilize both fiction and nonfiction.

4. Plan and conduct a prereading discussion. Activate and build students' prior knowledge by introducing key concepts, asking provocative questions, and posing critical problem situations ("What would you do if. . . ?"). Do not single out the child or children actually confronting the problem.

5. Introduce the books on a silent-reading or read-aloud basis, depending on the age and ability of the children, the length of the books, and so forth. Consider combining read-alouds with silent reading.

6. Plan and conduct a postreading discussion. Do not be overly convergent or heavy-handed in the questions you ask, even though you may hope that students arrive at certain conclusions and judgments. Make sure to discuss each book after it has been read in addition to holding a general discussion after all of the books have been read and discussed. Again, do not single out the child or children you have targeted.

7. Provide for additional ways of responding to the books. Consider writing activities (journal entries, comparisons of the books, book reviews), art projects, and the like.

8. If neither the postreading discussion nor the response activities convinces you that the bibliotherapy has been successful for the troubled child or children, arrange for private conferences during which to explore the issue individually. Consider asking for assistance from appropriate specialists (Grindler, Stratton, McKenna, & Smith, 1995).

Cautions

In closing, we offer a few cautionary notes. Teachers may wish to consult with the school psychologist or counselor as well as the media specialist prior to implementing a program of bibliotherapy. Professionals working together strengthen any educational program, but the added guidance by counselors may lend an extra boost to insecure or novice teachers.

Moreover, if books are going to be used to help children cope with their problems, teachers should not force the selections on them. Various books should be made available; a wide selection of materials from which boys and girls can choose is a better strategy than using a single selection. This will require patience on the part of the adult, but the intent is to be part of the solution and not to compound the problem.

During postreading discussions, children should be given the opportunity to talk about their feelings, their insights into the character's actions, the consequences of their decisions, and so on. At no time should a reader be forced to add to the discussion. The child should also be allowed to agree or disagree with the character's resolution of the problem.

After students have read the books, adults should be available for private discussion or listening. This may also be the appropriate time to call on professional advice or counsel from others who are trained in this area. Wisdom, not pride, should prevail in a teacher's decision to seek additional help.

At times, it may be necessary for the adult not to intervene with a formal discussion but simply to be available during a period of incubation or "think time" while students ponder seriously what was read. The students at times may be the ones who call for discussion.

Chapter 4

The Data Base

Each entry in the data base contains the book's title, author, publisher, length in pages, age appropriateness, publication date, main character, other topics addressed, and a brief overview. Under each category—for example, "adoption"—the books are listed in alphabetical order by book title.

Several issues arose during the development of the data base, and we believe we have addressed them in ways that will make it easy to use. It is important to understand our approach to these matters, and we outline it here.

Length. The book lengths are often listed as 32 pages, which is the standard length of picture books. The book length entry may help the reader determine the appropriateness of the selection for the target audience.

Age. We have used the term "age" to provide recommendations for the social and intellectual appropriateness of materials. We believe this approach is preferable to categorizing books according to the older notion of readability. Since many of these titles will be read aloud to children by their teacher or parents, this policy seems especially prudent. We acknowledge that some of the age ranges we have provided are extensive, but we suggest that these are not only appropriate for the titles they accompany but that using fairly extensive ranges is common practice within the retail book industry. See, for example, *The Fall of Freddie the Leaf* by Leo Buscaglia.

Date. Some publication dates may raise the issue of whether all titles are in print. Since teachers are in a position to use their school libraries and since many library holdings are in fact out of print, this issue is not overly important. Attempting to limit a resource of this nature to titles that are currently in print would be self-defeating because of the rapidity of change. The older titles which *are* included tend to be classics that remain in print or that are periodically released.

Main Character. Main characters are identified by both gender and ethnicity. Given the extensive research literature underlying children's tendency to identify with protagonists on the basis of both gender and ethnicity, this dimension may serve as a highly important avenue into the entries. Teachers and parents might find it useful in narrowing the range of acceptable books. This category does not pertain to nonfiction entries, which are few in number and have simply been coded N/A (not applicable).

Other Topics. The "Other Topics" category allows teachers and parents to anticipate secondary issues that may be addressed in the selection. For example, the main topic might be "loneliness," but elements of "sibling rivalry" may play a minor role.

Overview. A very brief overview concludes each entry. We have opted for more titles and less description in order to increase the likelihood that just the right match between a given child and a given title may be found.

The Issue of Quality. The question of the *quality* of the children's literature included is one that we have not dismissed. Certainly children's literature impacts on young readers, and *what* children read does matter. We feel, however, that a critique of the literature should not be limited to a consideration of the literary merit of a piece alone but also should consider the potential impact of the work, as an instructional tool, on the child's developing self. In other words, in some instances, we have included works that cannot be judged solely on the basis of literary quality or merit but that must also be viewed on the basis of their value in addressing, more holistically, the needs of children: physical, social, and emotional. To impose the restriction of only including the highest quality of literature (based inevitably on some arbitrary checklist) would jeopardize our purpose of matching children with books that meet their individual needs.

About the Reference Software

This book includes two disks with files that contain all the information on each book listed in the text. These files will help you search through the books to locate those that meet your needs. The following is a description of the files on the disks with instructions on how to use them.

Reference Disk 1

Reference Disk 1 is DOS formatted and will run on any IBM-compatible that will accept a high-density (1.4 mb) disk. In order to access the files on this disk you must have MS-Works 4.0 or a data base program that is capable of importing text files.

The Files

These are the files that you'll find on Reference Disk 1. Each file contains the topic, title, author, main character, other topics, age, length, overview, publication date, and publisher for each of the 1,236 books listed in the text.

BIBLIO.wdb   MS-Works 4.0 data base file

BIBLIO.txt   tab-separated text file

BIBLIO.slk   sylk formatted text file

BIBLIO.wdb.   If you have MS-Works 4.0, all you need to do is load MS-Works and tell the program to open BIBLIO.wdb located in drive a:>. You are now ready to use the functions of the program to search for books that meet your particular needs.

BIBLIO.txt and BIBLIO.slk.   If you do not have MS-Works you can create a data base file that you can use. In order to access the data you will need to import the data into a data base program. Almost all data base programs will allow you to do this.

Creating a Data Base

Follow the directions that came with your data base program for creating a new data base. The field names and sizes (not all data base programs require the use of the field size) are listed below.

size	field name
36	Topic
88	Title
58	Author
45	Main Character
65	Other Topics
8	Age
5	Length
256	Overview
5	Publication Date
33	Publisher

Once you have created the data base you will need to import the data from one of the two text files on Reference Disk 1. The documentation that came with your data base program will inform you how to perform this operation and which file to use, either the tab-separated text file or the sylk formatted text file.

Reference Disk 2

Reference Disk 2 is Macintosh formatted and will run on any Macintosh or compatible that will accept a high-density (1.4 mb) disk. In order to access the files on this disk you must have HyperCard Player, MS-Works 4.0, or a data base program that is capable of importing text files.

The Files

These are the files that you'll find on Reference Disk 2. Each file contains the topic, title, author, main character, other topics, age, length, overview, publication date, and publisher for each of the 1,236 books listed in the text.

BIBLIO.wdb	MS-Works 4.0 data base file
BIBLIO.txt	tab-separated text file
HyperReference	HyperCard stack

BIBLIO.wdb. If you have MS-Works 4.0, all you need to do is load MS-Works and tell the program to open the BIBLIO.wdb located on Reference Disk 2. You are now ready to use the functions of the program to search for books that meet your particular needs.

BIBLIO.txt. If you do not have MS-Works you can create a data base file that you can use. In order to access the data you will need to import the data into a data base program. Almost all data base programs will allow you to do this.

Creating a Data Base

Follow the directions that came with your data base program for creating a new data base. The field names and sizes (not all data base programs require the use of the field size) are listed below.

size	field name
36	Topic
88	Title
58	Author
45	Main Character
65	Other Topics
8	Age
5	Length
256	Overview
5	Publication Date
33	Publisher

Once you have created the data base you will need to import the data from one of the two text files on Reference Disk 2. The documentation that came with your data base program will inform you how to perform this operation and which file to use, either the tab-separated text file or the sylk formatted text file.

HyperReference Stack. HyperReference is a HyperCard stack that contains all the information on each of the 1,236 books listed in the text. Using this stack you may search for keywords located in the topic, title, author, main character, or overview fields, which makes it possible to find titles of interest so that they may be marked for future reference or printed.

Loading the Stack

In order to use the stack, you need to have either HyperCard or HyperCard Player. HyperCard Player comes with every Macintosh computer. To use the stack, copy it from the floppy disk and place it in the same folder that contains HyperCard or HyperCard Player. Double-clicking on the HyperReference stack icon will start the program.

Navigating the Stack

The buttons on each book card allow navigation through the stack and perform various functions such as sorting, finding, printing, viewing, and deleting information.

Browsing

There are a number of different ways that the data in this stack can be viewed. The simplest way to go from card to card, or to the next book entry, is to click on the left and right arrows located at the bottom of each card. One click advances one card. Hold down the mouse button, and the display continues until the mouse button is released. The first card ("The Right Book, The Right Time: Helping Children Cope") of the book list cannot be removed. It is the first card in the list and a number of functions end by returning to this card. If the text bothers you, select and change it to whatever you would like. A quick way to return to this card is to click the arrow pointing to a hollow line, positioned near the upper right-hand corner of each card.

New Entry

To enter a book that is not already in the list choose the "New Entry" button by clicking it. A blank card will be added to the stack, and the cursor will be placed in the topic field, ready for typing. Use the tab key to advance to the next field, which is for the title. Extra-long names will not show on screen. If you happen to type the full title, and it disappears, know that it will be transferred if and when the information is sent to disk for printing. It is very important to get into the habit of tabbing between fields rather than doing a return. The return key will only take you to the next line in that particular field. You can stop entering information wherever you want by clicking outside of a field. Your information is automatically saved. Corrections may be made at any time by selecting words that need to be changed.

Sorting

To sort the books, choose the "Sort" button by clicking it. You may sort the books by author, title, and/or topic. Click on the category or categories that you want to sort by, then click on ascending (alphabetical) or descending (reverse alphabetical) order. When you are ready, click on the "Sort it" button. Once the books have been sorted to your parameters, you will be returned to the first book in the stack.

Find

To find a particular book, choose the "Find" button by clicking it. The "Find" button presents more choices: (1) Enter the word (word string) to search for; (2) click where to look (find desired text in title, author, topic, or overview); and (3) click on the "Find it" button. The program will search each card of the book list for the particular text string that you have chosen. When it finds a match it will stop and display that card. To see the next card that meets your find parameters, push the return key. This will continue in a loop until you exit by clicking anywhere on the card. If the word is not found, a dialog box will appear. If the return key doesn't seem to move to the next entry, it means this find happens to be the only such word (for the parameters chosen) in the whole stack.

Mark This Book

After doing a search by clicking between cards, or doing a find, you may wish to mark a book for later retrieval or printing. Checking the "Mark This Book" box will mark the book for later use. Clicking the "Show Marked Books" box in the "View" page will allow you to return to all of the books that have been marked. After the first one appears on the screen, push return to go to the next marked book. This will continue in a loop until you exit by clicking anywhere on the card.

View

The "View" button will allow you to toggle between all the books that you have previously marked by selecting the "Show Marked Books" button. There is also a button that allows you to reset all of the Book Marks that you have checked. This button changes all of the marked books to the unmarked state.

Delete

The "Delete" button allows you to delete one or more entries in the book list. To delete a book, first mark the book and then choose "Delete Marked Books" from the "Delete" page. The "Delete" button also presents the choice of "Mark all Books." This will put a mark in all the boxes, so when "Delete Marked Books" is chosen, the stack is returned to a virgin state, with no entries at all. This is a powerful feature, so use it with caution. It is recommended that you make a backup of this stack, either by duplicating it or copying the stack to another disk.

Compact

After any sorts, insertions, or deletions, use the "Compact" button to get rid of the wasted space set aside by HyperCard. This will help keep the stack to a manageable size.

Print

The "Print" button allows you to print a list of one or more books contained in the stack. To print, you need to decide what information you want to include in your output. Once you have selected the fields to print, click on the "Print it" button. The program does not actually send the information to a printer; instead, it saves it to a text file located in the HyperCard folder. This text file can then be imported into any word processing program for formatting and printing.

Quit

When you have finished using the HyperReference stack, select the "Quit" button. This will (1) automatically save any changes that you have made to the stack, (2) take you out of HyperCard, and (3) return you to the Macintosh Desktop.

References

Agness, P. (1980). Effects of bibliotherapy on fourth and fifth graders' perception of physically disabled individuals (Doctoral dissertation, Ball State University, 1980).

Altman, H., & Nielsen, B. (1974). The influence of bibliotherapy on self-esteem. *Cornell Journal of Social Relations, 53,* 193–198.

Baruth, L. G., & Phillips, M. W. (1976). Bibliotherapy and the school counselor. *The School Counselor, 23,* 191–199.

Beardsley, D. (1979). The effects of using fiction in bibliotherapy to alter the attitudes of regular third-grade students toward their handicapped peers (Doctoral dissertation, University of Missouri-Columbia, 1979).

Borden, E., Hansen, R., Hall, S., & Hall, R. (1976). Use of programmed instruction in teaching self-management skills to overweight adults. *Behavior Therapy, 7,* 366–373.

Bromley, K. D. (1992). *Language arts: Exploring connections* (2nd ed.). Boston: Allyn & Bacon.

Brownell, K., Heckerman, C., & Westlake, R. (1978). Therapist and group contact as variables in the behavioral treatment of obesity. *Journal of Consulting and Clinical Psychology, 46,* 593–594.

Ciancolo, P. (1965). Children's literature can affect coping behavior. *Personnel and Guidance Journal, 43,* 897–903.

Cornett, C. E., & Cornett, C. (1980). *Bibliotherapy: The right book at the right time.* Phi Delta Kappan.

Crowder, J., & Thornten, D. (1970). Effects of systematic desensitization, programmed fantasy and bibliotherapy on a specific fear. *Behavior Research and Therapy, 8,* 35–41.

Dixon, J. (1974). The effects of four methods of group reading therapy on the level of reading, manifest anxiety, self-concept, and personal–social adjustment among fifth- and sixth-grade children in a central school setting (Doctoral dissertation, State University of New York, Buffalo, 1974).

Fisher, F. (1965). The influences of reading and discussion on the attitudes of fifth graders toward American Indians (Doctoral dissertation, University of California-Berkeley, 1965).

Fordyce, M. (1977). Development of a program to increase personal happiness. *Journal of Counseling Psychology, 24,* 511–520.

Girodo, M., & Henry, D. (1976). Cognitive, physiological and behavioral components of anxiety in flooding. *Canadian Journal of Behavioral Science, 8,* 224–231.

Grindler, M. C., Stratton, B. D., & McKenna, M. C. (1994, November). The effectiveness of bibliotherapy in altering kindergartners' beliefs about books. Paper presented at the meeting of the College Reading Association, New Orleans.

Grindler, M. C., Stratton, B. D., McKenna, M. C., & Smith, P. (1995). Bookmatching in the classroom: How action research reached the lives of children through books. *Action in Teacher Education, 16*(4), 50–58.

Hagen, R. (1974). Group therapy versus bibliotherapy in weight reduction. *Behavior Therapy, 5,* 222–234.

Hogan, R., & Kirchner, J. (1968). Implosive, eclectic verbal and bibliotherapy in the treatment of fears of snakes. *Behavior Research and Therapy, 6,* 167–171.

Hopkins, L. (1979). "Normal" kids have problems, too. *Teacher, 96,* 32–34.

Huck, C. S. (1987). *Children's literature in the elementary school* (4th ed.). New York: Holt, Rinehart & Winston.

Jalengo, M. (1983). Bibliotherapy: Literature to promote socio-emotional growth. *The Reading Teacher, 36,* 796–802.

Jeffrey, D., & Christensen, E. (1972). The relative efficacy of behavior therapy, will power and no-treatment control procedures for weight loss. Paper presented at the annual meeting of the Association for the Advancement of Behavior Therapy, New York.

Kanaan, J. (1975).The application of adjuvant bibliotherapeutic techniques in resolving peer acceptance problems (Doctoral dissertation, University of Pittsburgh, 1975).

Kimoto, C. (1974). The effects of a juvenile literature-based program on majority group attitudes toward black Americans (Doctoral dissertation, Washington State University, 1974).

King, N. (1972). The effects of group bibliocounseling on selected fourth-grade students who are underachieving in reading (Doctoral dissertation, University of the Pacific, 1972).

Litcher, J., & Johnson, D. (1969). Changes in attitudes toward Negroes of white elementary students after use of multiethnic readers. *Journal of Educational Psychology, 60,* 148–152.

Lundstein, S. (1972). A thinking improvement program through literature. *Elementary English, 49,* 505–512.

Mathewson, G. C. (1994). Model of attitude influence upon reading and learning to read. In R. B. Ruddell & M. R. Ruddell (Eds.), *Theoretical models and processes of reading* (4th ed., pp. 1131–1161). Newark, DE: International Reading Association.

McKenna, M.C. (1994). Toward a model of reading attitude acquisition. In E. H. Cramer & M. Castle (Eds.), *Fostering the life-long love of reading: The affective domain in reading education* (pp. 18–40). Newark, DE: International Reading Association.

Meyers, J. (1976). Werewolves in literature for children. *Language Arts, 53,* 552–556.

Ongoa, E. (1979). The effects of bibliotherapy through listening in reducing fears of young children (Doctoral dissertation, Ball State University, 1979).

Ouzts, D. T. (1991). The emergence of bibliotherapy as a discipline. *Reading Horizons, 31,* 199–206.

Ouzts, D. T., & Hewett, S. M. (1993, November). Bibliotherapeutic literature: A key facet of whole language instruction for the at-risk student. Paper presented at the annual meeting of the College Reading Association, Richmond, VA.

Ponder, V. (1969). An investigation of the effects of bibliotherapy and teachers' self-others acceptance on pupils' self-acceptance and reading achievement scores (Doctoral dissertation, University of Southern Mississippi, 1968).

Rich, A., & Bernstein, J. (October, 1975). The picture book image of entering school. *Language Arts, 52,* 978–982.

Roach, L. (1975). The effects of realistic fiction literature upon the self-concept of elementary school students exposed to a bibliotherapeutic situation (Doctoral dissertation, University of Akron, 1975).

Robinson, D. (1980). A bibliotherapy program for special education students. *Top of the News, 36,* 189–193.

Russell, D. (1970). *The dynamics of reading.* Waltham, MA: Ginn.

Russell, A., & Russell, W. (1979). Using bibliotherapy with emotionally disturbed children. *Teaching Exceptional Children, 11,* 168–169.

Schrank, F. (1977). A semantic differential study concerning attitude change of fourth-grade children toward slow-learning children utilizing imaginative literature as a psychological field. Published educational specialist thesis, University of Tennessee, 1977.

Schrank, F., Engles, D. W., & Silke, J. R. (1983). Using bibliotherapy in the elementary school: What does the research say? *Wisconsin State Reading Association Journal, 27*(2), 23–29.

Schultheis, M. (1970). A study of the effects of selected readings upon children's academic performances and social adjustment (Doctoral dissertation, Ball State University, 1969).

Shearon, E. (1975). The effects of psychodrama treatment on the professed and inferred self-concepts of selected fourth graders in one elementary school (Doctoral dissertation, University of Florida, 1975).

Shrodes, C. (1949). Bibliotherapy: A theoretical and clinical experimental study (Doctoral dissertation, University of California, Berkeley.)

Stanley, F., & Stanley, N. (1970). An experimental use of black literature at a predominantly white university. *Research in Teaching of English, 4*, 139–148.

Stevens, M. J., & Pfost, K. S. (1982). Bibliotherapy: Medicine for the soul? *Psychology, 4*, 21–25.

Tartagni, D. (1976). Using bibliotherapy with adolescents. *The School Counselor, 24*, 28–35.

Tauran, R. (1967). The influences of reading on the attitudes of third graders toward Eskimos (Doctoral dissertation, University of Maryland, 1967).

Watson, J. (1979). Bibliotherapy for abused children. *The School Counselor, 27*, 204–208.

Webster, J. (1961). Using books to reduce the fears of first-grade children. *The Reading Teacher, 14*, 159–162.

Yawkey, T. (1973). Attitudes toward black Americans held by rural and urban white early childhood subjects based on multi-ethnic social studies materials. *Journal of Negro Education, 42*, 164–169.

Zaccaria, J., & Moses, H. (1968). *Facilitating human development through reading.* Champaign, IL: Stripes Publishing Co.

List of Children's Books

Adoption

A Koala for Katie: An Adoption Story

Author: Jonathan London
Publisher: Albert Whitman and Co.
Length: 24 **Age:** 3–6 **Date:** 1993
Main Character: white female
Other Topics: N/A
Overview: Katie questions why her birth mother didn't want her.

A Look at Adoption

Author: Margaret S. Pursell
Publisher: Lerner Publications Co.
Length: 32 **Age:** 4–7 **Date:** 1978
Main Character: Asian female
Other Topics: N/A
Overview: Text and photographs answer many questions about adoption. The author tells about the adoption of her two Asian daughters.

Abby

Author: Jeannette Caines
Publisher: Harper
Length: 32 **Age:** 3–6 **Date:** 1973

Abby (cont.)

Main Character: African American female
Other Topics: Sibling Rivalry
Overview: Abby is adopted. Her big brother Kevin helps her to read her own baby book. They remember the day she was adopted and how close they became. She even goes to Kevin's school as his show-and-tell.

Adopted

Author: Judith E. Greenberg and Helen H. Carey
Publisher: Franklin Watts
Length: 32 **Age:** 5–8 **Date:** 1987
Main Character: white male and female
Other Topics: N/A
Overview: Sarah and her new brother are adopted. Sarah's mother, father, and grandfather explain what adoption is all about.

Adoption Is for Always

Author: Linda Girard
Publisher: Albert Whitman
Length: 32 **Age:** 5–8 **Date:** 1986
Main Character: white female

Adoption <small>(cont.)</small>

Adoption Is for Always (cont.)

Other Topics: N/A
Overview: At age six, Celia begins to better understand the concept of her adoption.

Being Adopted

Author: Maxine Rosenberg
Publisher: Lothrop
Length: 41 **Age:** 8–10 **Date:** 1984
Main Character: multicultural males and females
Other Topics: N/A
Overview: The story of what it's like to be adopted by a family of a different race.

Coping with Being Adopted

Author: Shari Cohen
Publisher: Rosen Publishing Group, Inc.
Length: 126 **Age:** 10–12 **Date:** 1988
Main Character: N/A
Other Topics: N/A
Overview: Discusses questions and feelings associated with being adopted. This is an excellent book for adolescents.

Her Own Song

Author: Ellen Howard
Publisher: Atheneum
Length: 176 **Age:** 8–12 **Date:** 1988
Main Character: Chinese American male and white female
Other Topics: Racism, Prejudice
Overview: An adopted girl finds out that she was once a member of the hated local community in turn-of-the-century Oregon.

How It Feels to Be Adopted

Author: Jill Krementz
Publisher: Knopf
Length: 107 **Age:** 9–12 **Date:** 1982
Main Character: multicultural males and females
Other Topics: N/A
Overview: Children ages 8–16 are interviewed. Photographs show the children and their adoptive families.

I Am Adopted

Author: Susan Lapsley
Publisher: Bradbury
Length: 23 **Age:** 2–5 **Date:** 1974
Main Character: white male and female
Other Topics: N/A
Overview: A small boy discusses his adoption into a warm and loving family.

Just as Long as We're Together

Author: Judy Blume
Publisher: Orchard/Watts
Length: 296 **Age:** 10–12 **Date:** 1987
Main Character: white female and Vietnamese female
Other Topics: Friendship
Overview: Two preadolescents befriend a Vietnamese adoptee.

Me, Mop, and Moondance Kid

Author: Walter Dean Myers
Publisher: Delacorte
Length: 154 **Age:** 9–12 **Date:** 1988
Main Character: African American male
Other Topics: Friendship
Overview: When eleven-year-old T.J. and younger brother Billy are adopted, they worry about leaving Mop at the orphanage. They plot to get Mop adopted.

Miracle of Time: Adopting a Sister

Author: Jane C. Miner
Publisher: Crestwood House
Length: 63 **Age:** 8–10 **Date:** 1982
Main Character: Asian American female
Other Topics: Shyness
Overview: A family adopts a withdrawn and shy five-year-old Vietnamese orphan.

Moonshadow of Cherry Mountain

Author: Doris Buchanan Smith
Publisher: Four Winds Press
Length: 154 **Age:** 8–12 **Date:** 1982
Main Character: white male
Other Topics: Adjusting to Change
Overview: The story of a mountain family and their adopted children.

Riding the Waves

Author: Teresa Tomlinson
Publisher: Macmillan Publishing Co.
Length: 144 **Age:** 8–12 **Date:** 1993
Main Character: white male
Other Topics: Intergenerational
Overview: Matts befriends an elderly lady who helps him adjust to being adopted.

Tall Boy's Journey

Author: Joanna H. Kraus
Publisher: Carolrhoda
Length: 48 **Age:** 6–8 **Date:** 1992
Main Character: Korean male
Other Topics: N/A
Overview: After his grandmother dies, an orphaned Korean boy is adopted by an American couple. With the help of an understanding Korean American man, Kim Moo Young adjusts to America and his new family.

The Adopted One: An Open Family Book for Parents and Children Together

Author: Sara B. Stein
Publisher: Walker and Co.
Length: 47 **Age:** 3–18 **Date:** 1979
Main Character: white male
Other Topics: N/A
Overview: This book is written with dual texts, one for adults, the other for children. Conflicting feelings of an adopted child are discussed.

The Boy Who Wanted a Family

Author: S. Gordon
Publisher: Harper
Length: 89 **Age:** 9–12 **Date:** 1980
Main Character: white male
Other Topics: N/A
Overview: Explores the hopes, fears, and experiences of a young boy and his new mom during the one-year waiting period before he can be legally adopted.

The Chosen Baby

Author: Valentina Wasson
Publisher: Lippincott
Length: 40 **Age:** 4–6 **Date:** 1977
Main Character: white male and female
Other Topics: N/A
Overview: Story of what it means to be adopted. A couple adopts first a boy and later a girl.

The Facts About Adoption

Author: Gail Stewart
Publisher: Macmillan
Length: 48 **Age:** 8–12 **Date:** 1989
Main Character: multicultural males and females
Other Topics: N/A

Adoption (cont.)

The Facts About Adoption (cont.)

Overview: This informative, factual text discusses the process by which people can adopt, who adopts, sources for adoption, and other aspects of adoption as seen from both children's and adults' perspectives.

The Pretty House That Found Happiness

Author: Eleanor Eisenburg
Publisher: Steck-Vaughn Co.
Length: 32 **Age:** 4–6 **Date:** 1974
Main Character: white male
Other Topics: N/A
Overview: This book is designed to be read by parents to young children about adoption.

Through Moon and Stars and Night Skies

Author: Ann Turner
Publisher: Harper
Length: 28 **Age:** 4–6 **Date:** 1990
Main Character: Asian male
Other Topics: Moving
Overview: A warm, loving story about the adoption of a little Asian boy.

Tuck Triumphant

Author: Theodore Taylor
Publisher: Doubleday
Length: 150 **Age:** 8–12 **Date:** 1991
Main Character: white female
Other Topics: Deaf/Hearing Impaired
Overview: Fourteen-year-old Helen owns a blind dog named Friar Tuck. She and her family face some challenges when they adopt a six-year-old Korean boy who is deaf.

We Adopted You, Benjamin Koo

Author: Linda Walvoord Girard
Publisher: Whitman
Length: 32 **Age:** 7–9 **Date:** 1989
Main Character: Korean male
Other Topics: Racism, Prejudice
Overview: A nine-year-old Korean, Benjamin, tells about being adopted by parents from another culture.

AIDS

AIDS: How It Works in the Body

Author: Lorna Greenberg
Publisher: Franklin Watts
Length: 64 **Age:** 8–12 **Date:** 1992
Main Character: N/A
Other Topics: N/A
Overview: This book of nonfiction examines how the AIDS virus invades the body and affects its immune system.

Alex, the Kid with AIDS

Author: Linda Girard
Publisher: Albert Whitman
Length: 32 **Age:** 6–10 **Date:** 1991
Main Character: white male
Other Topics: N/A
Overview: The story of a child with AIDS and how he and his classmates adjust.

Be a Friend: Children Who Live with HIV Speak

Author: Lori Wiener, Aprille Best, and Philip Pizzo
Publisher: Albert Whitman and Co.
Length: 40 **Age:** 8–12 **Date:** 1994
Main Character: multicultural males and females

Be a Friend: Children Who Live with HIV Speak (cont.)

Other Topics: N/A
Overview: Children with HIV infection and AIDS from the National Cancer Institute in Bethesda, Maryland, tell their stories. The book is illustrated by the children.

Children and the AIDS Virus

Author: Rosmarie Hausherr
Publisher: Clarion
Length: 48 **Age:** 7–10 **Date:** 1989
Main Character: multicultural males and females
Other Topics: N/A
Overview: An interesting format with two types of print: large print for younger readers and small print for adults.

Come Sit by Me

Author: Margaret Merrifield
Publisher: Gryphon House
Length: 32 **Age:** 4–8 **Date:** 1990
Main Character: multicultural males and females
Other Topics: N/A
Overview: This educational storybook was written by a medical doctor about AIDS and HIV infection. A special section for adults will help them answer children's questions.

Coping with AIDS: Facts and Fears

Author: Morton L. Kurland, M.D.
Publisher: Rosen Publishing Group
Length: 134 **Age:** 10–12 **Date:** 1990
Main Character: N/A
Other Topics: N/A
Overview: A thorough discussion of AIDS is presented, including a glossary, bibliography, and a list of Crisis Centers.

Everything You Need To Know About AIDS

Author: Barbara Taylor
Publisher: Rosen Publishing Group
Length: 64 **Age:** 10–18 **Date:** 1988
Main Character: multicultural males and females
Other Topics: N/A
Overview: This factual book discusses the AIDS virus, its discovery, causes, transmission, treatment, and how to protect oneself from contracting the disease.

Know About AIDS

Author: Margaret Hyde and Elizabeth Forsyth
Publisher: Walker
Length: 102 **Age:** 9–13 **Date:** 1990
Main Character: N/A
Other Topics: N/A
Overview: This book contains facts and myths about AIDS.

Losing Uncle Tim

Author: Marykate Jordan
Publisher: Albert Whitman and Co.
Length: 32 **Age:** 4–8 **Date:** 1989
Main Character: white male
Other Topics: N/A
Overview: Uncle Tim dies of AIDS.

Real Heroes

Author: Marilyn Kaye
Publisher: Harcourt Brace Jovanovich
Length: 144 **Age:** 10–14 **Date:** 1993
Main Character: white male
Other Topics: N/A
Overview: Kevin is torn between loyalty to his family and his sixth grade teacher when his parents demonstrate against a teacher who is HIV positive.

AIDS (cont.)

Ryan White: My Own Story

Author: Ryan White and Ann Marie Cunningham
Publisher: Dial
Length: 144 **Age:** 10–18 **Date:** 1991
Main Character: white male
Other Topics: Death (General)
Overview: Ryan was a thirteen-year-old boy who contracted AIDS through contaminated blood. This is his personal account of his struggle.

Understanding and Preventing AIDS

Author: Warren Colman
Publisher: Children's Press
Length: 123 **Age:** 10–18 **Date:** 1988
Main Character: multicultural males and females
Other Topics: N/A
Overview: This nonfiction book surveys the history and symptoms of AIDS. It also discusses how it spreads, how it may be prevented, and how it may eventually be cured.

Alcoholism

A Day at a Time: Dealing with an Alcoholic

Author: Jane C. Miner
Publisher: Crestwood House
Length: 64 **Age:** 10–12 **Date:** 1982
Main Character: white female
Other Topics: N/A
Overview: When her father abuses alcohol, Ellen decides to attend an Alateen meeting.

A Look at Alcoholism

Author: Rebecca Anders
Publisher: Lerner Publications
Length: 32 **Age:** 6–10 **Date:** 1978
Main Character: white males and females
Other Topics: N/A
Overview: Photographs and text describe the problems of alcohol abuse.

Alcohol—What It Is, What It Does

Author: Judith Seixas
Publisher: Greenwillow Books
Length: 56 **Age:** 6–10 **Date:** 1977
Main Character: cartoon characters
Other Topics: N/A
Overview: This easy-to-read book introduces young readers to facts about alcohol.

Everything You Need to Know About Alcohol

Author: Barbara Taylor
Publisher: Rosen Publishing Group Inc.
Length: 64 **Age:** 10–12 **Date:** 1989
Main Character: multicultural males and females
Other Topics: N/A
Overview: A description of the effect of alcohol on body and mind is presented. Treatment programs are also discussed.

Everything You Need to Know About an Alcoholic Parent

Author: Nancy Shuker
Publisher: Rosen Publishing Group, Inc.
Length: 64 **Age:** 8–12 **Date:** 1990
Main Character: multicultural males and females
Other Topics: N/A
Overview: Advice on how to deal with an alcoholic parent and where to go for help is offered.

Hannah in Between

Author: Colby Rodowsky
Publisher: Farrar-Straus-Giroux
Length: 176 **Age:** 12–18 **Date:** 1994
Main Character: white female
Other Topics: N/A
Overview: Twelve-year-old Hannah's life is comfortable and predictable. But Hannah is keeping a secret—her mother might be an alcoholic.

I Wish Daddy Didn't Drink So Much

Author: Judith Vigna
Publisher: Albert Whitman
Length: 32 **Age:** 3–9 **Date:** 1988
Main Character: white male
Other Topics: N/A
Overview: A sensitive and straightforward discussion of an alcoholic parent.

Kids and Alcohol, the Deadliest Drug

Author: Stanley Englebardt
Publisher: Lothrop, Lee and Shepard
Length: 64 **Age:** 9–12 **Date:** 1975
Main Character: N/A
Other Topics: N/A
Overview: This introductory book about alcohol discusses what it is, how it affects the body, why some people become alcoholics, and how to prevent the problem.

Living with a Parent Who Drinks Too Much

Author: Judith S. Seixas
Publisher: Greenwillow
Length: 116 **Age:** 10–18 **Date:** 1979
Main Character: N/A
Other Topics: N/A
Overview: The book describes alcoholism, alcoholic behavior, and family problems.

Toughboy and Sister

Author: Kirkpatrick Hill
Publisher: McElderry
Length: 121 **Age:** 9–12 **Date:** 1990
Main Character: Native American male and female
Other Topics: Survival, Death
Overview: Eleven-year-old Toughboy, an Athabascan Indian, and his sister are suddenly on their own at the family summer fish camp in Canada's Yukon Territory after their widowed father, an alcoholic, drinks himself to death.

Why Do People Drink Alcohol?

Author: Pete Sanders
Publisher: Aladdin Books
Length: 32 **Age:** 8–12 **Date:** 1989
Main Character: multicultural males and females
Other Topics: N/A
Overview: An elementary but excellent discussion of the use and abuse of alcohol.

You Can Say No To a Drink or a Drug

Author: Susan Newman
Publisher: Putnam
Length: 128 **Age:** 10–12 **Date:** 1986
Main Character: multicultural males and females
Other Topics: N/A
Overview: This book shows preteens and teens how to resist alcohol and drug-related situations in ten photo essays.

Allergies, Asthma

AH-CHOO

Author: Mercer Mayer
Publisher: Dial Press
Length: 32 **Age:** 6–8 **Date:** 1976
Main Character: elephant
Other Topics: N/A
Overview: A funny book about an elephant with an allergy.

All About Allergies

Author: Susan Neiburg Terkel
Publisher: Lodestar Books
Length: 58 **Age:** 6–10 **Date:** 1993
Main Character: multicultural males and females
Other Topics: N/A
Overview: Information about various kinds of allergies, their symptoms, diagnosis, and treatments is given.

All About Asthma

Author: William Ostrow and Vivian Ostrow
Publisher: Albert Whitman
Length: 32 **Age:** 6–10 **Date:** 1989
Main Character: white male
Other Topics: N/A
Overview: A young boy uses his own experiences to give a clear and thorough picture of living with asthma.

Allergies

Author: Dr. Alvin Silverstein and Virginia Silverstein
Publisher: Lippincott
Length: 128 **Age:** 10–18 **Date:** 1977
Main Character: N/A

Allergies (cont.)

Other Topics: N/A
Overview: This book explains the various types of allergies, their symptoms, causes, and treatment and discusses research being conducted to find cures for allergic diseases.

Furry

Author: Holly Keller
Publisher: Greenwillow
Length: 24 **Age:** 3–8 **Date:** 1992
Main Character: white female
Other Topics: N/A
Overview: Laura wheezed and sneezed and itched whenever she was around a furry pet. Her brother Alfie brings home a chameleon.

I'll Never Love Anything Ever Again

Author: Judy Delton
Publisher: Albert Whitman
Length: 32 **Age:** 4–6 **Date:** 1985
Main Character: white male
Other Topics: N/A
Overview: The family doctor discovers a young boy is allergic to animals and must say good-bye to his pet dog.

Itch, Sniffle, and Sneeze

Author: Dr. Alvin Silverstein and Virginia Silverstein
Publisher: Four Winds
Length: 44 **Age:** 6–10 **Date:** 1978
Main Character: cartoon characters
Other Topics: N/A
Overview: This book discusses what allergies are, the body's reaction to them, things people are allergic to, and how to cope with allergies.

Knight on Horseback

Author: Ann Rabinowitz
Publisher: Macmillan
Length: 176 **Age:** 8–12 **Date:** 1987
Main Character: white male
Other Topics: N/A
Overview: This fantasy tale describes how thirteen-year-old Eddy Newby, who has asthma, must come to terms with himself and his family.

Luke Has Asthma, Too

Author: Alison Rogers
Publisher: Waterfront
Length: 31 **Age:** 3–7 **Date:** 1987
Main Character: white male
Other Topics: N/A
Overview: A very upbeat story about a young boy with asthma, an illness that affects one of every twenty children.

Marathon Miranda

Author: Elizabeth Winthrop
Publisher: Bantom Skylark
Length: 116 **Age:** 9–11 **Date:** 1979
Main Character: white female
Other Topics: N/A
Overview: Even though Miranda has asthma, she decides to train for the Central Park Marathon with her friend Phoebe.

Alzheimer's Disease

A Beautiful Pearl

Author: Nancy Whitelaw
Publisher: Albert Whitman
Length: 32 **Age:** 7–10 **Date:** 1991

A Beautiful Pearl (cont.)

Main Character: white female
Other Topics: Intergenerational
Overview: Every year Lisa receives a beautiful pearl from Grandmother. When Lisa is ten, she worries that Alzheimer's disease is affecting Grandmother's mind.

Always Gramma

Author: Vaunda Nelson
Publisher: Putnam
Length: 32 **Age:** 6–8 **Date:** 1988
Main Character: white female
Other Topics: Intergenerational
Overview: This informational book is narrated from the child's viewpoint.

My Grandma's in a Nursing Home

Author: Judy Delton and Dorothy Tucker
Publisher: Albert Whitman
Length: 32 **Age:** 6–8 **Date:** 1986
Main Character: white male and female
Other Topics: N/A
Overview: Jason learns that his visits to the nursing home help his grandmother and the other patients.

Anger

A Family That Fights

Author: Sharon C. Bernstein
Publisher: Albert Whitman
Length: 32 **Age:** 6–10 **Date:** 1991
Main Character: white male
Other Topics: Fear
Overview: Siblings Henry, Claire, and Joe hate it when their parents fight. Sometimes Dad even hits Mom. The children feel afraid.

Anger (cont.)

All the Animals Were Angry

Author: William Wondriska
Publisher: Holt, Rinehart and Winston
Length: 30 **Age:** 4–6 **Date:** 1970
Main Character: animal
Other Topics: N/A
Overview: On a hot day in the jungle the animals had nothing to do so they became angry.

And My Mean Old Mother Will Be Sorry, Blackboard Bear

Author: Martha Alexander
Publisher: Dial
Length: 29 **Age:** 4–8 **Date:** 1972
Main Character: white male
Other Topics: Invisible Friend
Overview: A young boy argues with his mother and runs away to live in the woods with his friend Blackboard Bear.

Atilla the Angry

Author: Marjorie W. Sharmat
Publisher: Holiday House
Length: 32 **Age:** 5–8 **Date:** 1985
Main Character: animal
Other Topics: N/A
Overview: Atilla the Squirrel must learn to control his anger.

Boy, Was I Mad!

Author: Kathryn Hitte
Publisher: Parent's Magazine Press
Length: 29 **Age:** 4–8 **Date:** 1969
Main Character: white male
Other Topics: N/A
Overview: A young cowboy is so mad that he runs away. But he has such a good time that he forgets his anger and goes home again to a hot supper and warm bed.

Chucky Bellman Was So Bad

Author: Phyllis Green
Publisher: Albert Whitman
Length: 32 **Age:** 6–8 **Date:** 1991
Main Character: white male
Other Topics: N/A
Overview: No one wants to babysit Chucky because he throws temper tantrums. Finally, Mrs. Bellman finds Gaby Bipsey, who is really a treesitter.

He Lost It—Let's Find It

Author: Nathan Kravetz
Publisher: Henry Z. Walck
Length: 30 **Age:** 4–8 **Date:** 1969
Main Character: cartoon characters
Other Topics: N/A
Overview: The whole town is looking for what two young men lost. What is it? Their tempers!

Helen the Hungry Bear

Author: Marilyn MacGregor
Publisher: Four Winds Press
Length: 32 **Age:** 4–7 **Date:** 1987
Main Character: animal
Other Topics: N/A
Overview: Helen is usually well behaved, until she gets hungry. Then she gets angry!

I Was So Mad!

Author: Norma Simon
Publisher: Albert Whitman and Co.
Length: 32 **Age:** 4–7 **Date:** 1974
Main Character: white female
Other Topics: N/A
Overview: This book describes situations which provoke anger in young children—frustration, anxiety, humiliation, and loss of control.

I'll Fix Anthony

Author: Judith Viorst
Publisher: Harper
Length: 32 **Age:** 5–8 **Date:** 1969
Main Character: white male
Other Topics: Sibling Rivalry
Overview: A younger brother dreams of revenge, planning all the different ways he can think of to "fix Anthony," his older brother.

Let's Talk About Throwing Tantrums

Author: Joy Wilt Berry
Publisher: Children's Press
Length: 32 **Age:** 3–6 **Date:** 1984
Main Character: multicultural males and females
Other Topics: N/A
Overview: This easy-to-read picture book describes what happens when people become angry and lose their tempers. Helpful suggestions are also included.

Sometimes I Get Angry

Author: Jane Werner Watson
Publisher: Western Publishing Co.
Length: 28 **Age:** 3–6 **Date:** 1971
Main Character: cartoon characters
Other Topics: Growing Up
Overview: This is a read-together book for parents and children. A note to parents discusses the growing up processes of young children.

Spinky Sulks

Author: William Steig
Publisher: Farrar
Length: 30 **Age:** 6–8 **Date:** 1988
Main Character: white male
Other Topics: N/A
Overview: Spinky is sullen and unforgiving.

The Quarreling Book

Author: Charlotte Zolotow
Publisher: Harper and Row
Length: 25 **Age:** 4–8 **Date:** 1963
Main Character: cartoon characters
Other Topics: Friendship
Overview: It's a bad day for everyone when a father forgets to kiss his wife good-bye.

The Temper Tantrum Book

Author: Edna Preston and Rainey Bennett
Publisher: Penguin
Length: 40 **Age:** 4–7 **Date:** 1976
Main Character: animal
Other Topics: N/A
Overview: Even animals can have temper tantrums. The animals explain what makes them so angry.

Arthritis

Jodie's Journey
Author: Colin Thiele
Publisher: HarperCollins
Length: 176 **Age:** 9–12 **Date:** 1990
Main Character: white female
Other Topics: Wheelchair
Overview: Jodie enjoys training and riding her horse until she discovers that she has rheumatoid arthritis. She learns to use a wheelchair but misses her horse.

Autism

He Is Your Brother

Author: Richard Parker
Publisher: Thomas Nelson
Length: 98 **Age:** 9–13 **Date:** 1974

Autism (cont.)

He Is Your Brother (cont.)

Main Character: white male
Other Topics: N/A
Overview: Mike draws his autistic brother Orry out of his shell by sharing his interest in railroads.

Inside Out

Author: Ann M. Martin
Publisher: Holiday House
Length: 160 **Age:** 9–12 **Date:** 1984
Main Character: white male
Other Topics: N/A
Overview: This is the story of a family with an autistic child.

Please Don't Say Hello

Author: Phyllis Gold
Publisher: Behavioral Publishers
Length: 47 **Age:** 9–12 **Date:** 1975
Main Character: white male
Other Topics: N/A
Overview: Phyllis Gold, the mother of an autistic child, describes the strange, frightening world of the severely disturbed child to other youngsters.

The Devil Hole

Author: Eleanor Spence
Publisher: Lothrop
Length: 215 **Age:** 11–14 **Date:** 1977
Main Character: white male
Other Topics: N/A
Overview: The story of a family and the impact of an autistic child.

Bad Day

Alexander and the Terrible, Horrible, No Good, Very Bad Day

Author: Judith Viorst
Publisher: Atheneum
Length: 28 **Age:** 4–8 **Date:** 1972
Main Character: white male
Other Topics: Sibling Rivalry
Overview: Alexander's day is one of the worst anyone can imagine.

Eleanora Mousie's Gray Day

Author: Ann Morris
Publisher: Macmillan
Length: 24 **Age:** 3–6 **Date:** 1987
Main Character: animal
Other Topics: N/A
Overview: Eleanora Mousie's day begins on a bad note but with the help of her friend Fiona and a little sunshine, things look better.

Frosted Glass

Author: Denys Cazet
Publisher: Bradbury
Length: 32 **Age:** 4–7 **Date:** 1987
Main Character: animal
Other Topics: N/A
Overview: Gregory is having a bad day. This book illustrates the ups and downs of everyday life.

Grover's Bad, Awful Day

Author: Anna H. Dickson
Publisher: Western Publishing Co.
Length: 24 **Age:** 3–6 **Date:** 1986
Main Character: puppets
Other Topics: N/A
Overview: Grover is coping with a very bad day. His mother comforts him and explains that bad days happen to everyone.

I Hate It

Author: Miriam Schlein
Publisher: Albert Whitman and Co.
Length: 25 **Age:** 4–6 **Date:** 1978
Main Character: white male
Other Topics: N/A
Overview: Children identify various situations that they hate.

It's Not My Fault

Author: Franz Brandenberg
Publisher: Greenwillow Books
Length: 63 **Age:** 5–8 **Date:** 1980
Main Character: animal
Other Topics: N/A
Overview: The mouse family is very quarrelsome and is having a bad day. A big pot of soup serves as peacemaker.

Lisa and the Grompet

Author: Patricia Coombs
Publisher: Lothrop, Lee and Shepard
Length: 28 **Age:** 4–8 **Date:** 1970
Main Character: white female
Other Topics: Invisible Friends
Overview: Lisa got tired of being told what to do. It made her cross. Her problem is solved when she meets a grompet.

Max and the Great Blueness

Author: Lou Alpert
Publisher: Whispering Coyote Press, Inc.
Length: 30 **Age:** 3–7 **Date:** 1993
Main Character: white male
Other Topics: N/A
Overview: Max's big brother tries to help Max get rid of the Great Blueness that is ruining his day.

Search for Sidney's Smile

Author: Marc Kornblatt
Publisher: Simon and Schuster

Search for Sidney's Smile (cont.)

Length: 22 **Age:** 3–6 **Date:** 1993
Main Character: white male
Other Topics: N/A
Overview: When Sidney wakes up from his nap, his smile is gone. His father hunts for that smile the rest of their day together.

The Ornery Morning

Author: Patricia Brennan Demuth
Publisher: Dutton
Length: 24 **Age:** 2–6 **Date:** 1991
Main Character: white male
Other Topics: N/A
Overview: Farmer Bill knows he's in for trouble when all the farm animals are having an ornery morning.

Today Was a Terrible Day

Author: Patricia Reilly Giff
Publisher: Viking
Length: 26 **Age:** 3–8 **Date:** 1980
Main Character: white male
Other Topics: N/A
Overview: Ronald's day only gets worse as it progresses.

Bathing

Mother Makes a Mistake

Author: Ann Dorer
Publisher: Gareth Stevens Children's Books
Length: 30 **Age:** 4–8 **Date:** 1991
Main Character: white female
Other Topics: N/A
Overview: Kate would rather play than bathe. When mother makes a mistake and substitutes other words so many times, Kate would rather take a bath.

Bathing (cont.)

No Bath Tonight

Author: Jane Yolen
Publisher: Thomas Y. Crowell
Length: 28 **Age:** 3–6 **Date:** 1978
Main Character: white male
Other Topics: Intergenerational
Overview: A small boy refuses to take a bath until his grandmother shows him how to make kid tea.

No More Baths

Author: Brock Cole
Publisher: Doubleday
Length: 35 **Age:** 5–8 **Date:** 1980
Main Character: white female
Other Topics: N/A
Overview: When a little girl who hates to bathe is told by her mother to take a bath, she decides to run away.

Blind, Visually Impaired

A Cane in Her Hand

Author: Ada Litchfield
Publisher: Whitman
Length: 32 **Age:** 6–8 **Date:** 1977
Main Character: white female
Other Topics: N/A
Overview: Story of a visually impaired child and how she copes with her problem.

Apt. 3

Author: Ezra Jack Keats
Publisher: Macmillan

Apt. 3 (cont.)

Length: 32 **Age:** 3–8 **Date:** 1971
Main Character: African American male
Other Topics: N/A
Overview: A young boy and a blind man meet in an old apartment building.

Blind Outlaw

Author: Glen Rounds
Publisher: Scholastic
Length: 94 **Age:** 8–12 **Date:** 1980
Main Character: animal
Other Topics: Speech Impediment
Overview: A boy with a speech impediment spends the summer taming a blind range horse.

Carver

Author: Ruth Y. Radin
Publisher: Macmillan
Length: 80 **Age:** 9–12 **Date:** 1990
Main Character: white male
Other Topics: Death of a Parent
Overview: Jon loses both his vision and his father in a car accident. He turns to Carver, a sullen recluse, for support. Carver teaches Jon how to sculpt wooden birds.

Connie's New Eyes

Author: Bernard Wolf
Publisher: Lippincott
Length: 96 **Age:** 10–13 **Date:** 1976
Main Character: white female
Other Topics: N/A
Overview: Blythe becomes a seeing-eye dog for Connie, a teacher of handicapped children.

Follow My Leader

Author: James B. Garfield
Publisher: Apple
Length: 192 **Age:** 8–12 **Date:** 1957

Follow My Leader (cont.)

Main Character: white male
Other Topics: N/A
Overview: When Jimmy is blinded by a fire cracker, he must learn to follow the lead of his seeing-eye dog, Leader.

From Anna

Author: Jean Little
Publisher: Harper
Length: 201 **Age:** 10–12 **Date:** 1972
Main Character: white female
Other Topics: Moving
Overview: In 1933, the Solden family emigrated from Germany to Canada. Nine-year-old Anna is diagnosed as being visually impaired. She goes to a special school to learn English, relate to peers, and gain confidence.

Jenny's Magic Wand

Author: Helen and Bill Hermann
Publisher: Franklin Watts
Length: 27 **Age:** 5–8 **Date:** 1988
Main Character: white female
Other Topics: N/A
Overview: Since Jenny has only attended school with other blind children, she worries about going to school with regular classes in a public school until she learns that she is just one of the kids.

Knots on a Counting Rope

Author: Bill Martin, Jr
Publisher: Henry Holt
Length: 30 **Age:** 5–8 **Date:** 1987
Main Character: Native American male
Other Topics: Intergenerational
Overview: A young Native American boy and his grandfather sit by the campfire and tell stories. The young boy is blind.

Little by Little: A Writer's Education

Author: Jean Little
Publisher: Viking
Length: 224 **Age:** 9–12 **Date:** 1988
Main Character: white female
Other Topics: Growing Up
Overview: Author Jean Little recalls growing up visually disabled.

Mine for a Year

Author: Susan Kuklin
Publisher: Coward
Length: 77 **Age:** 9–11 **Date:** 1984
Main Character: white male
Other Topics: N/A
Overview: A boy takes care of a puppy that will be trained as a guide dog for the blind.

Mom Can't See Me

Author: Sally Hobart Alexander
Publisher: Macmillan
Length: 44 **Age:** 6–10 **Date:** 1990
Main Character: white female
Other Topics: N/A
Overview: Photographs show a family with a very active, blind mother.

One of Us

Author: Nikki Amdur
Publisher: Dial
Length: 133 **Age:** 9–12 **Date:** 1981
Main Character: white female
Other Topics: N/A
Overview: A blind boy helps a young girl adjust to a new school by allowing her to share in the responsibility of caring for a rabbit.

Ray Charles

Author: Sharon Mathis
Publisher: Thomas Y. Crowell

Blind, Visually Impaired (cont.)

Ray Charles (cont.)

Length: 34 **Age:** 6–8 **Date:** 1973
Main Character: African American male
Other Topics: N/A
Overview: This is a biography of an African American musician who became famous despite his blindness.

Red Thread Riddles

Author: Virginia Allen Jensen and Polly Edman
Publisher: Philomel
Length: 22 **Age:** 3–18 **Date:** 1980
Main Character: objects
Other Topics: N/A
Overview: Readers are asked to follow the raised red thread by sight and touch as a "together" experience for blind and sighted friends.

See You Tomorrow, Charles

Author: Miriam Cohen
Publisher: Greenwillow
Length: 28 **Age:** 5–8 **Date:** 1983
Main Character: white male
Other Topics: N/A
Overview: Charles's classmates don't know what to say or do since he is blind.

Seeing in Special Ways: Children Living with Blindness

Author: Thomas Bergman
Publisher: Gareth Stevens
Length: 54 **Age:** 5–10 **Date:** 1989
Main Character: multicultural males and females

Seeing in Special Ways: Children Living with Blindness (cont.)

Other Topics: N/A
Overview: Interviews with a group of blind and partially sighted children in Sweden show how they feel about their disability and the ways they use their other senses to help themselves.

The Cay

Author: Theodore Taylor
Publisher: Doubleday
Length: 137 **Age:** 10–13 **Date:** 1969
Main Character: African American male
Other Topics: Racism, Prejudice
Overview: A black sailor teaches an injured and temporarily blinded boy to be self-sufficient, which causes him to re-examine his prejudices.

The Gift

Author: Helen Coutant
Publisher: Knopf
Length: 30 **Age:** 8–10 **Date:** 1983
Main Character: Asian female
Other Topics: Shyness, Intergenerational
Overview: Ten-year-old Anna befriends an elderly neighbor who has just lost her sight.

The Seeing Stick

Author: Jane Yolen
Publisher: Crowell
Length: 24 **Age:** 5–8 **Date:** 1977
Main Character: Chinese male and female
Other Topics: Intergenerational
Overview: In this story set in ancient China, an old man carves pictures on a stick for a young blind girl.

Through Grandpa's Eyes

Author: Patricia MacLachlan
Publisher: Harper
Length: 34 **Age:** 5–8 **Date:** 1979
Main Character: white male
Other Topics: Intergenerational
Overview: A grandson learns from his blind grandfather to see without his eyes.

Body Safety

Close to Home

Author: Oralee Wachter
Publisher: Scholastic
Length: 48 **Age:** 5–8 **Date:** 1986
Main Character: multicultural males and females
Other Topics: N/A
Overview: This book informs children about how to be safe and how to stay safe.

Danger!

Author: Joy Wilt
Publisher: Weekly Reader Books
Length: 128 **Age:** 8–12 **Date:** 1979
Main Character: multicultural males and females
Other Topics: N/A
Overview: This book discusses handling fear and dangerous things, places, and situations.

Dinosaurs, Beware! A Safety Guide

Author: Marc Brown and Stephen Krensky
Publisher: Little, Brown, and Co.
Length: 32 **Age:** 4–8 **Date:** 1982
Main Character: animal
Other Topics: N/A
Overview: Sixty safety tips are demonstrated by dinosaurs in various situations.

Don't Panic: A Book about Handling Emergencies

Author: Jules Older
Publisher: Western Publishing Co., Inc.
Length: 25 **Age:** 4–8 **Date:** 1986
Main Character: multicultural males and females
Other Topics: N/A
Overview: This very basic book describes how to handle emergency situations.

It's My Body

Author: Lory Freeman
Publisher: Parenting Press
Length: 24 **Age:** 4–6 **Date:** 1986
Main Character: cartoon male
Other Topics: N/A
Overview: Teaches young children how to say "no" to unwanted touches.

It's Okay to Say "Don't!"

Author: Betty Boegehold
Publisher: Western Publishing Co., Inc.
Length: 24 **Age:** 5–8 **Date:** 1985
Main Character: multicultural
Other Topics: N/A
Overview: The purpose of this multisituational book is to help teach children how to use their judgment and common sense and how to get themselves out of difficult situations.

Keep an Eye on Kevin

Author: Genevieve Gray
Publisher: Lothrop, Lee and Shepard
Length: 34 **Age:** 6–9 **Date:** 1973
Main Character: white male and female
Other Topics: Sibling Rivalry
Overview: Accidents begin to happen when Lisa is left to look after her little brother. A list of safety rules for home is also included.

Body Safety (cont.)

Let's Talk About Being Careless

Author: Joy Berry
Publisher: Children's Press
Length: 32 **Age:** 4–6 **Date:** 1984
Main Character: cartoon characters
Other Topics: N/A
Overview: A candid discussion of what could happen if one is careless.

My Body Is Private

Author: Linda Walvoord Girard
Publisher: Albert Whitman and Co.
Length: 32 **Age:** 5–10 **Date:** 1984
Main Character: white female
Other Topics: N/A
Overview: Julie's parents teach her how to say no to unwanted touches.

Never Say Yes to a Stranger

Author: Susan Newman
Publisher: Putnam
Length: 127 **Age:** 7–10 **Date:** 1985
Main Character: white male and female
Other Topics: N/A
Overview: Twelve chapters with stories and photographs about specific incidents for being safe.

No More Secrets for Me

Author: Oralee Wachter
Publisher: Little, Brown
Length: 46 **Age:** 7–10 **Date:** 1983
Main Character: multicultural males and females
Other Topics: N/A
Overview: Four stories on child abuse that show children how to defend themselves.

The Berenstain Bears Learn about Strangers

Author: Stan and Jan Berenstain
Publisher: Random House
Length: 30 **Age:** 4–8 **Date:** 1985
Main Character: animal
Other Topics: N/A
Overview: The bears learn not to be too friendly to strangers. Children's safety rules are included on the last page.

Who Is a Stranger and What Should I Do?

Author: Linda Walvoord Girard
Publisher: Albert Whitman and Co.
Length: 32 **Age:** 6–10 **Date:** 1985
Main Character: white female
Other Topics: N/A
Overview: These two questions are often on the minds of children today. This book explains how to deal with strangers in many situations.

You Can Say "No": A Book About Protecting Yourself

Author: Betty Boegenhold
Publisher: Western Publishing Co.
Length: 22 **Age:** 5–8 **Date:** 1985
Main Character: multicultural males and females
Other Topics: N/A
Overview: This book offers six scenarios to help children learn about body safety.

Bossiness, Boasting, Bullies

Bootsie Barker Bites

Author: Barbara Bottner
Publisher: Putnam

Bootsie Barker Bites (cont.)

Length: 32 **Age:** 4–8 **Date:** 1992
Main Character: white female
Other Topics: N/A
Overview: Bootsie Barker not only bites but also wears cowboy boots so that she can kick better.

A Weekend with Wendell

Author: Kevin Henkes
Publisher: Greenwillow
Length: 30 **Age:** 5–8 **Date:** 1986
Main Character: animal
Other Topics: N/A
Overview: Wendell is bossy and full of practical jokes. Sophie teaches him a lesson.

Arthur's April Fool

Author: Marc Brown
Publisher: Little
Length: 31 **Age:** 6–7 **Date:** 1983
Main Character: animal
Other Topics: N/A
Overview: Arthur gets back at Binky Barnes, the class bully.

Bartholomew the Bossy

Author: Marjorie Weinman Sharmat
Publisher: Macmillan
Length: 32 **Age:** 4–8 **Date:** 1984
Main Character: animal
Other Topics: N/A
Overview: Just because Bartholomew Skunk is popular doesn't mean he can be bossy.

A Bundle of Sticks

Author: Pat R. Mauser
Publisher: Atheneum
Length: 176 **Age:** 9–12 **Date:** 1982
Main Character: white male

A Bundle of Sticks (cont.)

Other Topics: N/A
Overview: After being humiliated by a bully, an eleven-year-old decides to take self-defense lessons.

Bully Trouble

Author: Joanna Cole
Publisher: Random House
Length: 48 **Age:** 6–8 **Date:** 1989
Main Character: white male
Other Topics: N/A
Overview: Arlo and Robby are victims of a neighborhood bully. They make plans to discourage him.

Dazzle

Author: Diane Massie
Publisher: Parents' Magazine Press
Length: 46 **Age:** 5–8 **Date:** 1969
Main Character: peacock
Other Topics: N/A
Overview: Dazzle, the peacock, is convinced his beauty makes him Lord of the Jungle until the lion challenges his claim.

Ghosts in Fourth Grade

Author: Constance Hiser
Publisher: Holiday House
Length: 80 **Age:** 7–11 **Date:** 1991
Main Character: white male
Other Topics: N/A
Overview: When Mean Mitchell, the class bully, punches James in the eye, James and his friends develop a plan to get even.

Goggles!

Author: Ezra Jack Keats
Publisher: Macmillan
Length: 32 **Age:** 5–9 **Date:** 1969
Main Character: African American males

Bossiness, Boasting, Bullies (cont.)

Goggles! (cont.)

Other Topics: N/A
Overview: Two young boys escape from neighborhood bullies.

I Am Better Than You!

Author: Robert Lopshire
Publisher: Harper & Row
Length: 64 **Age:** 5–8 **Date:** 1968
Main Character: animals
Other Topics: N/A
Overview: Two lizards try to outdo each other. The loser fails because he tries to turn the colors of a comic strip.

James Will Never Die

Author: Joanne Oppenheim
Publisher: Dodd, Mead and Co.
Length: 30 **Age:** 5–8 **Date:** 1982
Main Character: white male
Other Topics: Sibling Rivalry, Youngest Child
Overview: The older brother always seems to come out ahead of his younger brother.

Luke's Bully

Author: Elizabeth Winthrop
Publisher: Puffin
Length: 64 **Age:** 6–11 **Date:** 1992
Main Character: white male
Other Topics: Weight Problem
Overview: Arthur is the bully in this chapter book.

Matilda Hippo Has a Big Mouth

Author: Dennis Panek
Publisher: Bradbury
Length: 32 **Age:** 5–7 **Date:** 1980
Main Character: animal
Other Topics: N/A
Overview: Sometimes Matilda's big mouth hurts her friends' feelings.

Seventh-Grade Weirdo

Author: Lee Wardlaw
Publisher: Scholastic
Length: 151 **Age:** 9–12 **Date:** 1992
Main Character: white male
Other Topics: N/A
Overview: Seventh grade is not so wonderful for Christopher Robin. He is embarrassed by his genius sister Winnie and tormented and teased by Shark, the school bully.

Sheila Rae, the Brave

Author: Kevin Henkes
Publisher: Greenwillow
Length: 28 **Age:** 4–8 **Date:** 1987
Main Character: animal
Other Topics: Fear
Overview: Afraid of nothing, Shelia Rae decides to take a different route home— and gets lost.

The Bluejay Boarders

Author: Harold Keith
Publisher: Thomas Y. Crowell
Length: 224 **Age:** 10–12 **Date:** 1972
Main Character: white males and females
Other Topics: N/A
Overview: Tom, Joey, and Susan befriend a bully, Beaky Callahan, and learn about caring for a nest of orphaned, newly hatched blue jays.

Braces

The Popcorn Dragon

Author: Jane Thayer
Publisher: William Morrow and Co.
Length: 48 **Age:** 5–8 **Date:** 1953
Main Character: animal
Other Topics: Jealousy
Overview: Dexter the Dragon brags that he can blow smoke and the other animals cannot. Since the other animals are so envious, they do not want to play with Dexter.

The Revenge of the Incredible Dr. Rancid and His Youthful Assistant, Jeffrey

Author: Ellen Conford
Publisher: Little, Brown, and Co.
Length: 119 **Age:** 10–18 **Date:** 1980
Main Character: white male
Other Topics: Weight Problem
Overview: A small, skinny boy finds a way to challenge the class bully.

Veronica the Show-Off

Author: Nancy K. Robinson
Publisher: Four Winds
Length: 128 **Age:** 8–12 **Date:** 1983
Main Character: white female
Other Topics: N/A
Overview: Veronica shows off in an effort to make friends.

What a Wimp!

Author: Carol Carrick
Publisher: Clarion Books
Length: 89 **Age:** 8–10 **Date:** 1983
Main Character: white male
Other Topics: Divorce
Overview: Barney struggles in dealing with a bully, Lenny.

Looking Good: Teeth and Braces

Author: Arlene Rourke
Publisher: Rourke Publications
Length: 32 **Age:** 8–12 **Date:** 1989
Main Character: multicultural males and females
Other Topics: N/A
Overview: This factual text discusses the function and care of teeth as well as information about how orthodontists straighten teeth with braces.

Smile! How to Cope with Braces

Author: Jeanne Betancourt
Publisher: Knopf
Length: 96 **Age:** 11–14 **Date:** 1982
Main Character: multicultural males and females
Other Topics: N/A
Overview: Advice about caring for braces as well as general information about having teeth straightened is given.

So You're Getting Braces: A Guide to Orthodontics

Author: Alvin and Virginia Silverstein
Publisher: Lippincott
Length: 112 **Age:** 10–14 **Date:** 1978
Main Character: white males and females
Other Topics: N/A
Overview: Facts and advice about the care of braces.

You Can't Put Braces on Spaces

Author: Alice Richter and Laura J. Numeroff
Publisher: Greenwillow Books
Length: 56 **Age:** 5–10 **Date:** 1979
Main Character: white male

Braces (cont.)

You Can't Put Braces on Spaces (cont.)

Other Topics: Jealousy, Sibling Rivalry
Overview: Neil has braces fitted on his teeth and his younger brother is jealous.

Cancer

Afraid to Ask: A Book for Families to Share About Cancer

Author: Judylaine Fine
Publisher: Lothrop, Lee and Shepard Books
Length: 178 **Age:** 10–14 **Date:** 1984
Main Character: N/A
Other Topics: N/A
Overview: The various types of cancer are discussed. Case histories are given as well as the physical and emotional problems involved.

Cancer

Author: Gail K. Haines
Publisher: Franklin Watts
Length: 64 **Age:** 8–12 **Date:** 1980
Main Character: N/A
Other Topics: N/A
Overview: This book investigates cancer, the types, warning signs, treatments, and the present state of research.

Cancer: A New True Book

Author: Dennis Fradin
Publisher: Children's Press
Length: 48 **Age:** 8–12 **Date:** 1988
Main Character: multicultural males and females
Other Topics: N/A

Cancer: A New True Book (cont.)

Overview: Various forms of cancer, their possible causes, treatments and a discussion of who gets cancer are included.

Cancer: The Whispered Word

Author: Judy H. Swenson and Roxanne Kunz
Publisher: Dillon Press
Length: 30 **Age:** 8–10 **Date:** 1986
Main Character: white male
Other Topics: N/A
Overview: Information is presented about cancer, emphasizing those things of particular interest to children and their families. Also included are an adult resource guide, glossary of terms, activities suggested for families, and easy recipes for snacks.

Hang Tough, Paul Mather

Author: Alfred Slote
Publisher: Lippincott
Length: 156 **Age:** 9–12 **Date:** 1973
Main Character: white male
Other Topics: N/A
Overview: Paul is a Little Leaguer who develops leukemia. The family moves from California to Michigan, where Paul will have special treatments. He longs to play baseball.

I Want to Grow Hair, I Want to Grow Up, I Want to Go to Boise

Author: Erma Bombeck
Publisher: Harper and Row
Length: 174 **Age:** 10–18 **Date:** 1989
Main Character: N/A
Other Topics: N/A
Overview: This is a heartwarming book about children surviving cancer.

Kathy's Hats: A Story of Hope

Author: Trudy Krisher
Publisher: Whitman
Length: 32 **Age:** 4–8 **Date:** 1992
Main Character: white female
Other Topics: N/A
Overview: A little girl hates the hats she must wear to cover the baldness caused by cancer, until her mother tells her she should also be wearing a thinking cap. She teaches her daughter that how one thinks about things is important.

My Book for Kids with Cancer

Author: Jason Gaes
Publisher: Houghton Mifflin
Length: 31 **Age:** 4–9 **Date:** 1987
Main Character: white male
Other Topics: N/A
Overview: A young cancer patient tells his story of chemotherapy, surgery, and remission in his battle with cancer.

One Day at a Time: Children Living with Luekemia

Author: Thomas Bergman
Publisher: Gareth Stevens
Length: 56 **Age:** 6–10 **Date:** 1989
Main Character: white males and females
Other Topics: N/A
Overview: This photo-essay focuses on children with leukemia and follows them as they are treated for their illness.

Patty Gets Well

Author: Patricia D. Frevert
Publisher: Creative Education
Length: 47 **Age:** 6–10 **Date:** 1983
Main Character: white female
Other Topics: N/A

Patty Gets Well (cont.)

Overview: This nonfiction story of the Ness family and how Patty survived cancer is very positive and a strong tribute to families.

Sadako and the Thousand Paper Cranes

Author: Eleanor Coerr
Publisher: Putnam
Length: 64 **Age:** 8–10 **Date:** 1977
Main Character: Japanese female
Other Topics: War
Overview: Twelve-year-old Sadako dies of leukemia ten years after the atomic bomb dropped on Hiroshima. During the last months of her life, she folds paper cranes with the hope that when she has folded one thousand she will be well again.

The Long Way Home

Author: Barbara Cohen
Publisher: Lothrop
Length: 170 **Age:** 11–14 **Date:** 1990
Main Character: white females
Other Topics: Weight Problem
Overview: Eleven-year-old twins Sally and Emily grow apart when their mother must undergo a mastectomy and chemotherapy treatments.

There's a Little Bit of Me in Jamey

Author: Diana Amadeo
Publisher: Albert Whitman
Length: 32 **Age:** 6–10 **Date:** 1989
Main Character: white male
Other Topics: Sibling Rivalry
Overview: Brian narrates this story of his ambivalence between his love for younger brother Jamey, a leukemia patient, and his irritation at how much time his parents must give to Jamey.

Cancer (cont.)

When Eric's Mom Fought Cancer

Author: Judith Vigna
Publisher: Albert Whitman and Co.
Length: 32 **Age:** 5–8 **Date:** 1993
Main Character: white male
Other Topics: N/A
Overview: Eric's mother has surgery for breast cancer and then undergoes debilitating chemotherapy.

Cerebral Palsy

A Contest

Author: Sherry N. Payne
Publisher: Carolrhoda Books
Length: 34 **Age:** 6–8 **Date:** 1982
Main Character: white male
Other Topics: Wheelchair
Overview: Mike has cerebral palsy but he can still be a winner in his class.

All by Self

Author: Ron Taylor
Publisher: Light On Publications
Length: 50 **Age:** 5–8 **Date:** 1991
Main Character: white male
Other Topics: Wheelchair
Overview: A father tells the story of his son, who has cerebral palsy. A separate story for adults is also included in the back of the book.

Barry's Sister

Author: Lois Metzger
Publisher: Atheneum
Length: 240 **Age:** 10–18 **Date:** 1992
Main Character: white female
Other Topics: Sibling Rivalry

Barry's Sister (cont.)

Overview: Ellen learns to live with and love a brother with cerebral palsy.

Going Places: Children Living with Cerebral Palsy

Author: Thomas Bergman
Publisher: Gareth Stevens
Length: 48 **Age:** 5–10 **Date:** 1991
Main Character: white male
Other Topics: Wheelchair, Deafness
Overview: Mathias is a charming six-year-old boy who has cerebral palsy. With his serious physical disability, he must use a wheelchair. He is almost totally deaf and requires extra time to learn to do things. Bibliography and index are included.

Howie Helps Himself

Author: Joan Fassler
Publisher: Albert Whitman
Length: 32 **Age:** 6–8 **Date:** 1975
Main Character: white male
Other Topics: Wheelchair
Overview: Howie triumphs when he is able to manipulate his wheelchair by himself.

Mine for Keeps

Author: Jean Little
Publisher: Little, Brown
Length: 186 **Age:** 9–12 **Date:** 1962
Main Character: white female
Other Topics: N/A
Overview: When Sally, who has cerebral palsy, returns from a special school to live at home, she attends regular school and faces many problems.

The Alfred Summer

Author: Jan Slepian
Publisher: Macmillan

The Alfred Summer (cont.)

Length: 119 **Age:** 11–14 **Date:** 1980
Main Character: white male
Other Topics: Mentally Handicapped
Overview: Lester is a fourteen-old
boy with cerebral palsy, an overly protec-
tive mother, and a father who ignores
him. He makes friends with Alfred, a
mentally handicapped boy.

Child Abuse

A Horse Named Sky

Author: Barbara Corcoran
Publisher: Atheneum
Length: 204 **Age:** 8–10 **Date:** 1986
Main Character: white female
Other Topics: Alcoholism
Overview: Georgia and her mother
move to Montana to escape Georgia's
abusive father. There Georgia buys a
horse, a wild mustang.

Child Abuse

Author: William A. Check
Publisher: Chelsea House Publishers
Length: 104 **Age:** 10–14 **Date:** 1989
Main Character: multicultural males
and females
Other Topics: N/A
Overview: The forms of child abuse, its
historical and cultural context, and meth-
ods for dealing with abuse are discussed.

Cracker Jackson

Author: Betsy Byars
Publisher: Viking
Length: 147 **Age:** 10–14 **Date:** 1985
Main Character: white male
Other Topics: N/A

Cracker Jackson (cont.)

Overview: Eleven-year-old Cracker
Jackson discovers that his former babysitter, Alma, is being abused by her hus-
band. He takes Alma to a shelter but she
returns home.

Daisy

Author: Sandy Powell
Publisher: Carolrhoda Books
Length: 38 **Age:** 6–9 **Date:** 1991
Main Character: white female
Other Topics: N/A
Overview: Daisy is being physically
abused by her father. Mrs. Calley, a vol-
unteer tutor, convinces Daisy to tell the
principal about the abuse.

Daphne's Book

Author: Mary Downing Hahn
Publisher: Clarion
Length: 192 **Age:** 11–14 **Date:** 1983
Main Character: white female
Other Topics: Friendship
Overview: Jessica agonizes over her
decision to intervene when she contacts
the Juvenile Authority about the
neglected Daphne and her little sister.

Don't Hurt Laurie!

Author: Willi Davis Roberts
Publisher: Atheneum
Length: 176 **Age:** 9–11 **Date:** 1977
Main Character: white female
Other Topics: N/A
Overview: This story of child abuse
ends on a note of promise and hope.

Don't Hurt Me, Mama

Author: Muriel Stanek
Publisher: Albert Whitman
Length: 32 **Age:** 5–8 **Date:** 1983

Child Abuse (cont.)

Don't Hurt Me, Mama (cont.)

Main Character: white female
Other Topics: Alcoholism
Overview: Acquaints children with the circumstances surrounding child abuse.

Everything You Need to Know About Family Violence

Author: Evan Stark
Publisher: Rosen Publishing Co.
Length: 64 **Age:** 8–10 **Date:** 1989
Main Character: white females
Other Topics: N/A
Overview: This informative book describes abuse against women and children. It also describes what abuse victims are doing to stop it.

Family Violence: How to Recognize and Survive It

Author: Janice Rench
Publisher: Lerner Publications
Length: 60 **Age:** 8–18 **Date:** 1992
Main Character: N/A
Other Topics: N/A
Overview: Information is given by professional counselors about violence in families.

Feeling Safe, Feeling Strong

Author: Susan N. Terkel and Janice Rench
Publisher: Lerner Publications
Length: 60 **Age:** 10–18 **Date:** 1984
Main Character: N/A
Other Topics: N/A
Overview: The authors discuss how to avoid sexual abuse and what to do if it does happen.

Good Night, Mr. Tom

Author: Michelle Magorian
Publisher: Harper
Length: 319 **Age:** 12–14 **Date:** 1981
Main Character: white male
Other Topics: War
Overview: An abused boy is evacuated from war-torn London to the home of a kind, old, country man.

Know About Abuse

Author: Margaret O. Hyde
Publisher: Walker
Length: 93 **Age:** 9–12 **Date:** 1992
Main Character: N/A
Other Topics: N/A
Overview: Hyde discusses the causes and effects of various abuses—prenatal drug use; sexual, physical, and emotional abuse.

Michael's Story: Emotional Abuse and Working with a Counselor

Author: Deborah Anderson and Martha Finne
Publisher: Dillon Press
Length: 46 **Age:** 5–8 **Date:** 1986
Main Character: white male
Other Topics: Weight Problem
Overview: A young boy is emotionally abused by his parents and classmates. He meets with a counselor. Sources of help for abused children are included.

Never, No Matter What

Author: Otto Maryleah
Publisher: Gryphon House
Length: 32 **Age:** 4–8 **Date:** 1992
Main Character: white male and female
Other Topics: N/A
Overview: Mark and Sara must leave an abusive situation. They leave home with their mother and move into a shelter.

No-No the Little Seal

Author: Sherri Patterson
Publisher: Random House
Length: 30 **Age:** 4–8 **Date:** 1986
Main Character: animal
Other Topics: N/A
Overview: This story about children's sexual abuse is for very young children. It was written by a marriage and family counselor as part of her Touch Safety program for Marin County, California, elementary schools.

Raymond

Author: Mark Geller
Publisher: Harper and Row
Length: 89 **Age:** 11–13 **Date:** 1988
Main Character: white male
Other Topics: N/A
Overview: Thirteen-year-old Raymond has endured years of abuse from his father. Finally, he decides to run away.

Robin's Story: Physical Abuse and Seeing the Doctor

Author: Deborah Anderson and Martha Finne
Publisher: Dillon Press
Length: 46 **Age:** 5–8 **Date:** 1986
Main Character: white female
Other Topics: N/A
Overview: A young girl is physically abused by her mother and must see a doctor. The book includes an adult resource guide and sources of help for children.

Silent Fear

Author: Nancy S. Levinson
Publisher: Crestwood House
Length: 64 **Age:** 8–12 **Date:** 1981
Main Character: white female
Other Topics: Foster Home

Silent Fear (cont.)

Overview: Although her social worker assures her that her foster home will be fine, Sara discovers that things could be better.

Slave Dancer

Author: Paula Fox
Publisher: Bradbury
Length: 176 **Age:** 10–12 **Date:** 1973
Main Character: white male
Other Topics: N/A
Overview: A young boy is abducted to serve as a piper on board a slave ship. He is appalled by the brutality he sees before he escapes.

The Facts About Child Abuse

Author: Gail B. Stewart
Publisher: Crestwood House
Length: 47 **Age:** 8–10 **Date:** 1989
Main Character: multicultural
Other Topics: N/A
Overview: This factual text surveys the changing attitudes toward child abuse over the years and discusses various sources of help. A glossary and index are included.

The Lottery Rose

Author: Irene Hunt
Publisher: Putnam
Length: 185 **Age:** 9–12 **Date:** 1976
Main Character: white male
Other Topics: Illiteracy, Reading Problems; Alcoholism, Foster Home
Overview: Seven-year-old Georgie Burgess is abused by his mother and her boyfriend. As a lonely child, he can't read, he sets fires, and acts mean. His greatest joy is found in looking at a book about roses.

Clumsiness

Don't Spill It Again, James

Author: Rosemary Wells
Publisher: Dial
Length: 48 **Age:** 3–8 **Date:** 1977
Main Character: animals
Other Topics: Bossiness
Overview: James is clumsy and his older brother is bossy.

I Was All Thumbs

Author: Bernard Waber
Publisher: Houghton
Length: 48 **Age:** 5–8 **Date:** 1975
Main Character: animal
Other Topics: N/A
Overview: A story of disasters.

Ooops!

Author: Suzy Cline
Publisher: Albert Whitman and Co.
Length: 28 **Age:** 2–6 **Date:** 1988
Main Character: white female
Other Topics: N/A
Overview: A little girl is feeling very clumsy when she trips over her cat, spills her juice, and drops her towel in her bath water. Then she notices that adults often have mishaps too.

What's the Matter, Sylvie, Can't You Ride?

Author: Karen B. Andersen
Publisher: Dial Press
Length: 26 **Age:** 5–8 **Date:** 1981
Main Character: white female
Other Topics: N/A
Overview: Sylvie struggles to learn how to ride her two-wheeler.

Copycat

Tell Me a Trudy

Author: Lore Segal
Publisher: Farrar, Straus and Giroux
Length: 35 **Age:** 5–8 **Date:** 1977
Main Character: white female
Other Topics: Sharing
Overview: In "Trudy and the Copycats," Trudy likes to copy what people say and do.

The Copycat

Author: Kathleen and Donald Hersom
Publisher: Atheneum
Length: 30 **Age:** 5–7 **Date:** 1989
Main Character: animals
Other Topics: N/A
Overview: A cat loves to imitate the sounds of other animals.

Cursing

Elbert's Bad Word

Author: Audrey and Don Wood
Publisher: Harcourt, Brace, and Jovanovich
Length: 29 **Age:** 4–8 **Date:** 1988
Main Character: white male
Other Topics: N/A
Overview: Elbert's bad word jumped out of his pocket and created chaos.

Max, the Bad-Talking Parrot

Author: Patricia B. Demuth
Publisher: Dutton
Length: 30 **Age:** 4–8 **Date:** 1986
Main Character: animal
Other Topics: N/A

Max, the Bad-Talking Parrot (cont.)

Overview: Max, the rhyming parrot, speaks very rudely.

Deaf, Hearing Impaired

A Button in Her Ear

Author: Ada Litchfield
Publisher: Whitman
Length: 32 **Age:** 5–8 **Date:** 1976
Main Character: white female
Other Topics: N/A
Overview: Angela relates how her hearing deficit is detected and corrected with a hearing aid.

A Dance to Still Music

Author: Barbara Corcoran
Publisher: Macmillan
Length: 192 **Age:** 10–14 **Date:** 1974
Main Character: white female
Other Topics: Friendship
Overview: When Margaret faces deafness, she becomes hurt, lonely, and distrustful. However, the arrival of a new and older friend helps her come to grips with her new situation.

A Deaf Child Listened

Author: Anne E. Neimark
Publisher: William Morrow
Length: 116 **Age:** 10–14 **Date:** 1983
Main Character: white male
Other Topics: N/A
Overview: This biography of Thomas Gallaudet describes his work in the education of deaf children in the early 1800s.

A Show of Hands

Author: Mary Beth Sullivan and Linda Bourke
Publisher: Harper and Row
Length: 96 **Age:** 8–10 **Date:** 1980
Main Character: cartoon characters
Other Topics: N/A
Overview: A lighthearted, cartoon-like presentation of the way we communicate with our hands. Finger spelling and methods of attracting the attention of the deaf are included.

Anna's Silent World

Author: Bernard Wolf
Publisher: Harper and Row
Length: 48 **Age:** 5–10 **Date:** 1977
Main Character: white female
Other Topics: N/A
Overview: Anna, who is deaf, attends school and makes friends. In this photo-documentary, Anna's deafness is explained. Lipreading, hearing aids, and other forms of therapy are described.

Apple Is My Sign

Author: Mary Riskind
Publisher: Houghton Mifflin
Length: 146 **Age:** 10–13 **Date:** 1981
Main Character: white male
Other Topics: Loneliness
Overview: Ten-year-old Harry Berger, nicknamed "Apple" because of his family's orchard, is sent to a school for the deaf in Philadelphia. While his whole family is deaf, Apple is the first one to go away and he is lonely.

Becky

Author: Karen Hirsch
Publisher: Carolrhoda Books
Length: 36 **Age:** 6–8 **Date:** 1981
Main Character: white female

Deaf, Hearing Impaired (cont.)

Becky (cont.)

Other Topics: N/A
Overview: Becky is deaf but lives with a hearing family so that she can attend a special school.

Cindy, A Hearing Ear Dog

Author: Patricia Curtis
Publisher: Dutton
Length: 64 **Age:** 8–11 **Date:** 1981
Main Character: white female
Other Topics: N/A
Overview: This book of photographs shows Cindy training as a Hearing Ear Dog.

Claire and Emma

Author: Diana Peter
Publisher: John Day Co.
Length: 32 **Age:** 4–8 **Date:** 1976
Main Character: white females
Other Topics: N/A
Overview: The mother of four-year-old Claire and two-year-old Emma describes their hearing aids and their lessons in lip-reading and lipspeaking. The book emphasizes the special communication skills needed by these two girls.

Dad and Me in the Morning

Author: Patricia Lakin
Publisher: Albert Whitman and Co.
Length: 32 **Age:** 6–8 **Date:** 1994
Main Character: white male
Other Topics: N/A
Overview: A young boy who is hearing impaired must wear hearing aids. He enjoys walking on the beach with his father.

Finding a Common Language: Children Living with Deafness

Author: Thomas Bergman
Publisher: Gareth Stevens
Length: 48 **Age:** 6–10 **Date:** 1987
Main Character: white female
Other Topics: N/A
Overview: This photo-essay follows the activities of a six-year-old Swedish girl as she attends a nursery school for the deaf. Bibliographical references and index are included.

Gideon Ahoy!

Author: William Mayne
Publisher: Delacorte
Length: 155 **Age:** 10–15 **Date:** 1989
Main Character: white male
Other Topics: N/A
Overview: An English family loves Gideon even though he is deaf and brain damaged. They encourage him to get and keep a job.

Handtalk: An ABC of Finger Spelling and Sign Language

Author: Remy Charlip and Mary Beth Miller
Publisher: Parents' Magazine Press
Length: 48 **Age:** 6–9 **Date:** 1974
Main Character: N/A
Other Topics: N/A
Overview: Photographs illustrate sign language in action.

Handtalk Birthday

Author: Remy Charlip and Mary Beth Miller
Publisher: Four Winds
Length: 48 **Age:** 4–18 **Date:** 1987
Main Character: white female
Other Topics: N/A

Handtalk Birthday (cont.)

Overview: This is a number and story book in sign language.

Handtalk School

Author: Mary Beth Miller and George Ancona
Publisher: Four Winds
Length: 31 **Age:** 8–12 **Date:** 1991
Main Character: N/A
Other Topics: N/A
Overview: Words and sign language depict a group of students involved in putting on a Thanksgiving play at a school for deaf children.

Handtalk Zoo

Author: George Ancona and Mary Beth Miller
Publisher: Fourwinds
Length: 28 **Age:** 4–18 **Date:** 1989
Main Character: multicultural males and females
Other Topics: N/A
Overview: This picture book uses photographs of children teaching sign language at a zoo.

I Have a Sister—My Sister Is Deaf

Author: Jeanne W. Peterson
Publisher: Harper and Row
Length: 30 **Age:** 3–8 **Date:** 1977
Main Character: Asian American female
Other Topics: N/A
Overview: A young girl describes how her younger deaf sister copes with everyday life.

I'm Deaf and It's Okay

Author: Lorraine Aseltine and E. Mueller
Publisher: Albert Whitman and Co.

I'm Deaf and It's Okay (cont.)

Length: 40 **Age:** 6–8 **Date:** 1986
Main Character: white male
Other Topics: N/A
Overview: A boy discusses his dilemmas with being deaf.

Lisa and Her Soundless World

Author: Edna Levine
Publisher: Behavioural Publications
Length: 30 **Age:** 8–10 **Date:** 1974
Main Character: white female
Other Topics: N/A
Overview: This book addresses the abilities and limitations of a hearing-impaired child.

Living with Deafness

Author: Barbara Taylor
Publisher: Franklin Watts
Length: 32 **Age:** 10–18 **Date:** 1989
Main Character: multicultural males and females
Other Topics: N/A
Overview: This book discusses various forms and degrees of deafness, how it may be caused, how it can be treated and how individuals cope with it.

Mandy

Author: Barbara Booth
Publisher: Lothrop, Lee and Shepard
Length: 32 **Age:** 5–8 **Date:** 1991
Main Character: white female
Other Topics: Fear
Overview: Mandy is hearing impaired and afraid of the dark. However, she is able to help her grandmother search for a pin in the grass.

Deaf, Hearing Impaired (cont.)

My First Book of Sign

Author: Pamela Baker
Publisher: Gallaudet Press
Length: 76 **Age:** 5–8 **Date:** 1986
Main Character: N/A
Other Topics: N/A
Overview: Cartoon pictures of children demonstrate the forming in sign language of 150 basic alphabetically arranged words, accompanied by illustrations of the words themselves.

The Bookseller's Advice

Author: Sue Breitner
Publisher: Viking
Length: 28 **Age:** 5–8 **Date:** 1981
Main Character: white male
Other Topics: Intergenerational
Overview: A hearing-impaired bookseller is much sought after for his knowledge and advice. However, he gets his clients' problems confused because of his inability to hear.

The Gift of the Girl Who Couldn't Hear

Author: Susan Shreve
Publisher: Tambourine
Length: 80 **Age:** 10–12 **Date:** 1991
Main Character: white female
Other Topics: friendship
Overview: Eliza is willing to help her deaf friend Lucy learn to sing.

The Handmade Alphabet

Author: Laura Rankin
Publisher: Dial Books
Length: 27 **Age:** 5–12 **Date:** 1991
Main Character: N/A

The Handmade Alphabet (cont.)

Other Topics: N/A
Overview: This "wordless" alphabet book introduces the manual alphabet of American Sign Language. Each picture shows the hand and finger positions for making a letter of the alphabet.

The Swing

Author: Emily Hanlon
Publisher: Bradbury
Length: 224 **Age:** 10–12 **Date:** 1979
Main Character: white female
Other Topics: N/A
Overview: Beth has been deaf since birth. The swing is a refuge for her and her neighbor Danny.

Where's Spot? Sign Language Edition

Author: Eric Hill
Publisher: G.P. Putnam's Sons
Length: 21 **Age:** 3–8 **Date:** 1980
Main Character: animal
Other Topics: N/A
Overview: This manipulative toy book follows Spot through his hiding places. Also included is sign language, produced in consultation with Gallaudet University Press.

Words in Our Hands

Author: Ada Litchfield
Publisher: Whitman
Length: 32 **Age:** 7–9 **Date:** 1980
Main Character: white male
Other Topics: Moving, Anger
Overview: Michael explains his family life with deaf parents. Also presented are facts about deafness and the language of signing.

Death (General)

About Dying: An Open Family Book for Parents and Children Together

Author: Sarah Bonnett Stein
Publisher: Walker and Co.
Length: 47 **Age:** 5–8 **Date:** 1974
Main Character: white male and female
Other Topics: Death of a Pet, Death of a Grandparent
Overview: This dual-text book is designed for both children and adults. The story for the child is accompanied by an informative text for adults. Jane and Eric have a pet bird named Snow who dies. Then their grandfather dies.

Beyond the Ridge

Author: Paul Goble
Publisher: Bradbury
Length: 32 **Age:** 10–12 **Date:** 1989
Main Character: Native American female
Other Topics: N/A
Overview: An elderly Plains Indian experiences an afterlife as believed by her people.

Coping with Death and Grief

Author: Marge E. Heegaard
Publisher: Lerner Publications Company
Length: 64 **Age:** 8–10 **Date:** 1990
Main Character: multicultural males and females
Other Topics: N/A
Overview: The author discusses death as a natural occurrence and ways to deal with the loss and grief.

Dealing with Death

Author: Norma Gaffon
Publisher: Lucent Book Inc.
Length: 111 **Age:** 9–14 **Date:** 1989
Main Character: N/A
Other Topics: N/A
Overview: A thorough explanation of the multiple aspects of death—biological, emotional, legal, and philosophical. Coping strategies are also suggested.

Jake and Honeybunch Go to Heaven

Author: Margot Zemach
Publisher: Farrar, Straus, & Giroux
Length: 39 **Age:** 8–11 **Date:** 1982
Main Character: African American male
Other Topics: N/A
Overview: This book deals with a literal interpretation of heaven. Two people die and enter heaven where they find ordinary people doing ordinary things. The story itself is based on a black folk tale.

Lifetimes

Author: Bryan Mellonie
Publisher: Bantam Books
Length: 40 **Age:** all **Date:** 1983
Main Character: N/A
Other Topics: N/A
Overview: Death is handled with grace and beauty as a universal end to the life cycle.

The Dead Tree

Author: Alvin Tresselt
Publisher: Parent's Magazine
Length: 28 **Age:** 4–8 **Date:** 1972
Main Character: object
Other Topics: N/A
Overview: A beautiful story about the natural death of a tree.

Death (General) (cont.)

The Fall of Freddie the Leaf

Author: Leo Buscaglia
Publisher: Slack
Length: 27 **Age:** 3–18 **Date:** 1982
Main Character: object
Other Topics: N/A
Overview: This book illustrates how death is a natural part of life.

The Kids' Book About Death and Dying: By and For Kids

Author: Eric E. Rofes (ed.)
Publisher: Little
Length: 119 **Age:** 10–14 **Date:** 1985
Main Character: multicultural males and females
Other Topics: N/A
Overview: Children share their stories of dealing and coping with death.

The Saddest Time

Author: Norma Simon
Publisher: Albert Whitman and Company
Length: 40 **Age:** 5–8 **Date:** 1986
Main Character: multicultural males and females
Other Topics: N/A
Overview: In three stories, Simon focuses on the powerful emotions children feel when death touches their lives.

When People Die

Author: Joanne E. Bernstein and Steven V. Gullo
Publisher: Dutton
Length: 40 **Age:** 5–8 **Date:** 1977
Main Character: N/A

When People Die (cont.)

Other Topics: N/A
Overview: A sensible yet comprehensive discussion of death.

Death of a Friend

A Ring of Endless Light

Author: Madeleine L'Engle
Publisher: Farrar, Straus, & Giroux
Length: 324 **Age:** 10–12 **Date:** 1980
Main Character: white female
Other Topics: Suicide, Intergenerational, Friendship
Overview: Vicky Austin begins her sixteenth summer at a funeral for a family friend who suffered a heart attack after rescuing a spoiled teenager from an attempted suicide.

A Taste of Blackberries

Author: Doris B. Smith
Publisher: Thomas Y. Crowell Co.
Length: 58 **Age:** 7–10 **Date:** 1973
Main Character: white male
Other Topics: Guilt, Allergies
Overview: The young narrator expresses denial, guilt, and grief concerning the unexpected death of his friend.

Bridge to Terabithia

Author: Katherine Paterson
Publisher: Harper
Length: 128 **Age:** 10–13 **Date:** 1977
Main Character: white male
Other Topics: Friendship
Overview: A boy must handle the sudden death of his best friend.

I Had a Friend Named Peter

Author: Janice Cohn
Publisher: William Morrow
Length: 30 **Age:** 4–8 **Date:** 1987
Main Character: white male
Other Topics: Friendship
Overview: Talking to children about the death of a friend. There is an introduction to adults by the author, a psychotherapist.

On My Honor

Author: Marion D. Bauer
Publisher: Houghton Mifflin
Length: 90 **Age:** 10–18 **Date:** 1986
Main Character: white male
Other Topics: N/A
Overview: Tony and Joel ride their bikes to the bluffs outside of town when they decide to stop for a swim. Tony is swept away and drowns. Joel is so horrified that when he returns home, he can't tell anyone what has happened but withdraws to his room.

Say Goodnight, Gracie

Author: Julie R. Deaver
Publisher: Harper
Length: 214 **Age:** 12–18 **Date:** 1988
Main Character: white male and female
Other Topics: Friendship
Overview: Morgan and Jimmy were friends growing up together. After an accident, Morgan has to face life alone. Without Jimmy, she feels like a part of her has died.

Thank You, Jackie Robinson

Author: Barbara Cohen
Publisher: Lothrop, Lee, and Shepard
Length: 125 **Age:** 9–11 **Date:** 1974
Main Character: African American male

Thank You, Jackie Robinson (cont.)

Other Topics: Racism, Prejudice, Loneliness
Overview: Sam is a lonely boy who has a strong passion for the Dodgers. He befriends Davey, the black cook at Davey's mother's country inn. Davey becomes ill, is hospitalized, and dies. Sam has memories of his own father's death and grieves.

The Class in Room 44

Author: Lynn Bennett Blackburn
Publisher: Centering Corporation
Length: 30 **Age:** 6–10 **Date:** 1991
Main Character: multicultural
Other Topics: N/A
Overview: Deals with the death of Tony and how his teacher and class dealt with the loss.

The Empty Window

Author: Eve Bunting
Publisher: Warne
Length: 48 **Age:** 7–10 **Date:** 1980
Main Character: white male
Other Topics: Friendship
Overview: C.G. must face the impending death of his friend, Joe, who lives downstairs in their inner-city apartment house. C.G. is afraid to visit Joe at first.

Timothy Duck

Author: Lynn Bennett Blackburn
Publisher: Centering Corp.
Length: 30 **Age:** 4–8 **Date:** 1987
Main Character: animal
Other Topics: N/A
Overview: A simple story of the death of a friend.

Death of a Friend (cont.)

Toothpick

Author: Kenneth E. Ethridge
Publisher: Holiday House
Length: 128 **Age:** 12–18 **Date:** 1985
Main Character: white male and female
Other Topics: N/A
Overview: Jamie is teased about his friendship with a girl who is terminally ill.

We Remember Philip

Author: Norma Simon
Publisher: Albert Whitman and Company
Length: 28 **Age:** 5–8 **Date:** 1979
Main Character: white male
Other Topics: N/A
Overview: Sam and his classmates are sad when their teacher's son accidentally dies.

Death of a Grandparent

After the Rain

Author: Norma Fox Mazer
Publisher: Morrow
Length: 249 **Age:** 11–14 **Date:** 1987
Main Character: white female
Other Topics: Aging
Overview: A girl develops a close relationship with her grandfather, then mourns his death.

Annie and the Old One

Author: Miska Miles
Publisher: Little
Length: 44 **Age:** 5–9 **Date:** 1972
Main Character: Native American female
Other Topics: Intergenerational
Overview: When Grandmother tells her family that she will die as soon as a hand-made rug is woven, Annie tries to hold back time by removing strands of yarn from the rug. Annie finally accepts her impending death.

Blackberries in the Dark

Author: Mavis Jukes
Publisher: Knopf
Length: 48 **Age:** 6–9 **Date:** 1985
Main Character: white male
Other Topics: N/A
Overview: Avis spends the summer on the farm with Grandma and is constantly reminded of his grandfather's absence. Together they try to come to terms with their loss.

Christmas Moon

Author: Denys Cazet
Publisher: Bradbury
Length: 32 **Age:** 4–7 **Date:** 1984
Main Character: animal
Other Topics: N/A
Overview: When Patrick, a small rabbit, can't sleep at night after his grandfather dies, his mother shows him the beautiful Christmas moon.

First Snow

Author: Helen Coutant
Publisher: Knopf
Length: 33 **Age:** 6–8 **Date:** 1974
Main Character: Vietnamese female
Other Topics: Intergenerational

First Snow (cont.)

Overview: A young Vietnamese girl struggles to understand her grandmother's impending death. Lien's grandmother helps her to understand the Buddhist view of life and death.

My Grandma Leonie

Author: Bijou Le Tord
Publisher: Bradbury Press
Length: 32   **Age:**   3–7   **Date:**   1987
Main Character: white female and male
Other Topics: N/A
Overview: A child tells of the loss of his grandmother.

My Grandpa Died Today

Author: Joan Fassler
Publisher: Behavioral Publishers
Length: 28   **Age:**   4–8   **Date:**   1971
Main Character: white male
Other Topics: Intergenerational
Overview: A young boy tells the story of his grandpa and how sad he felt when he died.

Nana Upstairs—Nana Downstairs

Author: Tomie de Paola
Publisher: Putnam
Length: 32   **Age:**   3–8   **Date:**   1973
Main Character: white male
Other Topics: Aging
Overview: A sensitive story about Tommy and the death of his grandmother.

The Great Change

Author: White Deer of Autumn
Publisher: Beyond Words
Length: 32   **Age:**   4–8   **Date:**   1992
Main Character: Native American female

The Great Change (cont.)

Other Topics: N/A
Overview: A Native American grandmother explains the meaning of death, or the Great Change, to her granddaughter.

The Key into Winter

Author: Janet Anderson
Publisher: Albert Whitman and Co.
Length: 32   **Age:**   7–10   **Date:**   1994
Main Character: African American female
Other Topics: Intergenerational
Overview: Mattie's beloved grandmother is dying and Mattie is determined to save her.

The Two of Them

Author: Aliki
Publisher: Greenwillow
Length: 26   **Age:**   4–7   **Date:**   1979
Main Character: white female
Other Topics: Intergenerational
Overview: This story relates the experiences of a little girl and her grandfather. He becomes ill and the girl must care for him. When he dies, she grieves but remembers the happy memories too.

Then I'll Be Home Free

Author: Phyllis Anderson Wood
Publisher: Dodd, Mead and Company
Length: 239   **Age:**   12–14   **Date:**   1986
Main Character: white female
Other Topics: N/A
Overview: When her beloved grandmother dies during Rosemary's junior year in high school, Rosemary tries to comfort her grandfather and form new relationships for herself.

Death of a Grandparent (cont.)

When Grandfather Journeys into Winter

Author: Craig Kee Strete
Publisher: Greenwillow
Length: 86 **Age:** 8–10 **Date:** 1979
Main Character: Native American male
Other Topics: Racism, Prejudice
Overview: Since his father's death, Little Thunder is very close to his grandfather, Tayhua. When Little Thunder learns his grandfather is ill, he is fearful. Little Thunder spends the last day of his grandfather's life with him as his grandfather describes life as a journey.

When Grandpa Died

Author: Margaret Stevens
Publisher: Children's Press
Length: 30 **Age:** 5–8 **Date:** 1979
Main Character: white female
Other Topics: Intergenerational
Overview: A young girl tries to deal with her grandfather's death.

Why Did He Die?

Author: Audrey Harris
Publisher: Lerner Publications Co.
Length: 28 **Age:** 5–8 **Date:** 1965
Main Character: white male
Other Topics: Intergenerational
Overview: This story, written in rhyming verse, tells about the death of Jim's grandfather. His father shows him that death is necessary in the natural order of things.

Death of a Parent

A Sound of Chariots

Author: Mollie Hunter
Publisher: Harper and Row
Length: 173 **Age:** 12–15 **Date:** 1972
Main Character: white female
Other Topics: N/A
Overview: This autobiography is the story of a young Scottish girl coming to terms with her father's death.

Everett Anderson's Goodbye

Author: Lucille Clifton
Publisher: Holt, Rinehart, and Winston
Length: 30 **Age:** 3–6 **Date:** 1983
Main Character: African American male
Other Topics: N/A
Overview: Winner of Coretta King Award—Everett eats, but what's the good of food after Dad dies. Each stage of grief is described.

Father Figure

Author: Richard Peck
Publisher: Viking
Length: 182 **Age:** 12–18 **Date:** 1992
Main Character: white male
Other Topics: Divorce
Overview: When their mother dies, two brothers get to know their father—who divorced their mother eight years previously.

Fourth Grade Wizards

Author: Barthe DeClements
Publisher: Puffin Books
Length: 122 **Age:** 8–12 **Date:** 1988
Main Character: white female
Other Topics: N/A

Fourth Grade Wizards (cont.)

Overview:　After her mother dies, Mari-anne becomes a daydreamer and falls behind in her schoolwork.

Geranium Morning

Author:　Sandy Powell
Publisher:　Carolrhoda Books
Length:　38 **Age:**　6–9 **Date:**　1990
Main Character:　white male and female
Other Topics:　N/A
Overview:　The death of a parent is sensitively addressed in this book for young readers.

Mama, Let's Dance

Author:　Patricia Hermes
Publisher:　Scholastic
Length:　168 **Age:**　8–12 **Date:**　1991
Main Character:　white male and females
Other Topics:　Honesty
Overview:　When Papa dies and Mama abandons them, Mary Belle decides to make up some lies so that she, her brother Ariel, and her sister Callie will not be separated.

Pennies for the Piper

Author:　Susan McLeon
Publisher:　Sunburst
Length:　160 **Age:**　10–18 **Date:**　1993
Main Character:　white female
Other Topics:　N/A
Overview:　Ten-year-old Bicks must move to her aunt's home in Iowa when her mother dies.

Saying Goodbye to Daddy

Author:　Judith Vigna
Publisher:　Albert Whitman
Length:　32 **Age:**　5–8 **Date:**　1991
Main Character:　white female

Saying Goodbye to Daddy (cont.)

Other Topics:　N/A
Overview:　Clare's daddy dies in a car accident and she experiences a wide range of emotions.

Seaward

Author:　Susan Cooper
Publisher:　Macmillan
Length:　180 **Age:**　11–14 **Date:**　1983
Main Character:　white male and female
Other Topics:　N/A
Overview:　Two teens try to adjust to the loss of their respective parents. West and Cally, who speak different languages and come from different countries, are torn from reality into a perilous world through which they must travel toward the sea.

The Princess in the Kitchen Garden

Author:　Annemie and Margriet Heymans
Publisher:　Farrar, Straus, and Giroux
Length:　48 **Age:**　5–8 **Date:**　1993
Main Character:　white female
Other Topics:　N/A
Overview:　Hannah mourns the loss of her mother by running away to her old garden.

There Are Two Kinds of Terrible

Author:　Peggy Mann
Publisher:　Doubleday
Length:　132 **Age:**　10–12 **Date:**　1977
Main Character:　white male
Other Topics:　Cancer, Loneliness
Overview:　At first, Robbie Farley felt that breaking his arm on the first day of summer vacation was the most terrible thing that could happen until his mother dies of cancer. He also must deal with the cool and quiet stranger who is his father.

Death of a Parent (cont.)

Tiger Eyes

Author: Judy Blume
Publisher: Bradbury
Length: 222 **Age:** 12–14 **Date:** 1981
Main Character: white female
Other Topics: Fear
Overview: Fifteen-year-old Davey tries to adjust to the death of her father, who was robbed and killed in a convenience store.

To Hell with Dying

Author: Alice Walker
Publisher: Harcourt, Brace, and Jovanovich
Length: 28 **Age:** 8–12 **Date:** 1967
Main Character: African American male
Other Topics: Intergenerational
Overview: The children are saddened by Mr. Sweet's death.

Upside Down

Author: Mary Jane Miller
Publisher: Viking
Length: 128 **Age:** 8–12 **Date:** 1991
Main Character: white female
Other Topics: N/A
Overview: Since her father's death, Sara's life has been turned upside down. Her brother spends more time with his girlfriend than he does with Sara, and her mother is dating again. Sara feels out of control.

Winter Camp

Author: Kirkpatrick Hill
Publisher: Margaret K. McElderry Books
Length: 185 **Age:** 10–12 **Date:** 1993
Main Character: Native American male and female
Other Topics: Survival
Overview: After their parents' deaths, eleven-year-old Toughboy and his younger sister must survive the winter at a friend's trapping camp in Alaska.

Death of a Pet

Do You Love Me?

Author: Dick Gackenbach
Publisher: Seabury Press
Length: 46 **Age:** 6–8 **Date:** 1975
Main Character: white male
Other Topics: N/A
Overview: The accidental death of a hummingbird helps Walter understand the different needs of animals. Not all animals make good pets.

Frog and the Birdsong

Author: Max Velthuijs
Publisher: Farrar, Straus, and Giroux
Length: 32 **Age:** 5–8 **Date:** 1991
Main Character: animal
Other Topics: N/A
Overview: Frog finds a dead bird and must bury it.

Growing Time

Author: Sandol S. Warburg
Publisher: Houghton Mifflin
Length: 44 **Age:** 5–8 **Date:** 1969

Growing Time (cont.)

Main Character: white male
Other Topics: Intergenerational
Overview: Jamie is very sad and bitter when his dog dies of old age. His grandmother explains that the spirit of something you love can never die. Jamie is then ready for a new puppy.

I'll Always Love You

Author: B. H. Wilhelm
Publisher: Scholastic
Length: 29 **Age:** 3–6 **Date:** 1985
Main Character: white male
Other Topics: N/A
Overview: This is the story of a boy and his dog Effie. Effie eventually grows old and can no longer do everything she once could. When she dies, the boy is comforted with the thought that he had told her he would always love her.

Jim's Dog Muffins

Author: Miriam Cohen
Publisher: Greenwillow
Length: 32 **Age:** 4–7 **Date:** 1984
Main Character: white male
Other Topics: Anger
Overview: Jim is upset when his dog is run over by a garbage truck. His classmates try to console him by writing a letter, but Jim needs time to be sad.

Old Yeller

Author: Fred Gipson
Publisher: First Perennial Library
Length: 184 **Age:** 9–12 **Date:** 1964
Main Character: white male
Other Topics: N/A
Overview: A boy is forced to shoot his rabid dog.

Petey

Author: Tobi Tobias
Publisher: Putnam
Length: 31 **Age:** 5–8 **Date:** 1978
Main Character: white female
Other Topics: N/A
Overview: Emily is sad when her pet gerbil Petey dies. Yet she begins to understand that life will continue and changes are inevitable.

Sunny, The Death of a Pet

Author: Judith Greenberg and Helen Carey
Publisher: Franklin Watts
Length: 32 **Age:** 4–7 **Date:** 1986
Main Character: white male
Other Topics: N/A
Overview: Bill is sad when his pet dog Sunny dies. Another puppy helps his grief.

The Accident

Author: Carol Carrick
Publisher: Clarion
Length: 32 **Age:** 5–8 **Date:** 1976
Main Character: white male
Other Topics: N/A
Overview: Story of the death of a pet. Christopher's dog Bodger is run over by a truck and killed.

The Black Dog Who Went into the Woods

Author: Edith Hurd
Publisher: Harper and Row
Length: 32 **Age:** 6–8 **Date:** 1980
Main Character: white male
Other Topics: N/A
Overview: Black Dog disappeared into the woods and Benjamen knows he has died. Yet during the night, Benjamen and his family have happy dreams about Black Dog.

Death of a Pet (cont.)

The Comeback Dog

Author: Jane Resh Thomas
Publisher: Clarion
Length: 62 **Age:** 8–11 **Date:** 1981
Main Character: white male
Other Topics: N/A
Overview: When Daniel's dog Captain dies, he is not sure he wants another pet, until he finds Lady.

The Dead Bird

Author: Margaret Wise Brown
Publisher: Addison-Wesley Co.
Length: 42 **Age:** 4–6 **Date:** 1938
Main Character: white males and females
Other Topics: N/A
Overview: Some young children find a dead bird and decide to bury it in the woods. They plan the funeral to include a song and a small marker. The children cry because the bird is dead and return to the site often to sing their song and to leave flowers.

The Foundling

Author: Carol and Donald Carrick
Publisher: Clarion
Length: 32 **Age:** 5–8 **Date:** 1977
Main Character: white male
Other Topics: N/A
Overview: In this sequel to *The Accident*, Christopher's dad takes him to the local animal shelter to get a new pet after Bodger is killed. Christopher feels unfaithful to Bodger's memory and initially won't select a dog.

The Tenth Good Thing About Barney

Author: Judith Viorst
Publisher: Atheneum
Length: 25 **Age:** 4–9 **Date:** 1971
Main Character: white male
Other Topics: N/A
Overview: Barney, the family cat, dies. At his funeral, his young owner can tell nine good things about Barney. After working in the garden with his father, the young narrator thinks of the tenth good thing about Barney.

The Trouble with Thirteen

Author: Betty Miles
Publisher: Knopf
Length: 108 **Age:** 10–12 **Date:** 1979
Main Character: white female
Other Topics: Growing Up
Overview: Annie is approaching her thirteenth birthday when her dog Nora dies.

The Yearling

Author: Marjorie K. Rawlings
Publisher: Scribner
Length: 405 **Age:** 12–18 **Date:** 1938
Main Character: white male
Other Topics: N/A
Overview: Jody is ordered to shoot his pet deer because it is ruining the family crops.

When Violet Died

Author: Mildred Kantrowitz
Publisher: Parents' Magazine Press
Length: 27 **Age:** 5–8 **Date:** 1973
Main Character: multicultural male and female
Other Topics: N/A
Overview: When their pet bird dies, the children have an elaborate funeral.

Whiskers, Once and Always

Author: Doris Orgel
Publisher: Viking
Length: 82 **Age:** 6–11 **Date:** 1986
Main Character: white female
Other Topics: Anger
Overview: Rebecca's cat Whiskers is badly injured and she must face his death. Rebecca finds it difficult to vent her anger and to accept her mother's comfort.

Death of a Relative

Circle of Gold

Author: Candy Dawson Boyd
Publisher: Apple
Length: 128 **Age:** 8–12 **Date:** 1984
Main Character: African American female
Other Topics: N/A
Overview: When Mattie's father dies, her mother seems to take it out on Mattie. Mattie decides to come up with a plan to bring her family back together again.

Cousins

Author: Virginia Hamilton
Publisher: Philomel
Length: 125 **Age:** 3–6 **Date:** 1990
Main Character: African American male
Other Topics: Intergenerational
Overview: Cammy is almost intolerant of her perfect cousin, Patricia Ann. She feels guilty about those feelings, however, when Patricia Ann accidentally drowns. Her grandmother helps Cammy understand her mixed feelings.

Death and Illness

Author: Leslie McGuire
Publisher: Rourke Corporation
Length: 62 **Age:** 10–14 **Date:** 1990
Main Character: multicultural males and females
Other Topics: N/A
Overview: This nonfiction book describes what it is like to have someone you love face a terminal illness and death.

Devil's Bridge

Author: Cynthia De Felice
Publisher: Macmillan
Length: 95 **Age:** 9–12 **Date:** 1992
Main Character: white male
Other Topics: Honesty
Overview: Twelve-year-old Ben Daggett discovers that someone is planning on cheating to win the annual Striped Bass Derby. Ben must cope with his father's death in this coming-of-age story.

Good-bye, Chicken Little

Author: Betsy Byars
Publisher: Harper and Row
Length: 101 **Age:** 10–12 **Date:** 1979
Main Character: white male
Other Topics: Alcoholism
Overview: Jimmie Little comes from a strange family. His Uncle Pete gets drunk one day and accidentally drowns in Jimmie's presence. Jimmie feels guilty and responsible.

Grover

Author: Vera and Bill Cleaver
Publisher: Lippincott
Length: 125 **Age:** 11–13 **Date:** 1970
Main Character: white male
Other Topics: Suicide, Cancer

Death of a Relative (cont.)

Grover (cont.)

Overview: A young boy feels anger and frustration following his mother's suicide. He also has a difficult time relating to his father.

How It Feels When a Parent Dies

Author: Jill Krementz
Publisher: Knopf
Length: 128 **Age:** 11–15 **Date:** 1981
Main Character: multicultural males and females
Other Topics: N/A
Overview: Intimate interviews, including true first-person statements, of children from diverse backgrounds and circumstances.

Learning to Say Good-bye: When a Parent Dies

Author: Eda LeShan
Publisher: Macmillan
Length: 96 **Age:** 7–10 **Date:** 1976
Main Character: multicultural males and females
Other Topics: N/A
Overview: Insightful book about children's feelings when their parents die. Also includes practical advice.

Night Swimmer

Author: Betsy Byars
Publisher: Delacorte
Length: 125 **Age:** 10–12 **Date:** 1980
Main Character: white female
Other Topics: Growing Up

Night Swimmer (cont.)

Overview: In a motherless home, Retta cares for her younger brothers but has trouble allowing them to become independent. They sneak into a neighbor's pool to swim one night and the youngest almost drowns.

Saying Goodbye to Grandma

Author: Jane Resh Thomas
Publisher: Clarion
Length: 48 **Age:** 8–10 **Date:** 1988
Main Character: white female
Other Topics: N/A
Overview: Shows a typical American funeral. Seven-year-old Suzie and her parents return to the small town where Mother grew up to attend Grandma's funeral.

Sister

Author: Eloise Greenfield
Publisher: Crowell
Length: 83 **Age:** 10–12 **Date:** 1974
Main Character: African American female
Other Topics: N/A
Overview: Doretha is ten and called "Sister" by her family. She keeps a diary in which she describes her father's sudden death.

That Julia Redfern

Author: Eleanor Cameron
Publisher: Dutton
Length: 133 **Age:** 8–10 **Date:** 1982
Main Character: white female
Other Topics: N/A
Overview: A girl develops a close relationship with her father, then accepts his death.

The Cat Next Door

Author: Betty Ren Wright
Publisher: Holiday House
Length: 32 **Age:** 4–8 **Date:** 1991
Main Character: white female
Other Topics: Intergenerational
Overview: A young girl copes with the death of her grandmother with the help of the cat next door.

The Edge of Next Year

Author: Mary Stolz
Publisher: Harper
Length: 195 **Age:** 10–13 **Date:** 1974
Main Character: white male
Other Topics: N/A
Overview: This book describes the problems a close family must face when one of them dies.

The Empty Chair

Author: Bess Kaplan
Publisher: Harper
Length: 243 **Age:** 11–13 **Date:** 1978
Main Character: Jewish female
Other Topics: Stepmother
Overview: Eleven-year-old Becky must adjust to the death of her mother and the acceptance of a stepmother.

The Happy Funeral

Author: Eve Bunting
Publisher: Harper &Row
Length: 40 **Age:** 5–8 **Date:** 1982
Main Character: Chinese American girl
Other Topics: Intergenerational
Overview: A young Chinese American girl describes her feelings as she attends the funeral of her grandfather. The family gives gifts for his trip to the spirit world and shares memories of Grandfather.

Tina's Chance

Author: Alison Leonard
Publisher: Viking Kestrel
Length: 187 **Age:** 12–14 **Date:** 1988
Main Character: white female
Other Topics: N/A
Overview: Tina's mother died when she was two. Tina searches for answers to questions she has about her mother.

Winter Holding Spring

Author: Crescent Dragonwagon
Publisher: Macmillan
Length: 31 **Age:** 9–11 **Date:** 1990
Main Character: white female
Other Topics: Loneliness
Overview: Eleven-year-old Sarah and her father find it difficult to talk about their feelings after Sarah's mother dies.

Death of a Sibling

A Family Project

Author: Sarah Ellis
Publisher: Macmillan
Length: 144 **Age:** 9–12 **Date:** 1988
Main Character: white female
Other Topics: N/A
Overview: Jessica and her brothers cope with their baby sister's crib death.

A Summer to Die

Author: Lois Lowry
Publisher: Houghton Mifflin
Length: 154 **Age:** 10–13 **Date:** 1977
Main Character: white female
Other Topics: Sibling Rivalry

Death of a Sibling (cont.)

A Summer to Die (cont.)

Overview: Two sisters quarrel constantly until the older one contracts leukemia. Meg must move through the stages of dealing with her sister's death.

Beat the Turtle Drum

Author: Constance Green
Publisher: Viking
Length: 120 **Age:** 9–11 **Date:** 1976
Main Character: white female
Other Topics: N/A
Overview: Thirteen-year-old Kate narrates this story about the summer that her sister Joss saved her money, rented a horse, and then died from a fall from a tree.

Belle Pruitt

Author: Vera Cleaver
Publisher: Lippincott
Length: 169 **Age:** 9–12 **Date:** 1988
Main Character: white female
Other Topics: N/A
Overview: Eleven-year-old Belle is overwhelmed when her baby brother dies.

By the Highway Home

Author: Mary Stolz
Publisher: Harper and Row
Length: 194 **Age:** 11–13 **Date:** 1971
Main Character: female
Other Topics: Sibling Rivalry, Moving, Intergenerational
Overview: Thirteen-year-old Catty is miserable. The prolonged grief for her brother, Beau, who was killed in VietNam, is caused by her family's inability to talk about Beau. She finally seeks solace from someone outside her family.

Eighty-Eight Steps to September

Author: Jan Marino
Publisher: Little, Brown
Length: 154 **Age:** 10–12 **Date:** 1989
Main Character: white female
Other Topics: Hospitalization, Doctor's Office
Overview: Amory's happy life changes when she learns her brother isn't coming home from the hospital.

Losing Someone You Love: When a Brother or Sister Dies

Author: Elizabeth Richter
Publisher: G.P. Putnam's Sons
Length: 80 **Age:** 8–12 **Date:** 1986
Main Character: multicultural males and females
Other Topics: N/A
Overview: Sixteen young people, ages 10–24, describe their feelings when a brother or sister dies.

My Twin Sister Erika

Author: Ilse-Margaret Vogel
Publisher: Harper and Row
Length: 54 **Age:** 6–9 **Date:** 1976
Main Character: white female
Other Topics: Twins
Overview: Inge is less assertive than her twin Erika. When Erika becomes ill and dies, Inge originally feels important because she is the only one. She regrets that feeling when she discovers how much her mother is grieving for Erika.

Simon and the Game of Chance

Author: Robert Burch
Publisher: Viking
Length: 128 **Age:** 8–10 **Date:** 1970
Main Character: white male
Other Topics: Mental Illness

Simon and the Game of Chance (cont.)

Overview: The Bradley family experiences two deaths. Mrs. Bradley has a baby girl who dies. Clarissa, Bradley's fiance, dies on the day of the wedding. However, the deaths strengthen the family.

Tawny

Author: Chas Carner
Publisher: Macmillan
Length: 148 **Age:** 10–18 **Date:** 1978
Main Character: white male
Other Topics: Twins
Overview: The Landry family suffers when poachers hunting on their farm accidentally kill Trey's twin brother Troy. Trey remembers his brother with respect through flashbacks.

Where's Jess?

Author: Joy and Marv Johnson
Publisher: Centering Corp.
Length: 30 **Age:** 4–8 **Date:** 1982
Main Character: white male
Other Topics: N/A
Overview: For small children who have a baby brother or sister die.

Developing Sexuality

Are You There, God? It's Me, Margaret ✳

Author: Judy Blume
Publisher: Bradbury
Length: 149 **Age:** 10–12 **Date:** 1970
Main Character: white female
Other Topics: N/A

Are You There, God? It's Me, Margaret (cont.)

Overview: Margaret prays for her first period to come because she doesn't want to be the last of her secret club to start menstruating. She also searches for a meaningful relationship with God.

The Goats

Author: Brock Cole
Publisher: Farrar
Length: 184 **Age:** 10–13 **Date:** 1987
Main Character: white male and female
Other Topics: Friendship
Overview: A boy and a girl are stripped of their clothes and left on an island in the night as a summer camp prank. The two outcasts ("goats") are humiliated and decide not to return to camp. They find a cabin and develop a friendship.

The Long Secret

Author: Louise Fitzhugh
Publisher: Harper
Length: 275 **Age:** 11–13 **Date:** 1965
Main Character: white female
Other Topics: N/A
Overview: This is the first story to discuss menstruation. In it, a girl explains menstruation to her friend in a matter-of-fact manner to correct misinformation the friend's grandmother had given her.

Then Again, Maybe I Won't

Author: Judy Blume
Publisher: Bradbury
Length: 127 **Age:** 10–12 **Date:** 1971
Main Character: white male
Other Topics: N/A
Overview: Tony is a thirteen-year-old boy who is embarrassed and concerned about erections and nocturnal emissions.

Diabetes

Even Little Kids Get Diabetes

Author: Connie W. Pirner
Publisher: Albert Whitman and Co.
Length: 24 **Age:** 3–7 **Date:** 1994
Main Character: cartoon characters
Other Topics: N/A
Overview: This simple book was written for children who have diabetes. It discusses symptoms, diagnostic procedures, and treatment. A "note to parents" is also included.

Meeting the Challenge: Children Living with Diabetes

Author: Thomas Bergman
Publisher: Gareth Stevens
Length: 48 **Age:** 6–10 **Date:** 1991
Main Character: white male
Other Topics: N/A
Overview: This photo-essay describes the medical problems and daily routine of a ten-year-old Swedish boy with diabetes and discusses the two main types of this chronic disease.

Runaway Sugar: About Diabetes

Author: Dr. Alvin and Virginia Silverstein
Publisher: Lippincott
Length: 34 **Age:** 12–14 **Date:** 1981
Main Character: cartoon characters
Other Topics: N/A
Overview: This book presents a discussion of diabetes—causes and treatments.

Tough Beans

Author: Betty Bates
Publisher: Holiday House
Length: 96 **Age:** 8–12 **Date:** 1988
Main Character: white male

Tough Beans (cont.)

Other Topics: Bullies
Overview: Fourth-grader Nat Berger has two problems. First, he discovers that he has diabetes, a condition that is permanent. Second, Jasper Denletter is the fourth-grade bully and a real challenge to Nat.

Disobedience

Feather Fin

Author: Stephen Cosgrove
Publisher: Price/Stern/Sloan
Length: 26 **Age:** 5–8 **Date:** 1983
Main Character: animal
Other Topics: N/A
Overview: Feather Fin disobeys his mother and finds himself in trouble.

In the Rabbitgarden

Author: Leo Lionni
Publisher: Pantheon
Length: 28 **Age:** 4–6 **Date:** 1975
Main Character: animal
Other Topics: N/A
Overview: Two little rabbits disobey the command not to eat the apples.

Joshua Disobeys

Author: Dennis Vollmer
Publisher: Landmark Editions
Length: 29 **Age:** 5–8 **Date:** 1988
Main Character: animal
Other Topics: N/A
Overview: Joshua the whale disobeyed his mother and swam too close to the shore.

Nadia the Willful

Author: Sue Alexander
Publisher: Pantheon
Length: 44 **Age:** 8–10 **Date:** 1983
Main Character: white female
Other Topics: Temper
Overview: When her favorite brother disappears in the desert forever, Nadia refuses to let him be forgotten, despite her father's order that his name should not be spoken.

Tale of Peter Rabbit

Author: Beatrix Potter
Publisher: Warne
Length: 30 **Age:** 4–7 **Date:** 1902
Main Character: animal
Other Topics: N/A
Overview: Story of Peter Rabbit's adventures in Mr. MacGregor's garden.

The Good Master

Author: Kate Seredy
Publisher: Viking
Length: 196 **Age:** 9–11 **Date:** 1935
Main Character: white male and female
Other Topics: N/A
Overview: Cousin Kate is sent to the country to stay with her uncle. Her father describes Kate as "impossible, incredible, disobedient, and headstrong."

Where the Wild Things Are

Author: Maurice Sendak
Publisher: Harper
Length: 37 **Age:** 4–7 **Date:** 1962
Main Character: white male
Other Topics: N/A
Overview: A small boy is sent to his room to think about his misbehavior where he conjures up a crowd of grotesque monsters.

Diverse Families

All Kinds of Families

Author: Norma Simon
Publisher: Whitman
Length: 32 **Age:** 5–8 **Date:** 1976
Main Character: multicultural males and females
Other Topics: N/A
Overview: All kinds of families are discussed in this concept book. It acknowledges that families are not always composed in the traditional way.

Beginnings: How Families Come To Be

Author: Virginia Kroll
Publisher: Albert Whitman and Co.
Length: 32 **Age:** 4–9 **Date:** 1994
Main Character: multicultural males and females
Other Topics: Wheelchair, Adoption
Overview: Simple and moving stories about various children from varied backgrounds.

Black Is Brown Is Tan

Author: Arnold Adoff
Publisher: Harper
Length: 32 **Age:** 3–18 **Date:** 1973
Main Character: multicultural males and females
Other Topics: N/A
Overview: This story-poem describes a family of different races growing up happily in a house full of love.

Daddy's Roommate

Author: Michael Willhoite
Publisher: Alyson Publications
Length: 32 **Age:** 6–9 **Date:** 1990
Main Character: white males
Other Topics: N/A

Diverse Families (cont.)

Daddy's Roommate (cont.)

Overview: This is the first book written for children of gay men. A young boy, his father, and his father's lover take part in activities familiar to all families.

Families Are Different

Author: Nina Pellegrini
Publisher: Holiday House
Length: 32 **Age:** 4–8 **Date:** 1991
Main Character: Korean females
Other Topics: Adoption
Overview: Nico and Angel are Korean sisters who are adopted by a white mom and dad.

Family Pose

Author: Dean Hughes
Publisher: Atheneum
Length: 184 **Age:** 10–12 **Date:** 1989
Main Character: white male
Other Topics: Alcoholism, Foster Home
Overview: Eleven-year-old David runs away from his foster home and ends up at the Hotel Jefferson. He meets Paul, a bellboy and recovering alcoholic, who encourages David to seek help.

Heather Has Two Mommies

Author: Leslea Newman
Publisher: Alyson Publications
Length: 32 **Age:** 6–9 **Date:** 1989
Main Character: white female
Other Topics: N/A
Overview: Heather has two mommies—Mama Kate and Mama Jane, both lesbians—who are raising her.

Homecoming

Author: Cynthia Voigt
Publisher: Macmillan
Length: 320 **Age:** 10–14 **Date:** 1981
Main Character: white female
Other Topics: Abandonment, Mental Illness
Overview: Thirteen-year-old Dicey, along with her younger siblings, has been abandoned in the parking lot of a shopping mall by her mentally ill mother. Despite all odds, Dicey takes the family to their grandmother's home.

Living in Two Worlds

Author: Maxine B. Rosenberg
Publisher: Lothrop
Length: 46 **Age:** 7–10 **Date:** 1986
Main Character: multicultural males and females
Other Topics: N/A
Overview: Photographs show children from four biracial families describing the pleasures and problems of living in two cultures.

Mom, the Wolfman and Me

Author: Norma Klein
Publisher: Pantheon
Length: 156 **Age:** 10–13 **Date:** 1972
Main Character: white male
Other Topics: Illegitimacy
Overview: Brett is an illegitimate child, living alone with his mother, until the "wolfman" comes along.

Seventh Grade Weirdo

Author: Lee Wardlaw
Publisher: Scholastic
Length: 149 **Age:** 10–18 **Date:** 1992
Main Character: white male
Other Topics: Hating Your Name, Growing Up, Giftedness

Seventh Grade Weirdo (cont.)

Overview: Rob is embarrassed about his family. He hates his name, his mother runs a mail-order business called Hef-falump House, his father is a famous former surfing champion, and his five-year-old sister is gifted.

The Kids' Book About Parents

Author: Students at Fayerweather Street School and Eric E. Rofes
Publisher: Houghton Mifflin
Length: 204 **Age:** 8–12 **Date:** 1984
Main Character: multicultural males and females
Other Topics: N/A
Overview: Thirty-one children, ages 11–14, share their stories about their family situations.

The Not-Just-Anybody Family

Author: Betsy Byars
Publisher: Delacorte Press
Length: 149 **Age:** 10–12 **Date:** 1986
Main Character: white male and female
Other Topics: Incarceration
Overview: Maggie and Vern try to settle family problems. It is not so easy with grandfather in jail, a brother in the hospital; and a mother on the rodeo circuit.

William

Author: Irene Hunt
Publisher: Scribner's
Length: 192 **Age:** 10–12 **Date:** 1977
Main Character: white males and females
Other Topics: Illegitimacy, Orphans
Overview: This family unit consists of an unmarried mother, her daughter, and three orphaned neighbor children.

Divorce

A Book for Jodan

Author: Marcia Newfield
Publisher: Atheneum
Length: 40 **Age:** 7–11 **Date:** 1975
Main Character: white female
Other Topics: N/A
Overview: When nine-year-old Jodan learns that her parents are separating, she worries that she may be the reason.

A Father Like That

Author: Charlotte Zolotow
Publisher: Harper and Row
Length: 29 **Age:** 5–7 **Date:** 1971
Main Character: white male
Other Topics: N/A
Overview: The mother of a fatherless child listens to the dreams of her son, who wishes for an ideal father. She tells him that he can be a father like that.

A Friend Can Help

Author: Terry Berger
Publisher: Raintree Publishers, Ltd.
Length: 32 **Age:** 4–6 **Date:** 1974
Main Character: white female
Other Topics: N/A
Overview: Susan becomes a good listener for her friend, whose parents have divorced.

A Girl Called Al

Author: Constance Greene
Publisher: Viking
Length: 128 **Age:** 10–13 **Date:** 1969
Main Character: white female
Other Topics: Weight Problem

Divorce (cont.)

A Girl Called Al (cont.)

Overview: Al's parents are divorced. She doesn't love her mother very much but she does love her father, who sends her presents. A new friendship begins when Al moves into the apartment building with Isobel.

A Look at Divorce

Author: Margaret S. Pursell
Publisher: Lerner Publications
Length: 30 **Age:** 4–6 **Date:** 1977
Main Character: multicultural males and females
Other Topics: N/A
Overview: Both text and photographs describe problems faced by both children and parents when a divorce occurs.

At Daddy's on Saturdays

Author: Linda Girard
Publisher: Albert Whitman
Length: 32 **Age:** 5–8 **Date:** 1987
Main Character: white female
Other Topics: N/A
Overview: Daddy moves out one Saturday and young Katie feels concern, anger, and sadness.

Beauty

Author: Bill Wallace
Publisher: Holiday House
Length: 240 **Age:** 8–12 **Date:** 1988
Main Character: white male
Other Topics: Moving
Overview: Eleven-year-old Luke is unhappy about his parents' divorce and the move he must make to his grandfather's farm with his mother. He befriends Beauty, the old white horse his mother rode as a child.

Dear Angie, Your Family's Getting a Divorce

Author: Carol Nelson
Publisher: Chariot Books
Length: 119 **Age:** 10–12 **Date:** 1980
Main Character: white female
Other Topics: N/A
Overview: Angie is concerned about her parents' not getting along and their arguing, which might end in divorce.

Dear Dad, Love Laurie

Author: Susan Beth Pfeffer
Publisher: Apple
Length: 128 **Age:** 8–12 **Date:** 1989
Main Character: white female
Other Topics: N/A
Overview: Sixth-grader Laurie writes letters to her divorced father.

Dear Mr. Henshaw

Author: Beverly Cleary
Publisher: Morrow
Length: 144 **Age:** 8–12 **Date:** 1983
Main Character: white male
Other Topics: New School
Overview: A young boy recounts his story through a series of real and pretend letters to his favorite children's author as he tries to work through the problems of his parents' divorce and the adjustments of attending a new school.

DeDe Takes Charge

Author: Johanna Hurwitz
Publisher: Morrow
Length: 144 **Age:** 8–12 **Date:** 1984
Main Character: white female
Other Topics: N/A
Overview: When DeDe's parents got divorced, everything changed. Her mother works odd hours, her father has a telephone answering machine. DeDe decides to take charge.

Dinosaur's Divorce

Author: Laurence Brown and Marc Brown
Publisher: Little, Brown, and Co.
Length: 32 **Age:** 5–8 **Date:** 1986
Main Character: animal
Other Topics: N/A
Overview: An excellent book about divorce and what it means. A glossary is included. The comic book format is non-threatening.

Divorce Can Happen to the Nicest People

Author: Peter Mayle
Publisher: Macmillan
Length: 27 **Age:** 6–12 **Date:** 1979
Main Character: cartoon characters
Other Topics: N/A
Overview: This unique handbook offers reassurance and answers on how to cope with a family that's breaking up.

Don't Make Me Smile

Author: Barbara Park
Publisher: Knopf
Length: 112 **Age:** 9–12 **Date:** 1981
Main Character: white male
Other Topics: N/A
Overview: A ten-year-old boy reacts to his parents' divorce.

Ellen Grae

Author: Vera and Bill Cleaver
Publisher: Lipppincott
Length: 89 **Age:** 9–11 **Date:** 1964
Main Character: white female
Other Topics: Honesty
Overview: Ellen Grae tells her story about the effects of her parents' divorce. She learns that a parent's love and responsibility are not changed by divorce.

Emily and the Klunky Baby and the Next-Door Dog

Author: Joan Lexau
Publisher: Dial Press
Length: 35 **Age:** 4–8 **Date:** 1972
Main Character: white female
Other Topics: N/A
Overview: When her parents divorce, Emily takes her baby brother and searches for their absent father.

Everything You Need to Know About Your Parents' Divorce

Author: Linda C. Johnson
Publisher: Rosen Publishing Group, Inc.
Length: 64 **Age:** 12–14 **Date:** 1989
Main Character: multicultural males and females
Other Topics: Suicide, Stepfamilies, Anger
Overview: This book discusses divorce as the beginning of a different kind of family life.

Hideaway

Author: Eloise McGraw
Publisher: Atheneum
Length: 217 **Age:** 10–12 **Date:** 1983
Main Character: white male
Other Topics: Friendship, Rejection
Overview: Jerry is rejected by both of his divorced parents but befriends an older girl in a vacant house.

How It Feels When Parents Divorce

Author: Jill Krementz
Publisher: Knopf
Length: 115 **Age:** 9–13 **Date:** 1984
Main Character: multicultural males and females
Other Topics: N/A
Overview: Children discuss living through a divorce.

Divorce (cont.)

I Won't Go Without a Father

Author: Muriel Stanek
Publisher: Albert Whitman and Co.
Length: 32 **Age:** 7–9 **Date:** 1972
Main Character: white male
Other Topics: N/A
Overview: Realistic discussion of one-parent homes.

It's Not the End of the World

Author: Judy Blume
Publisher: Bradbury
Length: 174 **Age:** 10–12 **Date:** 1972
Main Character: white female
Other Topics: N/A
Overview: Karen Newman thinks it is the end of the world when her father decides to go to Las Vegas to get a divorce. She decides to plot to keep her parents together.

Just Like Sisters

Author: Lou Ann Galddent
Publisher: Dutton
Length: 90 **Age:** 8–12 **Date:** 1981
Main Character: white female
Other Topics: Only Child
Overview: Carrie Clark is an only child. Her cousin Kate moves into the Clarks' home when her parents divorce. Kate is very depressed and difficult to live with.

Mama and Her Boys

Author: Lee Bennett Hopkins
Publisher: Harper and Row
Length: 149 **Age:** 9–12 **Date:** 1981
Main Character: white males
Other Topics: N/A

Mama and Her Boys (cont.)

Overview: Since her divorce, Mama must raise her two boys alone. When Mr. Jacobs, her boss at the laundry, proposes, she asks Mark and Chris how they feel.

Mom and Dad Don't Live Together Anymore

Author: Kathy Stinson
Publisher: Annick Press
Length: 24 **Age:** 4–7 **Date:** 1984
Main Character: white female
Other Topics: N/A
Overview: A young girl slowly accepts the fact that her parents do not live together anymore. She also realizes that both parents still love her.

Mommy and Daddy Are Divorced

Author: Patricia Perry and Marietta Lynch
Publisher: Dial Books
Length: 26 **Age:** 4–8 **Date:** 1985
Main Character: white male
Other Topics: N/A
Overview: Ned and Joey's parents are recently divorced. The boys must learn to cope with this changed family situation.

My Dad Lives in a Downtown Hotel

Author: Peggy Mann
Publisher: Doubleday
Length: 92 **Age:** 7–10 **Date:** 1973
Main Character: white male
Other Topics: N/A
Overview: A boy discovers his parents are divorcing and experiences a variety of feelings.

My Mother Is Not Married to My Father

Author: Jean D. Okimoto
Publisher: G.P. Putnam

My Mother Is Not Married to My Father (cont.)

Length: 109 **Age:** 10–14 **Date:** 1979
Main Character: white female
Other Topics: N/A
Overview: Eleven-year-old Cynthia and her sister must adjust to their parents' divorce.

My Mother's House, My Father's House

Author: C.B. Christiansen
Publisher: Atheneum
Length: 32 **Age:** 3–8 **Date:** 1989
Main Character: white female
Other Topics: N/A
Overview: A little girl lives with her mother during the week and with her father on the weekends.

On Divorce

Author: Sara B. Stein
Publisher: Walker and Co.
Length: 47 **Age:** 4–6 **Date:** 1979
Main Character: white female
Other Topics: N/A
Overview: Separate texts for both parents and children explain the emotions experienced by divorce.

Pig-Out Inn

Author: Lois Ruby
Publisher: Houghton Mifflin Co.
Length: 171 **Age:** 10–14 **Date:** 1987
Main Character: white female
Other Topics: Abandonment
Overview: Fourteen-year-old Dovi spends a summer helping her mother run a truckstop diner. She becomes involved in a custody battle when both parents want to hold on to her after a divorce.

Pillow of Clouds

Author: Marc Talbert
Publisher: Dial
Length: 208 **Age:** 10–18 **Date:** 1991
Main Character: white male
Other Topics: N/A
Overview: Chester is faced with a difficult decision—which of his divorced parents he should live with.

Puppy Love

Author: Jeanne Betancourt
Publisher: Avon Camelot
Length: 89 **Age:** 8–12 **Date:** 1986
Main Character: white female
Other Topics: Death of a Pet, Sibling Rivalry
Overview: Aviva has a lot of things going on her eighth-grade year. Her parents are divorced, her mother has remarried and had a baby boy, her father moves in with his girlfriend, and her dog dies.

Son for a Day

Author: Corinne Gerson
Publisher: Scholastic
Length: 140 **Age:** 9–11 **Date:** 1980
Main Character: white male
Other Topics: Loneliness
Overview: A lonely eleven-year-old boy frequently visits the zoo, where he helps recently divorced fathers with their "weekend only" sons.

The Boys' and Girls' Book about Divorce

Author: Richard Gardner, M.D.
Publisher: Bantam Books
Length: 155 **Age:** 10–14 **Date:** 1970
Main Character: N/A
Other Topics: Anger, Fear
Overview: This book was written for both children and their divorced parents. An introduction for parents is included.

Divorce (cont.)

The Divorce Express

Author: Paula Danziger
Publisher: Delacorte
Length: 128 **Age:** 11–14 **Date:** 1982
Main Character: white female
Other Topics: N/A
Overview: Phoebe has problems after her parents' divorce—two homes, a new school, and new friends.

The Fox Steals Home

Author: Matt Christopher
Publisher: Little, Brown
Length: 178 **Age:** 8–12 **Date:** 1978
Main Character: white male
Other Topics: N/A
Overview: A boy's interest in baseball helps overcome his concern about his parents' divorce.

The Hatchet

Author: Gary Paulsen
Publisher: Bradbury
Length: 195 **Age:** 11–14 **Date:** 1987
Main Character: white male
Other Topics: Survival
Overview: Brian Roberson is on his way to visit his father after his parents' divorce when the pilot suffers a heart attack and the plane crashes. Thirteen-year-old Brian is on his own in the Canadian wilderness with only a hatchet.

The Soloman System

Author: Phyllis Reynolds Naylor
Publisher: Atheneum
Length: 210 **Age:** 10–18 **Date:** 1983
Main Character: white male
Other Topics: N/A

The Soloman System (cont.)

Overview: Thirteen-year-old Ted Soloman is grateful to his older brother Nory when their parents are getting a divorce.

Two Homes to Live in: A Child's Eye View of Divorce

Author: Barbara Shook Hazen
Publisher: Human Sciences Press
Length: 36 **Age:** 4–6 **Date:** 1978
Main Character: white female
Other Topics: N/A
Overview: A little girl explains how she came to terms with her parents' divorce.

Two Places to Sleep

Author: Joan Schuchman
Publisher: Carolrhoda Books
Length: 28 **Age:** 4–6 **Date:** 1979
Main Character: white male
Other Topics: N/A
Overview: David describes living with his father and visiting his mother on weekends after his parents' divorce.

Veronica Ganz

Author: Marilyn Sachs
Publisher: Doubleday
Length: 156 **Age:** 10–12 **Date:** 1968
Main Character: white female
Other Topics: Bullies
Overview: A bully becomes friends with the smallest boy in the class. Veronica has a difficult time adjusting to her divorced father and his new wife.

What's Going to Happen to Me: When Parents Separate or Divorce

Author: Eda LeShan
Publisher: Four Winds
Length: 144 **Age:** 8–11 **Date:** 1978
Main Character: white male

What's Going to Happen to Me: When Parents Separate or Divorce (cont.)

Other Topics: N/A
Overview: Feelings are discussed in this book about divorce or separation. The author answers many questions children may have. She also suggests ways of coping with personal and family problems that often accompany the divorce.

When Mom and Dad Divorce

Author: Steven Nichman
Publisher: Messner
Length: 76 **Age:** 6–12 **Date:** 1986
Main Character: N/A
Other Topics: N/A
Overview: The author, a pediatrician and psychiatrist, uses anecdotes as discussions of coping with divorce and separation.

Where Is Daddy? The Story of a Divorce

Author: Beth Goff
Publisher: Beacon Press
Length: 28 **Age:** 3–5 **Date:** 1969
Main Character: white female
Other Topics: Intergenerational
Overview: A preschool child experiences feelings of guilt when her parents divorce. A grandmother provides support.

Win Me and You Lose

Author: Phyllis Anderson Wood
Publisher: Westminster Press
Length: 137 **Age:** 10–14 **Date:** 1977
Main Character: white male
Other Topics: N/A
Overview: A seventeen-year-old boy and his father become reacquainted after the divorce.

Down's Syndrome

A Little Time

Author: Anne N. Baldwin
Publisher: Viking
Length: 119 **Age:** 8–12 **Date:** 1978
Main Character: white female
Other Topics: N/A
Overview: Ten-year-old Sarah is one of five children. Her brother Matt is four years old and has Down's Syndrome. Sarah is exploring her feelings towards Matt and his handicap.

Between Friends

Author: Shelia Garrigue
Publisher: Bradbury
Length: 160 **Age:** 10–12 **Date:** 1978
Main Character: white female
Other Topics: Friendship, Moving
Overview: When ten-year-old Jill must move to a new neighborhood, she is desperate for a friend. She reluctantly befriends Dede who has Down's Syndrome.

Loving Ben

Author: Elizabeth Laird
Publisher: Delacorte Press
Length: 183 **Age:** 10–18 **Date:** 1988
Main Character: white male
Other Topics: N/A
Overview: Anna's teen years bring maturity and fulfillment as she experiences the truth about and death of a loving hydrocephalic brother, Ben. She also works with a Down's Syndrome child, Jackie.

Down's Syndrome (cont.)

Making Room for Uncle Joe

Author: Ada Litchfield
Publisher: Albert Whitman
Length: 32 **Age:** 5–12 **Date:** 1984
Main Character: white male
Other Topics: N/A
Overview: Since the state hospital is closing, Uncle Joe, a Down's Syndrome adult, comes to live with Dan and his family.

Our Brother Has Down's Syndrome

Author: Shelley Cairo
Publisher: Annick Press
Length: 20 **Age:** 5–9 **Date:** 1985
Main Character: white male
Other Topics: N/A
Overview: Tara and Jasmine tell the story of Jai, their little brother with Down's Syndrome. Photographs are used to describe Jai's daily routine. Emphasis is on similarities rather than differences.

The Man Who Loved Clowns

Author: June Rae Wood
Publisher: Putnam
Length: 224 **Age:** 10–15 **Date:** 1992
Main Character: white male
Other Topics: Shyness
Overview: A friend helps Delrita see that her uncle's Down's Syndrome is nothing to be ashamed of.

Thumbs Up, Rico!

Author: Maria Testa
Publisher: Albert Whitman and Co.
Length: 40 **Age:** 8–12 **Date:** 1994

Thumbs Up, Rico! (cont.)

Main Character: Hispanic American male
Other Topics: N/A
Overview: Three short stories tell Rico's trials and successes in dealing with Down's Syndrome.

Where's Chimpy?

Author: Bernice Raber
Publisher: Albert Whitman
Length: 32 **Age:** 4–7 **Date:** 1988
Main Character: white female
Other Topics: N/A
Overview: Misty is a little girl with Down's Syndrome. She likes to hold her toy monkey, Chimpy, when her father reads her a story.

Dwarfism

The Real Tom Thumb

Author: Helen Reeder Cross
Publisher: Four Winds
Length: 96 **Age:** 8–12 **Date:** 1980
Main Character: white male
Other Topics: N/A
Overview: A unique story of the famous dwarf, Tom Thumb.

Thinking Big: The Story of a Young Dwarf

Author: Susan Kuklin
Publisher: Lothrop
Length: 48 **Age:** 6–10 **Date:** 1986
Main Character: white female
Other Topics: Growing Up
Overview: This book of photographs illustrates the daily life of an eight-year-old dwarf, Jaime Osborne, who belongs to the Little People of America.

Dyslexia, Learning Disabilities

Coping with a Learning Disability

Author: Lawrence Clayton and Jaydene Morrison
Publisher: Rosen Publishing Group
Length: 115 **Age:** 10–14 **Date:** 1992
Main Character: N/A
Other Topics: N/A
Overview: The special problems associated with learning disabilities are discussed.

Dyslexia: Understanding Reading Problems

Author: John F. Savage
Publisher: Julian Messner
Length: 90 **Age:** 12–18 **Date:** 1985
Main Character: N/A
Other Topics: Illiteracy, Reading Problems
Overview: This nonfiction work describes the characteristics of dyslexia, its causes, how it affects children, and how dyslexic children can learn to read.

He's My Brother

Author: Joe Lasker
Publisher: Albert Whitman
Length: 35 **Age:** 5–8 **Date:** 1974
Main Character: white male
Other Topics: N/A
Overview: This is the story of Jamie's affection for his brother, who has difficulty learning.

It's George

Author: Miriam Cohen
Publisher: Greenwillow
Length: 29 **Age:** 5–8 **Date:** 1988
Main Character: white male
Other Topics: Intergenerational
Overview: George has a difficult time with his schoolwork. But his classmates are proud of him when he saves an elderly friend's life.

Kelly's Creek

Author: Doris Buchanan Smith
Publisher: Crowell
Length: 71 **Age:** 9–11 **Date:** 1975
Main Character: white male
Other Topics: N/A
Overview: Kelly is a boy with a learning disability which makes it hard for his eyes, hands, and brain to coordinate.

Learning Disabilities

Author: Jean McBee Knox
Publisher: Chelsea House Publishers
Length: 98 **Age:** 12–18 **Date:** 1989
Main Character: N/A
Other Topics: N/A
Overview: A discussion of the nature, possible causes, and treatment of learning disabilities.

When Learning Is Tough: Kids Talk About Learning Disabilities

Author: Cynthia Roby
Publisher: Albert Whitman and Co.
Length: 56 **Age:** 7–12 **Date:** 1993
Main Character: white males and females
Other Topics: N/A
Overview: Eight boys and girls talk about the challenge of being learning disabled.

Dyslexia, Learning Disabilities (cont.)

Will the Real Gertrude Hollings Please Stand Up?

Author: Shelia Greenwald
Publisher: Little, Brown
Length: 162 **Age:** 10–12 **Date:** 1983
Main Character: white female
Other Topics: Sibling Rivalry
Overview: Eleven-year-old Gertrude has a learning disability. She spends several weeks with her overachieving cousin Albert, teaching him how to be a brother.

Epilepsy

Edith Herself

Author: Ellen Howard
Publisher: Atheneum
Length: 144 **Age:** 7–10 **Date:** 1987
Main Character: white female
Other Topics: N/A
Overview: Set in the 1890s, this is the story of a girl with epilepsy who learns to value herself.

Halsey's Pride

Author: Lynn Hall
Publisher: Scribner's
Length: 128 **Age:** 10–12 **Date:** 1990
Main Character: white female
Other Topics: Moving
Overview: Thirteen-year-old March Halsey has epilepsy. She must begin a new life with her father in a small rural community.

Lee, The Rabbit with Epilepsy

Author: Deborah Moss
Publisher: Woodbine House
Length: 23 **Age:** 4–8 **Date:** 1993
Main Character: animal
Other Topics: N/A
Overview: Lee has epilepsy but knows how to deal with it.

Moments That Disappear: Children Living with Epilepsy

Author: Thomas Bergman
Publisher: Garth Stevens
Length: 48 **Age:** 8–12 **Date:** 1992
Main Character: white male
Other Topics: N/A
Overview: This photo-essay describes the medical problems and daily routine of a 12–year-old Swedish boy with epilepsy. Biographical references and index are included. (The author/photographer is the boy's father.)

What If They Knew?

Author: Patricia Hermes
Publisher: Dell
Length: 128 **Age:** 10–14 **Date:** 1980
Main Character: white female
Other Topics: N/A
Overview: Jeremy doesn't want anyone to know she is epileptic—not even her best friends. (The author was epileptic).

Fast-Track Families

H, My Name Is Henley

Author: Colby Rodowsky
Publisher: Farrar, Straus, and Giroux
Length: 192 **Age:** 8–12 **Date:** 1982

H, My Name Is Henley (cont.)

Main Character: white female
Other Topics: Growing Up
Overview: Twelve-year-old Henley has no other family but her fast-paced young mother, who is always on the go and dragging Henley with her.

Jellybean

Author: Tessa Duder
Publisher: Puffin
Length: 112 **Age:** 8–12 **Date:** 1985
Main Character: white female
Other Topics: N/A
Overview: Jellybean's mother is very involved with her musical career and has little time for her daughter.

My Mom and Our Dad

Author: Rose Impey
Publisher: Viking
Length: 32 **Age:** 3–8 **Date:** 1991
Main Character: white families
Other Topics: Twins
Overview: Sam's mom is always busy and rushing around. The twins next door have a different problem, but with their dad. He gets carried away with fun.

Noisy Nora

Author: Rosemary Wells
Publisher: Scholastic
Length: 33 **Age:** 3–6 **Date:** 1973
Main Character: animal
Other Topics: N/A
Overview: Noisy Nora is a little mouse who can't get the attention of her busy family.

Take Time to Relax

Author: Nancy Carlson
Publisher: Viking

Take Time to Relax (cont.)

Length: 32 **Age:** 3–8 **Date:** 1991
Main Character: animals
Other Topics: N/A
Overview: Tina's family is very busy with their many classes and activities. When a snowstorm makes them housebound, they discover the pleasures of popcorn, storytelling, and relaxation.

The Berenstain Bears and Too Much Pressure

Author: Stan and Jan Berenstain
Publisher: Random House
Length: 32 **Age:** 4–8 **Date:** 1992
Main Character: animal
Other Topics: N/A
Overview: The Berenstain Bears find themselves stress-ridden from an overwhelming list of after-school activities. The family re-evaluates their priorities when their car and Mama break down.

The Do-Something Day

Author: Joe Lasker
Publisher: Viking
Length: 30 **Age:** 5–8 **Date:** 1982
Main Character: white male
Other Topics: Running Away
Overview: Everyone in Bernie's family is too busy to pay any attention to him so he decides to run away.

Fear

A Dog on Barkham Street

Author: Mary Stolz
Publisher: Harper
Length: 184 **Age:** 10–12 **Date:** 1960
Main Character: white male
Other Topics: N/A

Fear *(cont.)*

A Dog on Barkham Street (cont.)

Overview: Edward is frightened of Martin, the bully next door, who threatens him every day. His uncle visits and teaches Edward how to handle a bully.

A Letter to Amy

Author: Ezra Jack Keats
Publisher: Harper
Length: 26 **Age:** 3–8 **Date:** 1968
Main Character: African American male
Other Topics: Sexism
Overview: Peter worries about two things: whether or not his friend Amy will attend his birthday party and whether or not the boys will tease him for inviting a girl. The party is a success when Amy finally arrives.

Barney's Horse

Author: Syd Hoff
Publisher: Harper and Row
Length: 32 **Age:** 4–8 **Date:** 1987
Main Character: white male
Other Topics: N/A
Overview: Barney's horse is frightened of the noisy new overhead trains in the city.

Bear and Mrs. Duck

Author: Elizabeth Winthrop
Publisher: Holiday House
Length: 29 **Age:** 3–6 **Date:** 1988
Main Character: white female
Other Topics: N/A
Overview: A bear is initially afraid when he has a new babysitter.

Brave Irene

Author: William Steig
Publisher: Farrar, Straus and Giroux
Length: 32 **Age:** 4–8 **Date:** 1986
Main Character: white female
Other Topics: N/A
Overview: Irene trudges through wind, snow, and ice to deliver a gown her mother had made to the duchess.

Call It Courage

Author: Armstrong Sterry
Publisher: Macmillan
Length: 95 **Age:** 10–13 **Date:** 1968
Main Character: Polynesian male
Other Topics: N/A
Overview: In this survival story, Mafatu tries to overcome his fear of the water by sailing to another island.

Clyde Monster

Author: Robert Crowe
Publisher: Dutton
Length: 26 **Age:** 4–8 **Date:** 1976
Main Character: animal
Other Topics: N/A
Overview: This "turnaround" tale tells of Clyde Monster who is afraid of people lurking around his cave at night.

Darkness and the Butterfly

Author: Ann Grifalconi
Publisher: Little, Brown
Length: 32 **Age:** 4–8 **Date:** 1987
Main Character: African American female
Other Topics: N/A
Overview: A little girl learns not to be afraid of the dark.

Every Kid's Guide to Understanding Nightmares

Author: Joy Berry
Publisher: Children's Press
Length: 48 **Age:** 6–8 **Date:** 1987
Main Character: African American male
Other Topics: N/A
Overview: This self-help book describes how nightmares affect you, what common nightmares are, how to understand nightmares, and how to cope with them.

Face Off

Author: Matt Christopher
Publisher: Little, Brown
Length: 131 **Age:** 8–12 **Date:** 1972
Main Character: white male
Other Topics: N/A
Overview: Scott Harrison must overcome a fear of a hockey player.

First Night Away from Home

Author: Myra Berry Brown
Publisher: Watts
Length: 52 **Age:** 4–7 **Date:** 1960
Main Character: white male
Other Topics: Separation Anxiety
Overview: Stevie was excited about going to Davey's house to spend the night. But things looked different when the lights went out. As a surprise, his mother brings his teddy bear.

Franklin in the Dark

Author: Paulette Bourgeois
Publisher: Scholastic
Length: 32 **Age:** 5–8 **Date:** 1987
Main Character: turtle
Other Topics: N/A
Overview: Franklin has a problem. He is a turtle who is afraid of the dark, so he cannot stay in his shell.

Frizzy the Fearful

Author: Marjorie W. Sharmat
Publisher: Holiday House
Length: 32 **Age:** 5–8 **Date:** 1983
Main Character: animal
Other Topics: N/A
Overview: Frizzy the Tiger is afraid of everything until he finds his friend in a frightful situation.

Ghost's Hour, Spook's Hour

Author: Eve Bunting
Publisher: Clarion
Length: 29 **Age:** 2–7 **Date:** 1987
Main Character: white male
Other Topics: N/A
Overview: A young boy is afraid when the lights go out and he cannot find his parents.

Ginger Jumps

Author: Lisa Cambell Ernst
Publisher: Bradbury Press
Length: 34 **Age:** 4–6 **Date:** 1990
Main Character: animal
Other Topics: Friendship
Overview: Ginger is a dog that loves performing in the circus. She is afraid to learn a new trick until she finds a friend to help her.

Harry and the Terrible Whatzit

Author: Dick Gackenbach
Publisher: Seabury Press
Length: 30 **Age:** 4–8 **Date:** 1977
Main Character: white male
Other Topics: N/A
Overview: Harry must go down to the cellar and confront the terrible two-headed whatzit when his mother doesn't return from there immediately.

Fear (cont.)

Harvey's Horrible Snake Disaster

Author: Eth Clifford
Publisher: Houghton
Length: 108 **Age:** 8–11 **Date:** 1984
Main Character: white male
Other Topics: Sharing
Overview: Harvey is unhappy about giving up his room when his cousin Nora comes to visit. He is also afraid to admit that he fears snakes, one of Nora's infatuations.

I Would If I Could

Author: Betty Miles
Publisher: Knopf
Length: 120 **Age:** 9–12 **Date:** 1982
Main Character: white female
Other Topics: N/A
Overview: Patty wants to learn to ride her new bike but she is afraid.

Laney's Last Momma

Author: Diane Johnston Hamm
Publisher: Albert Whitman
Length: 32 **Age:** 3–6 **Date:** 1991
Main Character: white female
Other Topics: N/A
Overview: Laney becomes separated from her mother in a department store.

Like Jake and Me

Author: Mavis Jukes
Publisher: Knopf
Length: 32 **Age:** 7–9 **Date:** 1984
Main Character: white male
Other Topics: N/A
Overview: Alex must adjust to his new stepfather, Jake, who wears Stetson hats and doubts Jake's ability to help out on the farm.

Lily Takes a Walk

Author: Satashi Kitamura
Publisher: Dutton
Length: 32 **Age:** 4–6 **Date:** 1991
Main Character: white female
Other Topics: Active Imagination
Overview: When Lily takes a walk, she simply observes stars and ducks. But Nicky, her dog, has an overly active imagination and sees sea serpents and vampires in the night.

My Mama Says There Aren't Any Zombies, Ghosts, Vampires, Creatures, Demons, Monsters, Fiends, Goblins or Things

Author: Judith Viorst
Publisher: Aladdin Books
Length: 40 **Age:** 4–8 **Date:** 1973
Main Character: white male
Other Topics: N/A
Overview: Since his mother has made other mistakes could Nick trust her when she says there are no zombies, ghosts, vampires, creatures, demons, monsters, fiends, goblins or things lurking in the dark?

Night Cry

Author: Phyllis Reynolds Naylor
Publisher: Atheneum
Length: 114 **Age:** 10–13 **Date:** 1984
Main Character: white female
Other Topics: Death of a Relative
Overview: Ellen is left alone on the farm while her salesman father travels. She copes with her fears when a nearby child is kidnapped and held for ransom.

Opening Night

Author: Rachel Isadora
Publisher: Putnam
Length: 32 **Age:** 5–8 **Date:** 1984

Opening Night (cont.)

Main Character: African American female
Other Topics: N/A
Overview: A young ballerina experiences both excitement and nervousness on the night of her first performance.

Otherwise Known as Shelia the Great

Author: Judy Blume
Publisher: Dutton
Length: 118 **Age:** 9–12 **Date:** 1972
Main Character: white female
Other Topics: N/A
Overview: Ten-year-old Shelia experiences a wonderful and exciting summer.

Sing to the Stars

Author: Mary Brigid Barrett
Publisher: Little, Brown
Length: 32 **Age:** 6–9 **Date:** 1994
Main Character: male
Other Topics: Blind, Visually Impaired
Overview: A young boy is afraid to play his violin on stage until he meets Flashing Fingers Washington, who is blind.

Sixth Grade Sleepover

Author: Eve Bunting
Publisher: Apple
Length: 112 **Age:** 8–12 **Date:** 1986
Main Character: white female
Other Topics: N/A
Overview: Janey is worried about the sixth-grade sleepover because she is afraid of the dark.

Sometimes I'm Afraid

Author: Jane Werner Watson
Publisher: Crown Publishers, Inc.
Length: 26 **Age:** 4–6 **Date:** 1986
Main Character: white male

Sometimes I'm Afraid (cont.)

Other Topics: N/A
Overview: A three-year-old boy describes some things he fears and how his parents help quiet those fears. A note to parents is included in the preface.

Swimmy

Author: Leo Lionni
Publisher: Pantheon Books, Inc.
Length: 28 **Age:** 5–8 **Date:** 1963
Main Character: animal
Other Topics: Loneliness, Adoption
Overview: Swimmy is a frightened and lonely little black fish who swims in the ocean, hunting for a family to adopt.

Sylvester and the Magic Pebble

Author: William Steig
Publisher: Simon and Schuster
Length: 29 **Age:** 5–7 **Date:** 1969
Main Character: animal
Other Topics: N/A
Overview: Sylvester Duncan is a young donkey who lives with his parents at Acorn Road in Oatsdale. A mishap with a magic pebble causes him to become separated from his parents.

The Bad Dream

Author: Jim Aylesworth
Publisher: Albert Whitman
Length: 32 **Age:** 5–8 **Date:** 1985
Main Character: white male
Other Topics: N/A
Overview: Comforting book for children with nightmares.

The Berenstain Bears Get Stage Fright

Author: Stan and Jan Berenstain
Publisher: Random House
Length: 29 **Age:** 4–8 **Date:** 1986

Fear (cont.)

The Berenstain Bears Get Stage Fright (cont.)

Main Character: animal
Other Topics: N/A
Overview: Sister Bear worries about remembering her lines in the school play.

The Brave Cowboy

Author: Joan Walsh Anglund
Publisher: Harcourt, Brace, and World, Inc.
Length: 36 **Age:** 3–7 **Date:** 1959
Main Character: white male
Other Topics: N/A
Overview: A young cowboy imagines what it is like to be brave.

The Courage of Sarah Noble

Author: Alice Dalgliesh
Publisher: Macmillan
Length: 64 **Age:** 7–8 **Date:** 1984
Main Character: white female
Other Topics: Death (General), Loneliness
Overview: This is a true story of eight-year-old Sarah, who accompanies her father into the wilderness to cook for him while he builds a cabin for their family. Sarah is left alone while her father returns to Massachusetts for the rest of the family.

? too young?

The Knight Who Was Afraid of the Dark

Author: Barbara Shook Hazen
Publisher: Puffin
Length: 32 **Age:** 4–8 **Date:** 1992
Main Character: white male
Other Topics: N/A
Overview: Sir Fred is a knight who is afraid of the dark.

The Little Old Lady Who Was Not Afraid of Anything

Author: Linda Williams
Publisher: Crowell
Length: 32 **Age:** 4–8 **Date:** 1986
Main Character: white female
Other Topics: N/A
Overview: One night the little old lady who was not afraid of anything had the scare of her life.

The Stone-Faced Boy

Author: Paula Fox
Publisher: Bradbury
Length: 106 **Age:** 9–12 **Date:** 1968
Main Character: white male
Other Topics: N/A
Overview: Gus overcomes his fear of the dark when he rescues a dog for his sister in the middle of the night.

There's a Monster in Your Closet! Understanding Phobias

Author: Brent Filson
Publisher: Simon and Schuster
Length: 78 **Age:** 8–12 **Date:** 1986
Main Character: cartoon characters
Other Topics: N/A
Overview: A description of various phobias, their causes, and treatments is provided.

There's a Nightmare in My Closet

Author: Mercer Mayer
Publisher: Dial
Length: 28 **Age:** 3–7 **Date:** 1968
Main Character: white male
Other Topics: N/A
Overview: A small boy ends up comforting a monster who has a nightmare. The ugly creature even crawls in bed with him.

There's Something in My Attic

Author: Mercer Mayer
Publisher: Dial
Length: 32 **Age:** 3–7 **Date:** 1988
Main Character: white female
Other Topics: N/A
Overview: A brave girl with a lasso confronts a nightmare in her attic.

Time of Wonder

Author: Robert McCloskey
Publisher: Viking Press
Length: 63 **Age:** 5–8 **Date:** 1957
Main Character: white family
Other Topics: N/A
Overview: Tells the story of life on a Maine island before and after a hurricane.

Timid Timothy: The Kitten Who Learned to Be Brave

Author: Gweneira Williams
Publisher: William R. Scott, Inc.
Length: 64 **Age:** 4–6 **Date:** 1954
Main Character: animal
Other Topics: N/A
Overview: Timothy was a little black kitten who was afraid of everything.

What's Under My Bed?

Author: James Stevenson
Publisher: Greenwillow
Length: 30 **Age:** 4–8 **Date:** 1983
Main Character: white male and female
Other Topics: Intergenerational
Overview: A humorous story of all the scary things that could frighten children.

Who Will Pick Me Up When I Fall?

Author: Dorothy Molnar
Publisher: Albert Whitman
Length: 32 **Age:** 4–7 **Date:** 1991
Main Character: white female

Who Will Pick Me Up When I Fall? (cont.)

Other Topics: N/A
Overview: Sarton is afraid she won't remember where to go or what to do after school. Perhaps her mother may even forget her.

Who's Afraid of Ernestine?

Author: Marjorie W. Scharmat
Publisher: Coward-McCann, Inc.
Length: 48 **Age:** 6–8 **Date:** 1986
Main Character: white male
Other Topics: N/A
Overview: Cecil hates to admit that he is afraid of his classmate, Ernestine.

Who's Afraid of the Dark?

Author: Crosby Bonsall
Publisher: Harper and Row
Length: 32 **Age:** 3–5 **Date:** 1980
Main Character: white male
Other Topics: N/A
Overview: A little boy projects his fear of the dark onto his dog.

Forgetfulness

Ollie Forgot

Author: Tedd Arnold
Publisher: Dial
Length: 28 **Age:** 4–8 **Date:** 1988
Main Character: white male
Other Topics: N/A
Overview: Ollie has a difficult time remembering anything.

Foster Home

Cady

Author: Lillian Eige
Publisher: Harper and Row
Length: 183 **Age:** 10–12 **Date:** 1987
Main Character: white male
Other Topics: Bravery
Overview: After having been passed from one relative to another, Cady finds love and acceptance in a foster home.

Fox Farm

Author: Eileen Dunlop
Publisher: Holt
Length: 149 **Age:** 10–12 **Date:** 1979
Main Character: white male
Other Topics: N/A
Overview: When Adam joined the Drake family as a foster child, he could not get along with son Richard until they saved a wounded animal.

Jason's Story: Going to a Foster Home

Author: Deborah Anderson and Martha Finne
Publisher: Dillon Press
Length: 45 **Age:** 6–10 **Date:** 1986
Main Character: African American male
Other Topics: N/A
Overview: Jason tells his story of living in a foster home. Also included are a glossary of terms related to the foster care system and an afterword for adults.

Mama One, and Mama Two

Author: Patricia MacLachlan
Publisher: Harper and Row
Length: 27 **Age:** 4–8 **Date:** 1982
Main Character: white female
Other Topics: Mental Illness

Mama One, and Mama Two (cont.)

Overview: A child is reassured by her foster mother that she will be loved and cared for until her real mother recovers from her mental depression.

My Little Foster Sister

Author: Muriel Stanek
Publisher: Whitman
Length: 29 **Age:** 4–8 **Date:** 1981
Main Character: white female
Other Topics: Jealousy
Overview: It's difficult to adjust to Penny, a new foster sister.

The Cat That Was Left Behind

Author: C. Adler
Publisher: Clarion
Length: 146 **Age:** 9–12 **Date:** 1981
Main Character: white male
Other Topics: N/A
Overview: Chad doesn't think his new foster family will be any better than the others he has known. He begins to change his mind during a summer at the Cape.

The Great Gilly Hopkins

Author: Katherine Paterson
Publisher: Crowell
Length: 148 **Age:** 10–13 **Date:** 1978
Main Character: white female
Other Topics: Illegitimacy
Overview: When Gilly is placed in yet another foster home, she can't stand the semiliterate Maime Trotter and her "retard" seven-year-old, Ward. Gilly steals from Maime and tries to get to her mother in California.

The Pinballs

Author: Betsy Byars
Publisher: Harper
Length: 136 **Age:** 10–18 **Date:** 1977

The Pinballs (cont.)

Main Character: white males and female
Other Topics: Alcoholism, Child Abuse
Overview: This story deals with three children who have been placed in a foster home. Carlie is a tough twelve-year-old who has been beaten up by her third stepfather. Harvey is in a wheelchair because his alcoholic father accidentally ran over him and broke both legs. Thomas J. is an eight-year-old who was raised by elderly twin spinsters who never sent him to school.

The Revolving Door Stops Here

Author: Phyllis A. Wood
Publisher: Cobbehill Books
Length: 187 **Age:** 10–12 **Date:** 1990
Main Character: white male
Other Topics: Death of a Parent
Overview: Seventeen-year-old Eric moves from one foster home to another.

The Secret Language of the SB

Author: Elizabeth Scarboro
Publisher: Puffin
Length: 128 **Age:** 8–12 **Date:** 1992
Main Character: Asian female, white male
Other Topics: N/A
Overview: Adam can't understand why his parents want an eleven-year-old foster child from Taiwan.

Three of a Kind

Author: Louise D. Rich
Publisher: Franklin Watts
Length: 151 **Age:** 8–12 **Date:** 1970
Main Character: white female
Other Topics: Jealousy

Three of a Kind (cont.)

Overview: Eleven-year-old Sally is an orphan. When she joins the Coopers, she really feels like a part of the family. When the Coopers' four-year-old grandson joins them, however, Sally feels jealous and resentful.

Toby Lived Here

Author: Hilma Wolitzer
Publisher: Farrar, Straus, and Giroux
Length: 92 **Age:** 10–18 **Date:** 1978
Main Character: white female
Other Topics: N/A
Overview: When Toby and Anne's mother becomes mentally ill, the girls must move into the Selwyns' foster home.

Trouble Maker

Author: Alberta Armer
Publisher: World Publishing Co.
Length: 191 **Age:** 10–12 **Date:** 1966
Main Character: white male
Other Topics: Incarceration
Overview: When his father goes to prison and his mother enters the hospital, twelve-year-old Joe is sent to a foster home.

Friendship

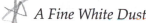

A Fine White Dust

Author: Cynthia Rylant
Publisher: Bradbury
Length: 106 **Age:** 11–18 **Date:** 1986
Main Character: white male
Other Topics: N/A

Friendship (cont.)

A Fine White Dust (cont.)

Overview: Peter Cassidy wishes his parents were more interested in religion. He befriends a Charismatic Preacher Man, who asks Peter to leave with him and become an itinerant preacher too. However, Preacher Man leaves without him.

A Friend Is Someone Who Likes You

Author: Joan W. Anglund
Publisher: Harcourt, Brace and World
Length: 26 **Age:** 2–18 **Date:** 1958
Main Character: white males and females
Other Topics: N/A
Overview: An enchanting little book about friendship, for all ages.

A Girl Called Al

Author: Constance Greene
Publisher: Viking
Length: 128 **Age:** 10–13 **Date:** 1969
Main Character: white female
Other Topics: Death of a Friend, Divorce, Growing Up
Overview: Two girls become fast friends and include Mr. Richards, the assistant superintendent of their building, in their friendship. They visit him in the hospital after his heart attack and mourn his death.

A Kid's Guide to Making Friends

Author: Joy Wilt
Publisher: Weekly Reader Books
Length: 128 **Age:** 6–9 **Date:** 1978
Main Character: N/A
Other Topics: N/A

A Kid's Guide to Making Friends (cont.)

Overview: This children's guide teaches the social skills of making friends.

A Secret Friend

Author: Marilyn Sachs
Publisher: Doubleday
Length: 111 **Age:** 8–12 **Date:** 1978
Main Character: white female
Other Topics: N/A
Overview: After many years as best friends, two best friends break the relationship.

Aldo Applesauce

Author: Johanna Hurwitz
Publisher: Morrow
Length: 127 **Age:** 8–10 **Date:** 1979
Main Character: white males
Other Topics: Divorce
Overview: Aldo Sossi and DeDe are two fifth-grade friends who tolerate each other's differences. DeDe has trouble accepting his parents' divorce and Aldo has decided to be a vegetarian.

Anything for a Friend

Author: Ellen Conford
Publisher: Little, Brown
Length: 180 **Age:** 10–14 **Date:** 1979
Main Character: white female
Other Topics: Moving
Overview: Wallis Greene has moved many times and hates the idea of trying to make friends in her new neighborhood. When she finally does make friends, the family must move again.

Best Friends

Author: Miriam Cohen
Publisher: Macmillan Co.
Length: 27 **Age:** 3–6 **Date:** 1971

Best Friends (cont.)

Main Character: white males
Other Topics: N/A
Overview: This story details the way Jim and Paul cement their friendship by working together on a class project.

Black Like Kyra, White Like Me

Author: Judith Vigna
Publisher: Whitman
Length: 32 **Age:** 4–8 **Date:** 1992
Main Character: African American female
Other Topics: N/A
Overview: This is a story of friendship between an African American girl and a white girl.

Buddies

Author: Barbara Park
Publisher: Knopf
Length: 119 **Age:** 10–18 **Date:** 1985
Main Character: white female
Other Topics: Growing Up
Overview: Thirteen-year-old Dinah Feeney is tired of being labeled "The Kind One." When she goes to summer camp she decides to lose that label. That proves difficult since Fern Wadley, a loser, attaches herself to Dinah.

Charlotte's Web

Author: E. B. White
Publisher: Harper
Length: 184 **Age:** 6–12 **Date:** 1952
Main Character: animal
Other Topics: Death of a Friend
Overview: Eight-year-old Fern can understand all of the animals in the barnyard but cannot communicate with them. Charlotte, a spider, is the true heroine of the story. She befriends Wilbur, the pig, and tries to keep him from being butchered.

Chester's Way

Author: Kevin Henkes
Publisher: Greenwillow
Length: 28 **Age:** 4–8 **Date:** 1988
Main Character: animal
Other Topics: Sharing
Overview: Chester and Wilson are best friends and enjoy doing things the same exact way. Lilly moves into the neighborhood and shows them new ways are fun too.

Do You Want to Be My Friend?

Author: Eric Carle
Publisher: Crowell
Length: 29 **Age:** 3–7 **Date:** 1971
Main Character: animal
Other Topics: N/A
Overview: In this wordless picture book, a mouse searches for a friend.

Fickle Barbara

Author: Satomi Ichikawa
Publisher: Philomel Books
Length: 30 **Age:** 4–8 **Date:** 1993
Main Character: animal
Other Topics: N/A
Overview: Ballerina Bear Barbara discovers that it is nice to make new friends, but old friends should not be forgotten.

Frog and Toad Are Friends

Author: Arnold Lobel
Publisher: Harper and Row
Length: 64 **Age:** 5–8 **Date:** 1970
Main Character: animal
Other Topics: N/A
Overview: A story of a friendship between Frog and Toad, told in five short stories.

Friendship (cont.)

Gabrielle and Selena

Author: Peter Desbarats
Publisher: Harcourt, Brace, and Jovanovich
Length: 27 **Age:** 5–8 **Date:** 1968
Main Character: multicultural females
Other Topics: N/A
Overview: This is the story of an interracial friendship between Gabrielle and Selena.

George and Martha Round and Round

Author: James Marshall
Publisher: Houghton Mifflin
Length: 48 **Age:** 4–6 **Date:** 1988
Main Character: animal
Other Topics: N/A
Overview: George and Martha survive tests of friendship with tolerance and exasperation.

Janey

Author: Charlotte Zolotow
Publisher: Harper and Row
Length: 24 **Age:** 4–8 **Date:** 1973
Main Character: white female
Other Topics: Moving
Overview: With simplicity and perception, the author tenderly evokes the special feeling of loss when Janey moves away.

Julian's Glorious Summer

Author: Ann Cameron
Publisher: Random House
Length: 62 **Age:** 8–10 **Date:** 1987
Main Character: African American male
Other Topics: Fear

Julian's Glorious Summer (cont.)

Overview: When his best friend, Gloria, receives a new bike, seven-year-old Julian hates to admit that he is afraid of bikes.

Let's Be Enemies

Author: Janice May Udry
Publisher: Harper and Brothers
Length: 28 **Age:** 4–6 **Date:** 1961
Main Character: white males
Other Topics: N/A
Overview: "James used to be my friend," begins John's story. This small book is about a friendship that fell apart and was mended again.

Libby on Wednesday

Author: Zilpha Keatley Snyder
Publisher: Delacorte
Length: 196 **Age:** 10–14 **Date:** 1990
Main Character: white female
Other Topics: Home Schooling, Cerebral Palsy, Alcoholism, Giftedness
Overview: Libby is an eleven-year-old who has been home schooled. When she returns to public school, she is placed in the eighth grade, where she is teased because of her height and intelligence. She joins a group of five young writers and in the process befriends children with their own problems.

Look Through My Window

Author: Jean Little
Publisher: Harper
Length: 258 **Age:** 9–11 **Date:** 1970
Main Character: white female
Other Topics: N/A
Overview: Emily Blair is an only child until her parents move into a large house and invite Emily's four cousins to live with them. Emily befriends Kate, who writes poetry, as she does.

Mike and Tony: Best Friends

Author: Harriet Ziefert
Publisher: Puffin Books
Length: 29 **Age:** 4–6 **Date:** 1987
Main Character: white males
Other Topics: N/A
Overview: This easy-to-read book shows how friends can argue and still be friends.

My Friend John

Author: Charlotte Zolotow
Publisher: Harper and Row
Length: 32 **Age:** 4–8 **Date:** 1968
Main Character: white males
Other Topics: N/A
Overview: John and his friend share everything with each other.

My Outrageous Friend Charlie

Author: Martha Alexander
Publisher: Dial
Length: 28 **Age:** 4–8 **Date:** 1989
Main Character: white male and female
Other Topics: N/A
Overview: Jessie Mae admires her friend Charlie because he is outrageous and can do anything. For her birthday, Charlie gives Jessie Mae a magic kit and she can do outrageous things too.

Old Friends, New Friends

Author: Emily North
Publisher: Children's Press
Length: 32 **Age:** 6–8 **Date:** 1980
Main Character: white female
Other Topics: N/A
Overview: Ann learns that she can keep her old friends when she makes new ones.

One to Teeter-Totter

Author: Edith Battles
Publisher: Albert Whitman and Co.
Length: 30 **Age:** 3–7 **Date:** 1973
Main Character: white male
Other Topics: N/A
Overview: A little boy discovers that he needs a friend to share his teeter-totter ride.

Other Bells for Us to Ring

Author: Robert Cormier
Publisher: Delacorte
Length: 136 **Age:** 8–10 **Date:** 1990
Main Character: white female
Other Topics: Alcoholism, Child Abuse
Overview: Eleven-year-old Darcy has never had a best friend until she meets Kathleen Mary O'Hara, who is Catholic.

Patrick and Ted

Author: Geoffrey Hayes
Publisher: Four Winds
Length: 32 **Age:** 3–5 **Date:** 1983
Main Character: animal
Other Topics: N/A
Overview: Two best friends experience their first fight. An excellent reference for children who are experiencing exclusive friendships.

Rosie and Michael

Author: Judith Viorst
Publisher: Atheneum
Length: 36 **Age:** 6–9 **Date:** 1974
Main Character: white male and female
Other Topics: N/A
Overview: Rosie and Michael are friends. They show how friendship can overcome all problems.

Friendship (cont.)

That's What a Friend Is

Author: P. K. Hallinan
Publisher: Children's Press
Length: 29 **Age:** 4–8 **Date:** 1977
Main Character: white males
Other Topics: N/A
Overview: Friendship is described in rhymed text.

The Cybil War

Author: Betsy Byars
Publisher: Viking
Length: 126 **Age:** 9–12 **Date:** 1981
Main Character: white female
Other Topics: N/A
Overview: Two fifth-grade friendships are presented: the first is between Simon Newton and Cybil Ackerman; the other is a rocky relationship between Simon and his boastful, lying friend, Tony Angotti.

The Egypt Game

Author: Zilpha Keatley Snyder
Publisher: Atheneum
Length: 215 **Age:** 9–12 **Date:** 1967
Main Character: African American male
Other Topics: N/A
Overview: Six children in a Berkeley, California, neighborhood set up an imaginary game in an abandoned yard, based on their studies of Egypt. Tragedy strikes when one child is attacked and another murdered.

The Friendship Book

Author: Woodleigh Hubbard
Publisher: Chronicle
Length: 26 **Age:** 4–8 **Date:** 1992
Main Character: animal

The Friendship Book (cont.)

Other Topics: N/A
Overview: Animals reveal a basic truth about friends and friendships.

The Giving Tree

Author: Shel Silverstein
Publisher: Harper and Row
Length: 52 **Age:** 3–18 **Date:** 1964
Main Character: white male
Other Topics: Sharing
Overview: The story of a boy who grows to be a man and of his friendship with a tree.

The Hating Book

Author: Charlotte Zolotow
Publisher: Harper and Row
Length: 32 **Age:** 4–8 **Date:** 1969
Main Character: white female
Other Topics: N/A
Overview: "I hate, hate, hated my friend," begins this small book. Two girls become enemies because of a misunderstanding. A mother encourages them to work out their differences.

The Hot and Cold Summer

Author: Johanna Hurwitz
Publisher: Apple
Length: 176 **Age:** 8–12 **Date:** 1984
Main Character: white male
Other Topics: Jealousy
Overview: Rory and Derek are best friends, until Bolivia comes to visit.

Two Is a Team

Author: Lorraine and Jerrold Beim
Publisher: Harcourt
Length: 56 **Age:** 5–8 **Date:** 1945
Main Character: African American male and white male

Two Is a Team (cont.)

Other Topics: N/A
Overview: An African American child and a white child learn to cooperate as a team.

Veronica the Show Off

Author: Nancy Robinson
Publisher: Four Winds
Length: 119 **Age:** 8–10 **Date:** 1981
Main Character: white female
Other Topics: Boasting
Overview: Veronica shows off in front of her classmates in an effort to gain friends.

We're Very Good Friends, My Brother and I

Author: P. K. Hallinan
Publisher: Children's Press
Length: 32 **Age:** 4–8 **Date:** 1973
Main Character: white males
Other Topics: Sibling Relationships
Overview: A boy explains why he is happy to have a brother for a friend.

When Kids Drive Kids Crazy

Author: Eda Leshan
Publisher: Dial Books
Length: 132 **Age:** 10–14 **Date:** 1990
Main Character: N/A
Other Topics: Growing Up
Overview: This nonfiction work discusses why some young people are brats, bullies, or are hurtful to others.

Giftedness

Been Clever Forever

Author: Bruce Stone
Publisher: Harper and Row

Been Clever Forever (cont.)

Length: 376 **Age:** 10–14 **Date:** 1988
Main Character: white male
Other Topics: Emotional Disturbance
Overview: A brilliant sixteen-year-old has trouble adjusting to a conventional high school setting.

Bravo Minski

Author: Arthur Yorinks
Publisher: Farrar, Straus, and Giroux
Length: 28 **Age:** 6–8 **Date:** 1988
Main Character: white male
Other Topics: N/A
Overview: Minski does everything better than anyone else.

First Grade Takes a Test

Author: Miriam Cohen
Publisher: Greenwillow
Length: 30 **Age:** 5–8 **Date:** 1983
Main Character: African American female
Other Topics: Test Anxiety, Jealousy
Overview: Anna Maria is moved to a class for the gifted and her jealous classmates in first grade begin to quarrel.

The Chalk Box Kid

Author: Clyde Robert Bulla
Publisher: Random House
Length: 58 **Age:** 7–9 **Date:** 1987
Main Character: white male
Other Topics: Poverty
Overview: Gregory's life changes when he is nine years old and his father loses his job. However, he is recognized for his artistic abilities when he attends a new school.

Giftedness (cont.)

The Gifted Kid's Survival Guide: For Ages Ten and Under

Author: Judy Galbraith
Publisher: Free Spirit Publishing
Length: 70 **Age:** 6–10 **Date:** 1984
Main Character: N/A
Other Topics: N/A
Overview: A uniquely organized instruction guide for gifted children, ages ten and under.

Glasses

Arthur's Eyes

Author: Marc Brown
Publisher: Little
Length: 30 **Age:** 6–7 **Date:** 1979
Main Character: animal
Other Topics: N/A
Overview: Arthur must wear glasses. Even though his friends tease him at first, Arthur wears them with pride.

Glasses and Contact Lenses

Author: Dr. Alvin and Virginia Silverstein
Publisher: Lippincott
Length: 135 **Age:** 10–14 **Date:** 1989
Main Character: N/A
Other Topics: N/A
Overview: A thorough investigation of how glasses and contact lenses correct vision problems.

Glasses (Who Needs 'Em?)

Author: Lane Smith
Publisher: Viking
Length: 32 **Age:** 3–8 **Date:** 1990

Glasses (Who Needs 'Em?) (cont.)

Main Character: white male
Other Topics: N/A
Overview: A young boy hates the idea of wearing glasses—until he visits the doctor.

Harry Four Eyes

Author: Nancy Kelton
Publisher: Raintree Editions
Length: 32 **Age:** 6–8 **Date:** 1977
Main Character: white male
Other Topics: N/A
Overview: Young Harry Truman is taunted by his friends when he must wear glasses.

Left, Right, Left, Right!

Author: Muriel Stanek
Publisher: Albert Whitman
Length: 29 **Age:** 5–8 **Date:** 1969
Main Character: white female
Other Topics: N/A
Overview: A small girl puts on her glasses the first thing every morning.

Little Hippo Gets Glasses

Author: Maryann MacDonald
Publisher: Dial
Length: 32 **Age:** 4–8 **Date:** 1992
Main Character: animal
Other Topics: N/A
Overview: Little Hippo is concerned about what his classmates will say when he gets glasses.

Spectacles

Author: Ellen Raskin
Publisher: Atheneum
Length: 48 **Age:** 5–7 **Date:** 1969
Main Character: white female
Other Topics: N/A

Spectacles (cont.)

Overview: A young girl finally gives in to wearing glasses.

Going to Bed

A Bedtime Story

Author: Joan G. Levin
Publisher: E. P. Dutton and Co.
Length: 26 **Age:** 4–6 **Date:** 1975
Main Character: white female
Other Topics: N/A
Overview: Since Arathusela hates going to bed so much, her parents let her put them to bed instead.

Bedtime for Bears

Author: Adelaide Hall
Publisher: Garrard
Length: 40 **Age:** 4–8 **Date:** 1973
Main Character: animal
Other Topics: N/A
Overview: Small Bear doesn't like going to bed. He likes to stay up and play.

First Pink Light

Author: Eloise Greenfield
Publisher: Thomas Crowell
Length: 36 **Age:** 4–8 **Date:** 1976
Main Character: African American male
Other Topics: N/A
Overview: A little boy does not want to go to bed. He is determined to stay up all night so he can welcome his father home in the morning.

Frances Face-Maker

Author: William Cole and Tomi Ungerer
Publisher: Collins

Frances Face-Maker (cont.)

Length: 28 **Age:** 4–8 **Date:** 1963
Main Character: white female
Other Topics: N/A
Overview: Frances McGee delays and postpones when it is time to go to bed.

I Want to Sleep in Your Bed!

Author: Harriet Ziefert
Publisher: HarperCollins
Length: 32 **Age:** 3–6 **Date:** 1990
Main Character: white female
Other Topics: N/A
Overview: Susan is hesitant about going to sleep in her own bed.

No Nap for Benjamen Badger

Author: Nancy W. Carlstrom
Publisher: Macmillan Publishing Co.
Length: 26 **Age:** 3–6 **Date:** 1991
Main Character: animal
Other Topics: N/A
Overview: Ben refuses to take a nap so his mother tells stories until they both fall asleep.

Rebecca's Nap

Author: Fred Burstein
Publisher: Bradbury Press
Length: 28 **Age:** 4–6 **Date:** 1988
Main Character: white female
Other Topics: N/A
Overview: Mommy, Daddy, and Rebecca all take separate naps.

Winifred's New Bed

Author: Lynn and Richard Howell
Publisher: Alfred A. Knopf
Length: 32 **Age:** 3–6 **Date:** 1985
Main Character: white female
Other Topics: N/A

Going to Bed (cont.)

Winifred's New Bed (cont.)

Overview: Winifred outgrows her crib and moves into a new bed.

Going to School

All Ready for School

Author: Leone Adelson
Publisher: David McKay
Length: 24 **Age:** 4–6 **Date:** 1957
Main Character: white female
Other Topics: N/A
Overview: Going to school for the first time is very exciting for Patty.

Annabelle Swift, Kindergartner

Author: Amy Schwartz
Publisher: Orchard Books
Length: 28 **Age:** 5–7 **Date:** 1988
Main Character: white female
Other Topics: N/A
Overview: Everything goes wrong when Annabelle Swift starts kindergarten. She is successful, however, with counting money—because her older sister has taught her. Mr. Blum even sends her to the lunchroom to bring back milk for the entire class.

Benji on His Own

Author: Joan Lexau
Publisher: Dial
Length: 34 **Age:** 5–8 **Date:** 1970
Main Character: African American male
Other Topics: N/A

Benji on His Own (cont.)

Overview: Granny meets Benji after school to walk him home. When she doesn't show up one day, Benji is afraid. Granny is sick. Benji learns that he can ask his neighbors for help.

Buzzy Bear's First Day at School

Author: Dorothy Marino
Publisher: Franklin Watts, Inc.
Length: 33 **Age:** 4–8 **Date:** 1970
Main Character: animal
Other Topics: N/A
Overview: Buzzy Bear learns to adjust to the demands of school.

Class Clown

Author: Joanna Hurwitz
Publisher: Morrow
Length: 112 **Age:** 8–10 **Date:** 1987
Main Character: white male
Other Topics: N/A
Overview: Lucus Cott is the third-grade cut-up and class clown. He learns to accept responsibility and make friends.

Come to School, Dear Dragon

Author: Margaret Hillert
Publisher: Modern Curriculum Press
Length: 32 **Age:** 4–6 **Date:** 1985
Main Character: white males
Other Topics: N/A
Overview: A young boy takes his pet dragon to school.

Come with Me to Nursery School

Author: Edith T. Hurd
Publisher: Coward-McCann, Inc.
Length: 42 **Age:** 4–6 **Date:** 1970
Main Character: multicultural males and females
Other Topics: N/A

Come with Me to Nursery School (cont.)

Overview: This book of photographs answers the question, "What will I do at my school?"

Did You Carry the Flag Today, Charley?

Author: Rebecca Caudill
Publisher: Holt
Length: 94 **Age:** 6–9 **Date:** 1971
Main Character: white male
Other Topics: N/A
Overview: A five-year-old Appalachian boy must adjust to the discipline of school.

First Day in School

Author: Bill Binzen
Publisher: Doubleday
Length: 30 **Age:** 4–6 **Date:** 1972
Main Character: multicultural males and females
Other Topics: N/A
Overview: The boys and girls are anxious about the first day of school.

First Day of School

Author: Myriam Deru and Paule Alen
Publisher: Derrydale Books
Length: 29 **Age:** 4–8 **Date:** 1988
Main Character: animal
Other Topics: N/A
Overview: A bilingual storyboard with side-by-side text in English and Spanish. Freddy the fox goes to school for the first time.

Herbie's Troubles

Author: Carol Chapman
Publisher: Dutton
Length: 29 **Age:** 4–6 **Date:** 1981
Main Character: white male
Other Topics: N/A

Herbie's Troubles (cont.)

Overview: Herbie liked school until he met Jimmy John, a bully. Herbie receives suggestions from his friends. Herbie's troubles are solved when he ignores Jimmy John.

I Don't Want to Go to School

Author: Elizabeth Bram
Publisher: Greenwillow
Length: 28 **Age:** 4–6 **Date:** 1977
Main Character: white female
Other Topics: Separation Anxiety
Overview: Jennifer is reluctant to go to kindergarten on the first day but soon changes her mind.

I Like School

Author: Bobbie Kalman
Publisher: Crabtree Publishing Co.
Length: 32 **Age:** 5–8 **Date:** 1985
Main Character: multicultural males and females
Other Topics: N/A
Overview: A picture book in chapter format describes various aspects of school.

I Like School

Author: Michaela Muntean
Publisher: Sesame Street/Golden Press
Length: 24 **Age:** 4–6 **Date:** 1980
Main Character: puppets
Other Topics: N/A
Overview: This informational book identifies everything one might encounter in the classroom.

I'd Rather Stay Home

Author: Carol Barking and Elizabeth James
Publisher: Raintree Editions

Going to School (cont.)

I'd Rather Stay Home (cont.)

Length: 32 **Age:** 4–6 **Date:** 1975
Main Character: African American male
Other Topics: Fear
Overview: A young boy is afraid to go to school. Mrs. Kimball makes him feel comfortable in the new setting.

Junie B. Jones and the Stupid Smelly Bus

Author: Barbara Park
Publisher: Random House
Length: 69 **Age:** 6–9 **Date:** 1992
Main Character: white female
Other Topics: N/A
Overview: Junie B. likes the first day of kindergarten. But then she hears horror stories of what happens on the bus ride home, so Junie B. hides out in a closet until everyone is gone. She's finally caught by the custodian.

Kitty in the Middle

Author: Judy Delton
Publisher: Houghton Mifflin
Length: 135 **Age:** 8–10 **Date:** 1979
Main Character: white female
Other Topics: War
Overview: Three best friends experience parochial school during WWII.

Little Monster at School

Author: Mercer Mayer
Publisher: Golden Press
Length: 25 **Age:** 4–7 **Date:** 1978
Main Character: cartoon characters
Other Topics: N/A

Little Monster at School (cont.)

Overview: Little Monster enjoys his first day of school.

Maybe Tomorrow I'll Have a Good Time

Author: Mary Sanderstrom
Publisher: Herman Sciences Press
Length: 27 **Age:** 4–8 **Date:** 1981
Main Character: white female
Other Topics: Working Mother
Overview: Marsha Lou is mad and sad about her first day at the daycare center. She tells her mother that maybe tomorrow she'll have a good time.

Monster Goes to School

Author: Virginia Mueller
Publisher: Albert Whitman
Length: 24 **Age:** 2–6 **Date:** 1991
Main Character: animal
Other Topics: N/A
Overview: Monster learns about time at school.

Morris Goes to School

Author: Bernard Wiseman
Publisher: Harper and Row
Length: 64 **Age:** 5–8 **Date:** 1970
Main Character: animal
Other Topics: N/A
Overview: When Morris the Moose cannot count, he decides to go to school to learn.

Move Over, Twerp

Author: Martha Alexander
Publisher: Dial
Length: 28 **Age:** 2–6 **Date:** 1981
Main Character: white male
Other Topics: Bossiness, Boasting, Bullies

Move Over, Twerp (cont.)

Overview: Jeffrey comes up with a plan when he encounters trouble on the school bus.

Never Spit on Your Shoes

Author: Denys Cazet
Publisher: Orchard Books
Length: 26 **Age:** 4–8 **Date:** 1990
Main Character: animal
Other Topics: N/A
Overview: A first grader describes his first day at school.

Only Jody

Author: Judy Delton
Publisher: Houghton Mifflin
Length: 95 **Age:** 8–12 **Date:** 1982
Main Character: white male
Other Topics: Sibling Rivalry, Hating Your Name
Overview: Fifth grader Jody is the only boy in his family, he hates his name, and must go to another new school—the eighth in his academic career.

Ramona Quimby, Age 8

Author: Beverly Cleary
Publisher: Morrow
Length: 190 **Age:** 7–9 **Date:** 1981
Main Character: white female
Other Topics: N/A
Overview: Ramona must adjust to a new teacher and a new school.

Ramona the Brave

Author: Beverly Cleary
Publisher: Morrow
Length: 190 **Age:** 8–10 **Date:** 1975
Main Character: white female
Other Topics: N/A

Ramona the Brave (cont.)

Overview: Ramona enters first grade, which she decides is boring.

Ramona the Pest

Author: Beverly Cleary
Publisher: Morrow
Length: 192 **Age:** 8–10 **Date:** 1968
Main Character: white female
Other Topics: N/A
Overview: Ramona is convinced that her teacher doesn't love her anymore so she decides to drop out of kindergarten.

Red Day, Green Day

Author: Edith Kunhardt
Publisher: Greenwillow
Length: 32 **Age:** 4–6 **Date:** 1992
Main Character: white male
Other Topics: Recognizing Colors
Overview: This picture book serves two purposes—reassuring children about starting kindergarten and introducing them to colors.

Russell Rides Again

Author: Johanna Hurwitz
Publisher: William Morrow
Length: 86 **Age:** 5–8 **Date:** 1985
Main Character: white male
Other Topics: N/A
Overview: Russell graduates from nursery school and enters kindergarten.

Russell Sprouts

Author: Johanna Hurwitz
Publisher: Morrow
Length: 68 **Age:** 3–8 **Date:** 1987
Main Character: white male
Other Topics: N/A
Overview: Russell receives a real report card in first grade.

Going to School (cont.)

Shawn Goes to School

Author: Petronella Breinberg
Publisher: Crowell
Length: 24 **Age:** 4–6 **Date:** 1973
Main Character: African American male
Other Topics: N/A
Overview: A small boy begins nursery school. At first, he is shy, but he soon adjusts.

Six New Students

Author: Franz Brandenberg
Publisher: Greenwillow
Length: 56 **Age:** 4–6 **Date:** 1978
Main Character: animal
Other Topics: N/A
Overview: In this easy-to-read book, six fieldmouse children find their new school more pleasurable than they expected.

Sometimes I Hate School

Author: Carol Barkin and Elizabeth James
Publisher: Raintree Editions
Length: 32 **Age:** 4–6 **Date:** 1975
Main Character: multicultural males and females
Other Topics: N/A
Overview: This book uses photographs to discuss a child's anxiety and distress about going to school when a substitute teacher is there.

Starting School

Author: Janet and Allan Ahlberg
Publisher: Viking
Length: 32 **Age:** 4–6 **Date:** 1988

Starting School (cont.)

Main Character: multicultural males and females
Other Topics: N/A
Overview: This picture storybook depicts the activities of eight children during their first four months of school. All aspects of school are introduced— bathrooms, P.E., activities, library.

Teach Me about School

Author: Joy Berry
Publisher: Children's Press
Length: 35 **Age:** 3–6 **Date:** 1986
Main Character: white female
Other Topics: N/A
Overview: This first introduction to school describes everything children are likely to encounter on the first day of attendance.

The First Day of School

Author: Patricia Relf
Publisher: Western Publishing Co.
Length: 20 **Age:** 4–6 **Date:** 1981
Main Character: multicultural males and females
Other Topics: N/A
Overview: Elizabeth is excited about going to school for the first time. At first she is scared, then she discovers she likes school!

The How: Making the Best of a Mistake

Author: Selma Boyd and Pauline Boyd
Publisher: Human Sciences Press
Length: 28 **Age:** 4–8 **Date:** 1981
Main Character: white male
Other Topics: Growing Up, Self-Confidence
Overview: A child finds a way to recover from an embarrassing mistake at school.

The School

Author: John Burningham
Publisher: Harper
Length: 18 **Age:** 4–6 **Date:** 1975
Main Character: white male
Other Topics: N/A
Overview: While at school, a young boy learns to read and write, paint, make friends, and play games.

The Secret Language

Author: Ursula Nordstrom
Publisher: Harper and Row
Length: 167 **Age:** 7–9 **Date:** 1960
Main Character: white female
Other Topics: Homesickness
Overview: A homesick child must adjust to life at boarding school.

Time for School, Nathan!

Author: Lulu Delacre
Publisher: Scholastic
Length: 30 **Age:** 4–6 **Date:** 1989
Main Character: animal
Other Topics: Jealousy
Overview: Nathan and Nicholas prepare for going to school.

We Like Kindergarten

Author: Clara Cassidy
Publisher: Golden Press
Length: 22 **Age:** 4–6 **Date:** 1965
Main Character: white female
Other Topics: N/A
Overview: Carol goes to kindergarten for the first time.

When You Go to Kindergarten

Author: James Howe
Publisher: Knopf
Length: 48 **Age:** 4–5 **Date:** 1986
Main Character: N/A

When You Go to Kindergarten (cont.)

Other Topics: N/A
Overview: These photographs will help children overcome their fears of going to real school.

Will I Have A Friend?

Author: Miriam Cohen
Publisher: Macmillan
Length: 32 **Age:** 5–7 **Date:** 1967
Main Character: white male
Other Topics: N/A
Overview: Even though Jim's father assures him that he will have a friend on the first day of school, Jim is doubtful. Jim does find a friend in Paul, who shows him his tiny truck.

Will You Come Back for Me?

Author: Anne Tompert
Publisher: Albert Whitman
Length: 32 **Age:** 4–6 **Date:** 1988
Main Character: Asian female
Other Topics: N/A
Overview: Four-year-old Suki must begin school when Mom goes to work for Dad in his office.

Willy Bear

Author: Mildred Kantrowitz
Publisher: Four Winds
Length: 40 **Age:** 4–6 **Date:** 1980
Main Character: white male
Other Topics: N/A
Overview: A little boy projects onto his teddy bear his anxieties about starting school the next day.

owing Up

Arthur's Honey Bear

Author: Lillian Hoban
Publisher: Harper and Row
Length: 64 **Age:** 5–8 **Date:** 1974
Main Character: animal
Other Topics: N/A
Overview: When Arthur sells his toy bear to his little sister, he must adjust to the fact that he still wants that bear.

Bearstone

Author: Will Hobbs
Publisher: Avon
Length: 154 **Age:** 8–12 **Date:** 1989
Main Character: Native American male
Other Topics: Illiteracy, Reading Problems, Intergenerational
Overview: Fourteen-year-old Cloyd had grown up without his parents, without school, and alone. His tribe sends him to a group home for boys. He finally discovers love when he spends a summer helping an elderly man on his ranch.

Big Boy, Little Boy

Author: Betty Jo Stanovich
Publisher: Lothrop, Lee and Shepard
Length: 28 **Age:** 4–6 **Date:** 1984
Main Character:: white male
Other Topics: Intergenerational
Overview: Four-year-old David has mixed feelings about growing up. His grandmother helps him remember when he was a "little boy."

Bingo Brown and the Language of Love

Author: Betsy Byars
Publisher: Viking
Length: 144 **Age:** 10–13 **Date:** 1989
Main Character: white male

Bingo Brown and the Language of Love (cont.)

Other Topics: N/A
Overview: Bingo's girlfriend Melissa has moved to Oklahoma and he has been running up huge phone bills. He is also confronted with the news that his mother is expecting another baby.

Captain Whiz-Bang

Author: Diane Stanley
Publisher: William Morrow
Length: 31 **Age:** 4–8 **Date:** 1987
Main Character: white female
Other Topics: N/A
Overview: Captain Whiz-Bang grows old gracefully with his owner Annie.

Come Sing, Jimmy Jo

Author: Katherine Paterson
Publisher: Dutton
Length: 197 **Age:** 11–14 **Date:** 1985
Main Character: white male
Other Topics: Loneliness, Giftedness, Friendship
Overview: James struggles to balance his singing talent with his need for quiet and security. He befriends Eleazer Jones, an African American classmate.

Dicey's Song

Author: Cynthia Voigt
Publisher: Macmillan
Length: 196 **Age:** 11–14 **Date:** 1982
Main Character: white female
Other Topics: Abandonment, Illiteracy, Reading Problems, Death, Mental Illness
Overview: This sequel to *Homecoming* shows thirteen-year-old Dicey learning to let her family change and become a family. Her changes parallel those of her grandmother.

Drop Dead

Author: Julia Cunningham
Publisher: Pantheon
Length: 88 **Age:** 8–10 **Date:** 1965
Main Character: white male
Other Topics: Orphan
Overview: Gilly Ground moves from an orphanage to Kobalt's house. He soon discovers that Kobalt is evil and cruel, and he is forced to escape.

Everybody Grows Up

Author: Mary McBurney Green
Publisher: Franklin Watts
Length: 44 **Age:** 4–6 **Date:** 1969
Main Character: animal
Other Topics: N/A
Overview: Rhythmic language about growing up.

Family Secrets: Five Very Important Stories

Author: Susan Shreve
Publisher: Alfred A. Knopf
Length: 56 **Age:** 8–12 **Date:** 1979
Main Character: white male
Other Topics: Death of a Pet, Death of a Grandparent, Divorce, Cancer
Overview: Sammy's growing up years include five stories of his dog's death, suicide, cheating on a test, divorce, and his grandmother's death with cancer.

Growing Up, Growing Older

Author: North Shore Committee on the Older Adult
Publisher: Holt, Rinehart, and Winston
Length: 42 **Age:** 4–8 **Date:** 1964
Main Character: white male
Other Topics: Intergenerational
Overview: The story of Johnny's life spans from age one week to sixty-five years.

I Am Not a Crybaby

Author: Norma Simon
Publisher: Puffin
Length: 32 **Age:** 4–8 **Date:** 1991
Main Character: multicultural males and females
Other Topics: N/A
Overview: Children talk about what makes them cry.

Journey

Author: Patricia MacLachlan
Publisher: Delacorte
Length: 83 **Age:** 8–11 **Date:** 1991
Main Character: white male
Other Topics: Intergenerational
Overview: When eleven-year-old Journey's mother leaves him and his sister with their grandparents, Journey feels rejected. Through photography, he learns about himself, his mother, and her past, and he slowly begins to accept her as she is.

Journey to an 800 Number

Author: E. L. Konigsburg
Publisher: Atheneum
Length: 138 **Age:** 10–13 **Date:** 1982
Main Character: white male
Other Topics: Divorce
Overview: Maximilian Stubbs is spending the summer with his father Woody while his mother remarries. Max feels disdain for his father, who gives camel rides at shopping centers.

Leo the Late Bloomer

Author: Robert Kraus
Publisher: Scholastic
Length: 28 **Age:** 4–8 **Date:** 1971
Main Character: animal
Other Topics: N/A

Growing Up (cont.)

Leo the Late Bloomer (cont.)

Overview: Leo felt that he couldn't do anything right. His mother assured him that he was just a late bloomer.

Old Yeller

Author: Fred Gipson
Publisher: Harper
Length: 158 **Age:** 10–14 **Date:** 1956
Main Character: white male
Other Topics: Death of a Pet
Overview: A brave dog helps a four-teen-year-old boy become the man of the family.

Park's Quest

Author: Katherine Paterson
Publisher: Dutton
Length: 147 **Age:** 10–13 **Date:** 1988
Main Character: white male
Other Topics: Death of a Parent
Overview: Park travels from his home near Washington, D.C., to his dead father's home in rural Virginia. Park is trying to discover who he is.

Red Sky at Morning

Author: Andrea Wyman
Publisher: Holiday House
Length: 160 **Age:** 8–12 **Date:** 1991
Main Character: white female
Other Topics: Death of a Parent, Child Abuse, Intergenerational
Overview: Callie Common's life in 1909 Indiana is not so common. She deals with the near death of her sister and grandfa-ther, the diphtheria epidemic, her aunt's abuse, and the death of her mother. She faces these challenges with courage and hope.

Scorpions

Author: Walter Dean Myers
Publisher: Harper
Length: 216 **Age:** 11–14 **Date:** 1988
Main Character: Hispanic male
Other Topics: Incarceration, Gangs
Overview: Twelve-year-old Jamal is reluctant to take his brother's place as leader of a Harlem gang.

Seven Long Years until College

Author: Mary Jane Auch
Publisher: Holiday House
Length: 160 **Age:** 8–12 **Date:** 1991
Main Character: white female
Other Topics: Stepfamilies
Overview: Natalie has three problems: her sister has gone away to college, her mother has remarried, and her best friend is moving. Natalie runs away to her sis-ter's college but discovers that she can't run away from her problems.

Shadow of a Bull

Author: Maia Wojciechowska
Publisher: Atheneum
Length: 165 **Age:** 12–15 **Date:** 1964
Main Character: Hispanic American male
Other Topics: N/A
Overview: Twelve-year-old Manolo is the son of a famous bullfighter. He is not certain if he wants to follow in his father's footsteps.

Simon

Author: Molly Cone
Publisher: Houghton Mifflin
Length: 102 **Age:** 10–12 **Date:** 1970
Main Character: white male
Other Topics: Blind, Mentally Handi-capped

Simon (cont.)

Overview: Simon is having a difficult time growing up. All he wants to do is escape until he meets a young mentally handicapped girl and an old blind man.

Sloppy Kisses

Author: Elizabeth Winthrop
Publisher: Macmillan
Length: 32 **Age:** 5–8 **Date:** 1980
Main Character: animal
Other Topics: N/A
Overview: Emmy Lou is from a kissing family but her school friend tells her kissing is for babies.

Someone New

Author: Charlotte Zolotow
Publisher: Harper and Row
Length: 32 **Age:** 4–8 **Date:** 1978
Main Character: white male
Other Topics: N/A
Overview: The young boy in this story is growing up and changing. He packs away his baby toys and takes a walk with his friend, Jack. He has become someone new.

The Broccoli Tapes

Author: Jan Slepian
Publisher: Putnam
Length: 157 **Age:** 10–12 **Date:** 1989
Main Character: white female
Other Topics: Intergenerational
Overview: Sara is a sixth grader whose father is a professor in Hawaii and whose mother is worried about the care of her sick mother. Sara is in charge of her brother Sam. She sends tape-recorded messages from Hawaii back to her class in Boston.

The Burning Questions of Bingo Brown

Author: Betsy Byars
Publisher: Viking
Length: 166 **Age:** 10–13 **Date:** 1988
Main Character: white male
Other Topics: Suicide
Overview: Bingo agonizes over which of the girls he should like in his sixth-grade class. He must also face a deeper issue—his teacher appears to have attempted suicide after an argument with a woman.

The 18th Emergency

Author: Betsy Byars
Publisher: Viking
Length: 128 **Age:** 9–11 **Date:** 1973
Main Character: white male
Other Topics: Fear, Bullies
Overview: Benjie (also known as Mouse) must face up to a beating by the school bully, Marr Hammerman.

The One-Eyed Cat

Author: Paula Fox
Publisher: Bradbury
Length: 216 **Age:** 12–14 **Date:** 1984
Main Character: white male
Other Topics: Death (General)
Overview: Eleven-year-old Ned Wallis receives an air rifle from his uncle. His father forbids it, but Ned slips into the attic, retrieves the gun, and shoots something out the window. He later finds a one-eyed cat that he feeds.

The Village by the Sea

Author: Paula Fox
Publisher: Orchard
Length: 147 **Age:** 10–18 **Date:** 1988
Main Character: white female
Other Topics: Ill Parent, Alcoholism, Intergenerational

Growing Up (cont.)

The Village by the Sea (cont.)

Overview: Emma spends two weeks with her aunt and uncle while her father undergoes heart bypass surgery. Her uncle is very friendly but her aunt is a sad and bitter woman. Emma grows to understand her aunt.

Who Hates Harold?

Author: Jules Older
Publisher: Western Publishing Co.
Length: 24 **Age:** 6–8 **Date:** 1986
Main Character: white male
Other Topics: Friendship, Loneliness
Overview: This book about peer pressure includes a note to parents.

Willie's Not the Hugging Kind

Author: Joyce Dunham Barrett
Publisher: Harper Trophy
Length: 32 **Age:** 5–8 **Date:** 1989
Main Character: African American male
Other Topics: Peer Pressure
Overview: Willie's best friend Jo Jo thinks hugging is silly, so Willie stops hugging too until he misses giving and receiving hugs.

Wish You Were Here

Author: Hilma Wolitzer
Publisher: Farrar, Straus, Giroux
Length: 180 **Age:** 10–14 **Date:** 1984
Main Character: white male
Other Topics: Intergenerational, Asthma, Divorce, Twins
Overview: Bernie Seagal needs money but his asthma prevents him from getting the jobs he likes. He settles for babysitting twins, coaching his sister for a play, and helping his mother's cheerful boyfriend.

Haircuts

Jeremy's First Haircut

Author: Linda Walvoord Girard
Publisher: Albert Whitman
Length: 21 **Age:** 4–6 **Date:** 1986
Main Character: white male
Other Topics: Fear
Overview: It takes both mommy's and daddy's help for Jeremy to see that a haircut is painless.

Mop Top

Author: Don Freeman
Publisher: Viking Press
Length: 48 **Age:** 4–6 **Date:** 1955
Main Character: white male
Other Topics: N/A
Overview: This is the story of a boy who never wanted to have his hair cut. Everyone called him "Moppy."

Hating Your Name

Anastasia Krupnik

Author: Lois Lowry
Publisher: Houghton Mifflin
Length: 114 **Age:** 10–12 **Date:** 1979
Main Character: white female
Other Topics: Sibling Rivalry
Overview: Anastasia Krupnik is the only girl in fourth grade whose name will not fit on the front of a sweatshirt. When a new baby joins the Krupnik family, Anastasia is allowed to choose his name—so she chooses the worst one possible.

But Names Will Never Hurt Me

Author: Bernard Waber
Publisher: Houghton Mifflin Co.
Length: 32 **Age:** 4–8 **Date:** 1976
Main Character: white female
Other Topics: N/A
Overview: Alison Wonderland learns how she got her name and how to live with it.

Chrysanthemum

Author: Kevin Henkes
Publisher: Greenwillow
Length: 30 **Age:** 4–8 **Date:** 1991
Main Character: animal
Other Topics: Going to School, Self-Worth
Overview: Chrysanthemum is a little mouse who loves her name, until she starts going to school, where she is teased. Her music teacher, Mrs. Twinkle, restores her love for her name.

I Hate My Name

Author: Eva Grant
Publisher: Raintree Publisher
Length: 32 **Age:** 6–8 **Date:** 1980
Main Character: white female
Other Topics: Going to School
Overview: Demelza dreads starting school because she hates her name, and she is afraid her classmates might ridicule her.

Sabrina

Author: Martha Alexander
Publisher: Dial
Length: 32 **Age:** 3–7 **Date:** 1991
Main Character: white female
Other Topics: Going to School
Overview: Sabrina liked her name until she started nursery school.

The Adventures of Ali Baba Bernstein

Author: Johanna Hurwitz
Publisher: Morrow
Length: 82 **Age:** 7–10 **Date:** 1985
Main Character: white male
Other Topics: N/A
Overview: Eight-year-old David Bernstein wants his life to be more exciting so he changes his name to Ali Baba Bernstein and things get a lot more exciting.

The Boy Who Would Not Say His Name

Author: Elizabeth Vreeken
Publisher: Follett
Length: 29 **Age:** 4–8 **Date:** 1959
Main Character: white male
Other Topics: N/A
Overview: This beginning-to-read book describes the problems that arise for Bobby Brown when he refuses to use his real name.

Time of the Bison

Author: Ann Turner
Publisher: Macmillan
Length: 64 **Age:** 7–11 **Date:** 1987
Main Character: Native American male
Other Topics: N/A
Overview: Young Scar Boy wants a more appropriate name.

Homeless

A Chance to Grow

Author: Sandy Powell
Publisher: Carolrhoda Books
Length: 38 **Age:** 6–9 **Date:** 1992
Main Character: white male
Other Topics: N/A

Homeless (cont.)

A Chance to Grow (cont.)

Overview: Joe, his mother, and little sister are evicted from their apartment and must find a place to live.

A Rose for Abby

Author: Donna Guthrie
Publisher: Abingdon Press
Length: 28 **Age:** 5–8 **Date:** 1988
Main Character: African American female
Other Topics: N/A
Overview: Abby sees a homeless woman searching the trash cans for food and wants to do something for the street people.

At the Sound of the Beep

Author: Mary Sachs
Publisher: Dutton
Length: 154 **Age:** 8–12 **Date:** 1990
Main Character: white male and female
Other Topics: Divorce, Twins
Overview: This mystery story depicts the homeless as real people in dire need. Twins Mathew and Mathilda Green run away from home when their parents split up and want to split the twins up. They take refuge in Golden Gate Park, a haven for the homeless.

Cara

Author: Dennis Fradin
Publisher: Regensteiner
Length: 31 **Age:** 5–8 **Date:** 1977
Main Character: African American male
Other Topics: N/A
Overview: A homeless cat finds a friend and a home.

December Stillness

Author: Mary Downing Hahn
Publisher: Clarion
Length: 181 **Age:** 10–18 **Date:** 1988
Main Character: white female
Other Topics: N/A
Overview: Thirteen-year-old Kelly tries to befriend Mr. Weems, a homeless Vietnam vet who spends his days in her surburban library, though he makes it clear that he wants to be left alone.

Fly Away Home

Author: Eve Bunting
Publisher: Clarion
Length: 32 **Age:** 5–8 **Date:** 1991
Main Character: white male
Other Topics: N/A
Overview: This affecting picture book is narrated by a young homeless boy who lives with his dad in an airport.

Home

Author: Michael J. Rosen, editor
Publisher: Harper Collins
Length: 26 **Age:** 6–10 **Date:** 1992
Main Character: multicultural males and females
Other Topics: N/A
Overview: Thirteen authors and seventeen illustrators celebrate the places and things that make up homes.

Homeless Children

Author: Karen O'Connor
Publisher: Lucent Books
Length: 79 **Age:** 10–18 **Date:** 1989
Main Character: multicultural males and females
Other Topics: N/A
Overview: This book of photographs and text illustrates the plight of the urban homeless.

Maniac Magee

Author: Jerry Spinelli
Publisher: Little, Brown
Length: 194 **Age:** 4–8 **Date:** 1990
Main Character: white male
Other Topics: Racism, Prejudice, Orphan
Overview: Jeffrey is an orphan who runs away. He lands in the segregated community of Two Mills where he touches people's lives.

Sam and the Moon Queen

Author: Alison C. Herzig and Jane L. Mali
Publisher: Puffin
Length: 176 **Age:** 8–12 **Date:** 1992
Main Character: white male and female
Other Topics: N/A
Overview: Sam finds a homeless girl living in the basement of his building.

Slake's Limbo

Author: Felice Holman
Publisher: Scribner
Length: 117 **Age:** 10–12 **Date:** 1974
Main Character: white male
Other Topics: Loneliness
Overview: Thirteen-year-old Aremis Slake takes refuge in the subway. He stays 121 days.

Sophie and the Sidewalk Man

Author: Stephanie S. Tollan
Publisher: Macmillan
Length: 75 **Age:** 7–10 **Date:** 1992
Main Character: white female
Other Topics: N/A
Overview: Sophie is torn between wanting to buy a toy and helping a hungry street person.

Taking Care of Terrific

Author: Lois Lowry
Publisher: Houghton Mifflin
Length: 168 **Age:** 10–12 **Date:** 1983
Main Character: white female
Other Topics: Hating Your Name
Overview: While babysitting, fourteen-year-old Enid meets a bag lady in the park.

The Crossing

Author: Gary Paulson
Publisher: Orchard Books
Length: 114 **Age:** 6–9 **Date:** 1987
Main Character: Hispanic male
Other Topics: Emotional Disturbance
Overview: Fourteen-year-old Manny, a street kid fighting for survival in a Mexican border town, develops a strange friendship with an emotionally disturbed American soldier who decides to help him get across the border.

The Facts about the Homeless

Author: Laurie Beckelman
Publisher: Crestwood House
Length: 48 **Age:** 8–10 **Date:** 1989
Main Character: multicultural males and females
Other Topics: Alcoholism, Poverty
Overview: This factual text discusses the problems and services available to the homeless in America. Myths, stereotypes, and ways to help the handicapped are also addressed. A glossary and index are included.

The Family under the Bridge

Author: Natalie Savage Carlson
Publisher: Harper
Length: 97 **Age:** 7–10 **Date:** 1958
Main Character: white male
Other Topics: N/A

Homeless (cont.)

The Family under the Bridge (cont.)

Overview: In post-World War II Paris, Armand becomes the adopted grandfather of a family living under a bridge.

The Fastest Friend in the West

Author: Vicki Grove
Publisher: Putnam
Length: 174 **Age:** 10–18 **Date:** 1990
Main Character: white female
Other Topics: Weight Problem, Friendship
Overview: When her best friend dumps her to be with the popular kids, overweight Lori shares an unusual but brief friendship with a homeless girl.

The Homeless

Author: Teresa O'Neill
Publisher: Greenhaven Press
Length: 32 **Age:** 10–18 **Date:** 1990
Main Character: multicultural male and female
Other Topics: N/A
Overview: This text offers opportunities for readers to apply critical thinking to understand society's attitude toward the homeless.

Honesty

A Crocodile's Tale

Author: Jose and Arianne Aruego
Publisher: Charles Scribner's Sons
Length: 32 **Age:** 6–8 **Date:** 1972
Main Character: Asian male
Other Topics: N/A

A Crocodile's Tale (cont.)

Overview: This Philippine folktale shows how Juan deals with a lying crocodile.

Charlotte Cheetham: Master of Disaster

Author: Barbara Ware Holmes
Publisher: Harper and Row
Length: 117 **Age:** 8–12 **Date:** 1985
Main Character: white female
Other Topics: Friendship
Overview: Ten-year-old Charlotte cannot keep from telling tales. She desperately wants to be a part of the group so she tells a really big lie.

Chicken Sunday

Author: Patricia Polacco
Publisher: Philomel
Length: 30 **Age:** 6–8 **Date:** 1992
Main Character: African American female
Other Topics: Loyalty, Responsibility
Overview: The author recalls the summer she and two neighbor boys sought a job from Mr. Kodinski so they could buy the boys' grandmother an Easter bonnet. Instead, the boys find themselves falsely accused of vandalism.

Ernie's Little Lie

Author: Don Elliott
Publisher: Random House
Length: 30 **Age:** 6–7 **Date:** 1983
Main Character: white male
Other Topics: N/A
Overview: Ernie enters a painting done by his cousin in a contest but is hesitant about telling a lie.

Fish Face

Author: Patricia Reilly Giff
Publisher: Delacorte Press

Fish Face (cont.)

Length: 75 **Age:** 5–8 **Date:** 1984
Main Character: white female
Other Topics: Friendship
Overview: When Dawn sits next to Emily at school, Emily discovers that Dawn is a thief.

Franklin Fibs

Author: Paulette Bourgeois
Publisher: Scholastic
Length: 30 **Age:** 4–8 **Date:** 1991
Main Character: animal
Other Topics: N/A
Overview: Franklin has a problem telling fibs to his friends.

Ivan the Great

Author: Isabel L. Cusack
Publisher: Thomas Y. Crowell
Length: 45 **Age:** 5–8 **Date:** 1978
Main Character: white male
Other Topics: N/A
Overview: Robby's pet parrot teaches him the difference between the truth and a lie.

Jamaica's Find

Author: Juanita Havill
Publisher: Houghton Mifflin
Length: 32 **Age:** 4–6 **Date:** 1986
Main Character: African American female
Other Topics: N/A
Overview: Jamaica discovers how good it makes her feel to return a lost possession.

John's Choice: A Story about Honesty

Author: Jane B. Moncure
Publisher: Children's Press
Length: 30 **Age:** 5–8 **Date:** 1982

John's Choice: A Story about Honesty (cont.)

Main Character: white male
Other Topics: N/A
Overview: After being overpaid, John contemplates using the money to buy candy.

Leprechauns Never Lie

Author: Lorna Balian
Publisher: Abingdon
Length: 29 **Age:** 4–8 **Date:** 1980
Main Character: white female
Other Topics: Intergenerational, Lazy
Overview: Ninny Nanny is too lazy to do chores so she catches a leprechaun to help. Since leprechauns never lie, Ninny Nanny follows all his directions and before she realizes it, all their chores are done.

Let's Talk about Breaking Promises

Author: Joy W. Berry
Publisher: Children's Press
Length: 32 **Age:** 4–6 **Date:** 1982
Main Character: white male
Other Topics: N/A
Overview: A discussion of breaking promises and how it makes you feel.

Matilda Who Told Lies

Author: Hilaire Belloc
Publisher: Puffin
Length: 32 **Age:** 5–8 **Date:** 1970
Main Character: white female
Other Topics: N/A
Overview: Matilda is not always honest.

Mean Streak

Author: Ilene Cooper
Publisher: Puffin
Length: 192 **Age:** 8–12 **Date:** 1992

Honesty (cont.)

Mean Streak (cont.)

Main Character: white female
Other Topics: Stepfamilies
Overview: Veronica Volner, sixth grader, talks a mean streak, especially when her father plans on remarrying.

One to Grow On

Author: Jean Little
Publisher: Puffin
Length: 144 **Age:** 8–12 **Date:** 1991
Main Character: white female
Other Topics: N/A
Overview: Janie has told so many stories that no one believes her anymore. She befriends Lisa, who is rich and famous.

Patti's Pet Gorilla

Author: Pat Rhoads Mauser
Publisher: Atheneum
Length: 64 **Age:** 7–9 **Date:** 1987
Main Character: white female
Other Topics: N/A
Overview: Patti tells a big fib—that she has a pet gorilla.

Pinocchio

Author: Carlo Collodi
Publisher: Children's Press
Length: 215 **Age:** 5–8 **Date:** 1968
Main Character: puppet
Other Topics: N/A
Overview: Old Geppetto carves a puppet out of wood and names him Pinocchio. Every time Pinocchio lies, his nose grows longer.

Puff in the Land of the Living Lies

Author: Romeo Muller
Publisher: Troll

Puff in the Land of the Living Lies (cont.)

Length: 62 **Age:** 5–8 **Date:** 1992
Main Character: animal
Other Topics: N/A
Overview: Puff the dragon helps Sandy learn the difference between honesty and lying.

Red Ribbon Rosie

Author: Jean Marzollo
Publisher: Random House
Length: 64 **Age:** 6–10 **Date:** 1988
Main Character: white female
Other Topics: Friendship
Overview: Rosie decides to cheat so that she can win a race with her best friend. The results are disastrous.

Sam, Bangs and Moonshine

Author: Evaline Ness
Publisher: Holt, Rinehart and Winston, Inc.
Length: 35 **Age:** 5–7 **Date:** 1966
Main Character: white female
Other Topics: Death of a Friend
Overview: Samantha (Sam) is highly imaginative. Her fantasies are responsible for the near loss of her friend, Thomas, when she sends him off to find a mermaid.

Shiloh

Author: Phyllis Reynolds Naylor
Publisher: Atheneum
Length: 144 **Age:** 8–12 **Date:** 1991
Main Character: white male
Other Topics: Pet Abuse
Overview: Marty is faced with an emotional dilemma when he takes in and hides a mistreated beagle that he knows belongs to someone else. In order to keep Shiloh, he finds himself telling an escalating series of lies.

The Bad Times of Irma Baumlein

Author: Carol Ryrie Brink
Publisher: Macmillan
Length: 144 **Age:** 9–11 **Date:** 1972
Main Character: white female
Other Topics: Bragging
Overview: In an effort to obtain a friend, Irma brags that she owns the biggest doll in the world, one as big as herself. But suddenly she is asked to display it.

The Boy Who Cried Wolf

Author: Tony Ross
Publisher: Puffin
Length: 32 **Age:** 5–8 **Date:** 1991
Main Character: white male
Other Topics: N/A
Overview: This classic Aesop fable is updated.

The Computer That Said Steal Me

Author: Elizabeth Levy
Publisher: Apple
Length: 160 **Age:** 8–12 **Date:** 1983
Main Character: white male
Other Topics: N/A
Overview: After Adam steals a computer game, his conscience bothers him.

The Gorilla Did It

Author: Barbara Hazen
Publisher: Atheneum
Length: 32 **Age:** 5–8 **Date:** 1974
Main Character: white male
Other Topics: Only Child, Imaginary Playmates
Overview: An only child has an imaginary playmate who receives the blame for everything wrong in his room.

The Thief's Daughter

Author: Alan Marks
Publisher: Farrar, Straus, and Giroux

The Thief's Daughter (cont.)

Length: 48 **Age:** 6–9 **Date:** 1994
Main Character: white female
Other Topics: N/A
Overview: Magpie learns the value of honesty and truth.

The Three Friends

Author: Susanne Kubler
Publisher: Macmillan
Length: 32 **Age:** 5–9 **Date:** 1985
Main Character: animal
Other Topics: Friendship
Overview: A bear, a rabbit, and a cat are friends. Does cat lie or does he just tell stories?

Hospitalization, Doctors' Offices

Curious George Goes to the Hospital

Author: H. A. Rey
Publisher: Houghton Mifflin
Length: 48 **Age:** 4–7 **Date:** 1966
Main Character: animal
Other Topics: N/A
Overview: When Curious George swallows a puzzle piece, he must go to the hospital for an operation.

Dilly Goes to the Dentist

Author: Tony Bradman
Publisher: Viking Penguin, Inc.
Length: 53 **Age:** 6–8 **Date:** 1986
Main Character: dinosaur
Other Topics: N/A
Overview: Dilly the dinosaur is hesitant about his first trip to the dentist.

Hospitalization, Doctors' Offices (cont.)

Elizabeth Gets Well

Author: Alfons Weber
Publisher: Crowell
Length: 29 **Age:** 4–8 **Date:** 1969
Main Character: white female
Other Topics: N/A
Overview: Elizabeth's stomachache turns out to be an inflamed appendix. The nurses and doctors at the hospital help her get well.

Emergency Mouse

Author: Bernard Stone
Publisher: Ray Rourke Publishing Co.
Length: 25 **Age:** 3–6 **Date:** 1982
Main Character: cartoon characters
Other Topics: N/A
Overview: When a young boy enters the hospital, he discovers that mice operate it.

Eric Needs Stitches

Author: Barbara Pavis Marino
Publisher: Addison-Wesley
Length: 26 **Age:** 5–8 **Date:** 1979
Main Character: white male
Other Topics: N/A
Overview: Even though he is very frightened, Eric goes to the hospital emergency room to get stitches in his knee.

Going to the Dentist

Author: Marianne Borgardt
Publisher: Simon and Schuster
Length: 10 **Age:** 3–6 **Date:** 1991
Main Character: white female
Other Topics: N/A

Going to the Dentist (cont.)

Overview: A pop-up book that explains what will happen on a visit to the dentist.

Going to the Dentist

Author: Fred Rogers
Publisher: G. P. Putman's Sons
Length: 25 **Age:** 4–6 **Date:** 1989
Main Character: multicultural males and females
Other Topics: N/A
Overview: This book of photographs and simple text prepares a child for a trip to the dentist for an examination.

Going to the Doctor

Author: Fred Rogers
Publisher: Putnam
Length: 30 **Age:** 4–8 **Date:** 1986
Main Character: multicultural males and females
Other Topics: N/A
Overview: Photographs help to describe a child's visit to the pediatrician.

Going to the Doctor

Author: Stacie Strong
Publisher: Simon and Schuster
Length: 10 **Age:** 3–6 **Date:** 1991
Main Character: white male
Other Topics: N/A
Overview: A pop-up book that presents what will happen in the doctor's office.

Gregory's Stitches

Author: Judith Vigna
Publisher: Albert Whitman
Length: 32 **Age:** 4–6 **Date:** 1974
Main Character: white male
Other Topics: N/A
Overview: Gregory must get six stitches in his forehead.

Honey, the Hospital Dog

Author: Hazel Edwards
Publisher: Gareth Stevens
Length: 32 **Age:** 4–8 **Date:** 1985
Main Character: animal
Other Topics: N/A
Overview: Honey is a hospital dog who is a friend to all the people in the hospital.

Hospital

Author: Brian Wood
Publisher: Silver Burdett Co.
Length: 48 **Age:** 10–12 **Date:** 1977
Main Character: N/A
Other Topics: N/A
Overview: A very sophisticated description of all aspects of the hospital is given.

I Know a Dentist

Author: Naomi Barnett
Publisher: G. P. Putnam's Sons
Length: 46 **Age:** 6–8 **Date:** 1977
Main Character: white female
Other Topics: N/A
Overview: A young girl learns about a dentist's work and how to best care for her teeth.

Itchy, Itchy Chicken Pox

Author: Grace Maccarone
Publisher: Scholastic
Length: 32 **Age:** 4–6 **Date:** 1992
Main Character: white male
Other Topics: N/A
Overview: A humorous easy-to-read rhyme about chicken pox.

Jeff's Hospital Book

Author: Harriet Langsam Sobol
Publisher: Walch
Length: 42 **Age:** 4–8 **Date:** 1975

Jeff's Hospital Book (cont.)

Main Character: white male
Other Topics: Strabismus (Crossed Eyes)
Overview: Jeff is going to the hospital to have an operation to fix his eyes. This book tells about the things that happen to Jeff in the hospital.

Learning about Love

Author: Jordan Jenkins
Publisher: Children's Press
Length: 32 **Age:** 4–7 **Date:** 1979
Main Character: white male
Other Topics: N/A
Overview: Eight-year-old Alan worries when his mother has to go to the hospital.

Let's Find out about the Clinic

Author: Robert Froman
Publisher: Franklin Watts
Length: 47 **Age:** 5–8 **Date:** 1968
Main Character: cartoon characters
Other Topics: N/A
Overview: This book illustrates what happens on a visit to the clinic.

Let's Find out about the Hospital

Author: Eleanor Kay, R.N.
Publisher: Franklin Watts, Inc.
Length: 48 **Age:** 6–8 **Date:** 1971
Main Character: white male
Other Topics: N/A
Overview: A description of what to expect in a hospital is given in easy-to-read text.

Madeline

Author: Ludwig Bemelmans
Publisher: Viking Press
Length: 44 **Age:** 5–8 **Date:** 1939
Main Character: French female

Hospitalization, Doctors' Offices (cont.)

Madeline (cont.)

Other Topics: N/A
Overview: Madeline lives in a Paris convent with eleven other girls. She is the envy of all the girls when an ambulance takes her to the hospital for an appendectomy.

Maggie and the Emergency Room

Author: Martine Davison
Publisher: Random House
Length: 32 **Age:** 4–8 **Date:** 1992
Main Character: white female
Other Topics: N/A
Overview: Maggie falls off her bike and needs X rays and stitches in the emergency room.

Michael and the Dentist

Author: Bernard Wolf
Publisher: Four Winds
Length: 48 **Age:** 4–8 **Date:** 1980
Main Character: Asian American male
Other Topics: N/A
Overview: Michael has four cavities and must return to the dentist's office.

Mom! I Broke My Arm!

Author: Angelika Wolff
Publisher: The Lion Press
Length: 44 **Age:** 6–8 **Date:** 1969
Main Character: white male
Other Topics: N/A
Overview: Steven breaks his arm and must go to the hospital for X rays and a cast.

My Dentist

Author: Harlow Rockwell
Publisher: Greenwillow Books
Length: 28 **Age:** 4–8 **Date:** 1975
Main Character: white female
Other Topics: N/A
Overview: Very simple text and pictures describe a trip to the dentist.

My Doctor

Author: Harlow Rockwell
Publisher: Macmillan
Length: 24 **Age:** 4–6 **Date:** 1973
Main Character: white male
Other Topics: N/A
Overview: This book explores a female doctor's office.

Robby Visits the Doctor

Author: Martine Davison
Publisher: Random House
Length: 32 **Age:** 4–7 **Date:** 1992
Main Character: African American male
Other Topics: N/A
Overview: When Robby wakes up with an earache, he must go to his doctor's office and take medicine.

Some Busy Hospital!

Author: Seymour Reit
Publisher: Western Publishing Co.
Length: 34 **Age:** 3–6 **Date:** 1985
Main Character: multicultural male and female
Other Topics: N/A
Overview: A detailed and colorful book about what goes on in a busy hospital.

The Get-Well Hotel

Author: Slim Goodbody
Publisher: McGraw Hill Book Co.
Length: 23 **Age:** 3–6 **Date:** 1980

The Get-Well Hotel (cont.)

Main Character: animal
Other Topics: N/A
Overview: A young alligator must check into a hospital.

The Hospital

Author: Daphne Butler
Publisher: Gareth Stevens, Inc.
Length: 32 **Age:** 4–8 **Date:** 1991
Main Character: multicultural males and females
Other Topics: N/A
Overview: Photographs and text that explain a variety of situations that occur in a hospital. A glossary and citations for similar references are included.

The Hospital Book

Author: James Howe
Publisher: Crown
Length: 94 **Age:** 8–11 **Date:** 1981
Main Character: multicultural males and females
Other Topics: N/A
Overview: This book of photographs shows children what to expect from a stay in the hospital.

What Happens When You Go to the Hospital

Author: Arthur Shay
Publisher: Reilly and Lee
Length: 27 **Age:** 4–8 **Date:** 1969
Main Character: multicultural male and female
Other Topics: N/A
Overview: This book strives to dispel some of the fear and uncertainty of going to the hospital.

When I See My Dentist

Author: Susan Kuklin
Publisher: Bradbury
Length: 32 **Age:** 3–6 **Date:** 1988
Main Character: white female
Other Topics: N/A
Overview: A photo-essay that explains most situations in a dentist's office.

When I See My Doctor

Author: Susan Kuklin
Publisher: Bradbury
Length: 32 **Age:** 3–6 **Date:** 1988
Main Character: Asian female
Other Topics: N/A
Overview: A photo-essay that explains most situations in a doctor's office.

Who's Sick Today?

Author: Lynne Cherry
Publisher: Dutton
Length: 22 **Age:** 4–8 **Date:** 1988
Main Character: animal
Other Topics: N/A
Overview: A fun look at common childhood illnesses.

Your World: Let's Visit the Hospital

Author: Billy N. Pope
Publisher: Taylor
Length: 32 **Age:** 5–8 **Date:** 1968
Main Character: multicultural males and females
Other Topics: N/A
Overview: Photographs are used to illustrate a trip to the hospital. A glossary of hospital-related words is included.

Hyperactivity

Shelley: The Hyperactive Turtle

Author: Deborah Moss
Publisher: Wooodbine House
Length: 20 **Age:** 4–8 **Date:** 1992
Main Character: animal
Other Topics: N/A
Overview: This book tells the story of Shelley and his family as they face the challenges of his hyperactivity.

Hypochondria

Lucretia the Unbearable

Author: Marjorie W. Sharmat
Publisher: Holiday House
Length: 36 **Age:** 5–8 **Date:** 1981
Main Character: animal
Other Topics: Friendship, Loneliness
Overview: The other animals don't enjoy being with Lucretia Bear because she is overly concerned about her health.

Illiteracy, Reading Problems

Arthur's Prize Reader

Author: Lillian Hoban
Publisher: Harper and Row
Length: 64 **Age:** 5–8 **Date:** 1978
Main Character: animal
Other Topics: N/A

Arthur's Prize Reader (cont.)

Overview: Arthur loses the Super Chimp Club contest, but his sister Violet wins the first-grade reading competition and a prize for them both.

Clara and the Book Wagon

Author: Nancy S. Levinson
Publisher: Harper
Length: 64 **Age:** 6–8 **Date:** 1988
Main Character: white female
Other Topics: N/A
Overview: During pioneer days, Clara ignores her father's objections and learns to read thanks to a traveling librarian.

Herbie Jones

Author: Suzy Kline
Publisher: Putnam
Length: 96 **Age:** 7–11 **Date:** 1985
Main Character: white male
Other Topics: N/A
Overview: Herbie Jones wants to move into a higher reading group.

Just Open a Book

Author: P. K. Hallinan
Publisher: Children's Press
Length: 30 **Age:** 4–8 **Date:** 1981
Main Character: white male
Other Topics: N/A
Overview: A verse about the value of reading.

Mitch and Amy

Author: Beverly Cleary
Publisher: Morrow
Length: 222 **Age:** 9–11 **Date:** 1967
Main Character: white male and female
Other Topics: Twins

Mitch and Amy (cont.)

Overview: Mitch and Amy are twins in the fourth grade. He is a slow reader; she is not. They are very competitive until Amy finds just the right book to help Mitch.

Mrs. Frisby and the Rats of NIMH

Author: Robert C. O'Brien
Publisher: Atheneum
Length: 233 **Age:** 8–12 **Date:** 1971
Main Character: animal
Other Topics: Death of a Relative
Overview: Mrs. Frisby asks for help from a group of rats who can read.

Muggie Maggie

Author: Beverly Cleary
Publisher: Morrow
Length: 70 **Age:** 7–10 **Date:** 1990
Main Character: white female
Other Topics: N/A
Overview: Maggie is a third grader who does not want to learn cursive writing.

My Mom Can't Read

Author: Muriel Stanek
Publisher: Albert Whitman
Length: 32 **Age:** 6–10 **Date:** 1986
Main Character: white female
Other Topics: Single Parent
Overview: A first grader struggling to learn to read discovers that her mother is illiterate.

Sixth Grade Can Really Kill You

Author: Berthe DeClements
Publisher: Scholastic
Length: 160 **Age:** 9–12 **Date:** 1985
Main Character: white female
Other Topics: N/A

Sixth Grade Can Really Kill You (cont.)

Overview: Helen has a severe reading problem and dislikes school. As a result, she enjoys pranks.

The Girl Who Knew It All

Author: Patricia Reilly Giff
Publisher: Yearling
Length: 118 **Age:** 9–12 **Date:** 1979
Main Character: white female
Other Topics: N/A
Overview: Tracy Matson sees a lonely summer looming ahead since she is the only girl her age in the small town. She also has another problem—she is a rotten reader.

The Wednesday Surprise

Author: Eve Bunting
Publisher: Houghton Mifflin
Length: 32 **Age:** 3–9 **Date:** 1989
Main Character: white female
Other Topics: Intergenerational
Overview: On Wednesday nights, Grandma rides a bus across town to sit with Anna, her granddaughter. She always brings a bag of books to read. The surprise is that Anna is teaching her grandmother to read.

When Will I Read?

Author: Miriam Cohen
Publisher: Greenwillow
Length: 28 **Age:** 5–7 **Date:** 1977
Main Character: white male
Other Topics: N/A
Overview: Jim worries about the skill of reading.

Yellow Bird and Me

Author: Joyce Hansen
Publisher: Clarion

Illiteracy, Reading Problems (cont.)

Yellow Bird and Me (cont.)

Length: 155 **Age:** 9–12 **Date:** 1986
Main Character: African American male
Other Topics: Sharing
Overview: Doris agrees to tutor the class clown, Yellow Bird, and find help for his learning disability.

Young Frederick Douglass: The Slave Who Learned to Read

Author: Linda W. Girard
Publisher: Albert Whitman and Co.
Length: 40 **Age:** 7–10 **Date:** 1994
Main Character: African American male
Other Topics: Racism, Prejudice
Overview: This is the story of young Frederick Douglass in 1826 Baltimore. He wants to learn to read and educate himself.

Incarceration

Monkey See, Monkey Do

Author: Barthe DeClements
Publisher: Delacorte
Length: 160 **Age:** 9–12 **Date:** 1990
Main Character: white male
Other Topics: N/A
Overview: When Jerry Johnson, Jr.'s father is out of prison and on parole, young Jerry wants to keep him that way. But he is challenged when his father's old buddies return with big plans.

One Thing for Sure

Author: David Gifaldi
Publisher: Clarion
Length: 172 **Age:** 9–12 **Date:** 1986
Main Character: white male
Other Topics: Bullies
Overview: Twelve-year-old Dylan's father is in prison for cutting timber illegally.

When Andy's Father Went to Prison

Author: Martha Whitmore Hickman
Publisher: Albert Whitman
Length: 40 **Age:** 7–10 **Date:** 1983
Main Character: white male
Other Topics: Separation Anxiety, Moving
Overview: A factual but sensitive book about a boy's father being sent to prison. Andy and his mother move so that they can be closer to him. Andy's first day at school is stressful until he meets Joel, whose father is seriously ill.

Insecurity, Self-Confidence

Be a Perfect Person in Just Three Days

Author: Stephen Manes
Publisher: Clarion
Length: 76 **Age:** 8–10 **Date:** 1982
Main Character: white male
Other Topics: N/A
Overview: Milo is tired of problems with his sister, parents, and friends so he finds a book to help him become perfect in three days.

Charley Skedaddle

Author: Patricia Beatty
Publisher: Morrow
Length: 208 **Age:** 11–14 **Date:** 1987
Main Character: white male
Other Topics: War
Overview: A boy under fire during battle deserts the battlefield and hides in the wilderness. In time, he restores his self-esteem.

Invisible Lissa

Author: Natalie Honeycutt
Publisher: Bradbury
Length: 168 **Age:** 8–10 **Date:** 1985
Main Character: white female
Other Topics: N/A
Overview: Lissa badly wants to get into Debra's exclusive fifth-grade lunch club, until she finds out what it is really like.

The Runt of Rodgers School

Author: Harold Verne Keith
Publisher: Lippincott
Length: 125 **Age:** 9–11 **Date:** 1971
Main Character: white male
Other Topics: Youngest Child, Smallest Child, Death of a Parent, New School
Overview: Bennie has a lot of problems: he is a runt, his father has died, and he must move to another state and start a new school.

The Smallest Boy in the Class

Author: Jerrold Beim
Publisher: Morrow
Length: 44 **Age:** 5–8 **Date:** 1949
Main Character: white male
Other Topics: N/A
Overview: Tiny is the smallest boy in the class. His real name is Jim and he hates being the smallest. To make up for his smallness, Tiny is loud and aggres-

The Smallest Boy in the Class (cont.)

sive, which makes the other children angry. When he shares his lunch with Priscilla, their teacher explains that there is more than one way to be big.

Intergenerational

A Figure of Speech

Author: Norma Fox Mazer
Publisher: Delacorte
Length: 197 **Age:** 11–14 **Date:** 1973
Main Character: white female
Other Topics: Death of a Grandparent
Overview: This touching story of Jenny's love for her grandfather, who is tolerated by his family and then pushed aside, ends in the death of the man.

A Special Trade

Author: Sally Whitman
Publisher: Harper
Length: 28 **Age:** 5–8 **Date:** 1978
Main Character: white female
Other Topics: Physical Disabilities
Overview: When Nell is small, her neighbor, Old Bartholomew, cares for her. He pushes her in her stroller, helps her learn to walk, then to skate. Nell must mirror his actions when Old Bartholomew falls down and must be in a wheelchair.

Anastasia Again!

Author: Lois Lowry
Publisher: Houghton Mifflin
Length: 145 **Age:** 8–12 **Date:** 1981
Main Character: white female
Other Topics: Moving
Overview: Anastasia devises a scheme for involving her grouchy neighbor with a group of lively senior citizens from the center.

Intergenerational

(cont.)

Anna and the Cat Lady

Author: Barbara M. Joose
Publisher: Harper Collins
Length: 170 **Age:** 8–10 **Date:** 1992
Main Character: white female
Other Topics: Allergies
Overview: Anna must give up her kitten because of her sister's allergic symptoms. She leaves it with Mrs. Sarafiny, who already owns six cats. Anna befriends Mrs. Sarafiny and soon discovers that she is a little crazy.

Applebaum's Garage

Author: Karen Lynn Williams
Publisher: Clarion
Length: 168 **Age:** 10–12 **Date:** 1993
Main Character: white male
Other Topics: Friendship
Overview: Ten-year-old Jeremy begins to spend time with old Mr. Applebaum, who lives next door.

Aunt Flossie's Hats and Crab Cake Letters

Author: Elizabeth Fitzgerald Howard
Publisher: Houghton Mifflin
Length: 31 **Age:** 6–9 **Date:** 1991
Main Character: African American female
Other Topics: N/A
Overview: Sarah and Susan hear the history behind Great-great Aunt Flossie's hats.

Bigmama's

Author: Donald Crews
Publisher: Greenwillow
Length: 33 **Age:** 5–8 **Date:** 1991

Bigmama's (cont.)

Main Character: African American male
Other Topics: N/A
Overview: Donald Crews recounts his memories of visiting his grandparents' farm as a child.

Blow Me a Kiss, Miss Lilly

Author: Nancy White Carlstrom
Publisher: Harper
Length: 30 **Age:** 4–6 **Date:** 1990
Main Character: white female
Other Topics: Death of a Friend
Overview: Sara befriends a very old lady who lives across the street from her. Miss Lilly eventually dies and Sara adopts her cat, visits her garden, and often "blows her a kiss."

Coco Can't Wait

Author: Taro Gomi
Publisher: Morrow
Length: 30 **Age:** 3–8 **Date:** 1984
Main Character: African American female
Other Topics: N/A
Overview: Coco and her grandmother travel back and forth one day until they finally meet in the middle.

Emma

Author: Wendy Kesselman
Publisher: Doubleday
Length: 30 **Age:** 4–8 **Date:** 1980
Main Character: white female
Other Topics: N/A
Overview: Emma becomes an artist in her late 80s.

Everywhere

Author: Bruce Brooks
Publisher: Harper
Length: 70 **Age:** 6–7 **Date:** 1990

Everywhere (cont.)

Main Character: white male
Other Topics: N/A
Overview: The ten-year-old narrator tells of his love for his grandfather, who may be dying from a heart attack.

Georgia Music

Author: Helen Griffith
Publisher: Greenwillow
Length: 22 **Age:** 4–8 **Date:** 1980
Main Character: white female
Other Topics: N/A
Overview: Janetta's grandfather must move to the city to live with her and her family when his health begins to fail. Janetta helps him accept his new situation.

Golden Days

Author: Gail Radley
Publisher: Macmillan
Length: 137 **Age:** 10–18 **Date:** 1991
Main Character: white male
Other Topics: Friendship, Foster Home
Overview: An eleven-year-old foster child befriends an old woman living in a nursing home. She longs for the days when she was a circus performer.

Granddaddy's Place

Author: Helen Griffith
Publisher: Greenwillow
Length: 35 **Age:** 4–8 **Date:** 1987
Main Character: white male
Other Topics: Fear
Overview: Janetta meets her granddaddy for the first time. She is apprehensive about staying at his house, which is out in the country. Her grandfather helps her make friends with all the animals on his place.

Grandma Didn't Wave Back

Author: Rose Blue
Publisher: Watts
Length: 62 **Age:** 8–10 **Date:** 1972
Main Character: white female
Other Topics: N/A
Overview: A child reluctantly accepts the idea that only a nursing home will be able to provide the needed care for Grandma.

Grandma's Joy

Author: Eloise Greenfield
Publisher: Collins
Length: 27 **Age:** 6–8 **Date:** 1980
Main Character: African American male
Other Topics: Poverty
Overview: Rhondy's grandmother can't afford to pay the rent anymore and they are going to have to move. They discover that as long as they have each other the move will not be so bad.

Grandma without Me

Author: Judith Vigna
Publisher: Albert Whitman
Length: 32 **Age:** 5–8 **Date:** 1984
Main Character: white male
Other Topics: Divorce
Overview: The story of a little boy who is cut off from his grandmother when his parents divorce.

Grandpa

Author: Barbara Borack
Publisher: Harper and Row
Length: 32 **Age:** 4–8 **Date:** 1967
Main Character: white male and female
Other Topics: N/A
Overview: Marilyn and Grandpa are best friends. They do wonderful things together.

Intergenerational

(cont.)

Grandpa

Author: John Burningham
Publisher: Crown
Length: 30 **Age:** 6–8 **Date:** 1984
Main Character: white female
Other Topics: Death of a Grandparent
Overview: A little girl shares many experiences with her grandfather—planting seeds, playing, sledding, and building sandcastles. The grandfather becomes ill and eventually dies.

Grandpappy

Author: Nancy White Carlstrom
Publisher: Little, Brown
Length: 29 **Age:** 7–10 **Date:** 1990
Main Character: white male
Other Topics: N/A
Overview: Nate enjoys visiting his Grandpappy and misses him when the visit is over.

Grandparents: A Special Kind of Love

Author: Eda LeShan
Publisher: Macmillan
Length: 112 **Age:** 8–10 **Date:** 1984
Main Character: multicultural males and females
Other Topics: N/A
Overview: Various grandparenting situations are explored—death of a grandparent, step-grandparents, grandparents living in the home.

Grandpa Putter and Granny Hoe

Author: Kimberly O. Fakih
Publisher: Farrar, Straus, Giroux
Length: 128 **Age:** 7–10 **Date:** 1993

Grandpa Putter and Granny Hoe (cont.)

Main Character: white male and female
Other Topics: Twins
Overview: Jazz and her twin brother, Koo, find themselves in the middle of a war between the grandparents when they vie for the twins' attention.

Grandpa's Face

Author: Eloise Greenfield
Publisher: Philomel
Length: 29 **Age:** 7–10 **Date:** 1988
Main Character: African American male
Other Topics: N/A
Overview: Tamika loves spending time with her grandfather. She is troubled one day as she sees a new expression on her grandpa's face while they rehearse for a play. Tamika learns that despite his many faces, she can always count on his love.

Grandpa's Too Good Garden

Author: James Stevenson
Publisher: Greenwillow
Length: 30 **Age:** 6–9 **Date:** 1989
Main Character: white male
Other Topics: N/A
Overview: Grandpa tells Louie and Mary Ann about a garden he and his brother had many years ago.

How Does It Feel to Be Old?

Author: Norma Farber
Publisher: Dutton
Length: 27 **Age:** 6–8 **Date:** 1979
Main Character: white female
Other Topics: N/A
Overview: A woman tells of her past and present in a poetic monologue.

I Dance in My Red Pajamas

Author: Edith T. Hurd
Publisher: Harper and Row

I Dance in My Red Pajamas (cont.)

Length: 28 **Age:** 3–7 **Date:** 1982
Main Character: white female
Other Topics: Deafness
Overview: A little girl enjoys a visit with her grandparents. Grandfather is deaf, and they have a jolly, noisy time together.

I Know a Lady

Author: Charlotte Zolotow
Publisher: Greenwillow
Length: 21 **Age:** 4–8 **Date:** 1984
Main Character: white female
Other Topics: N/A
Overview: An old lady makes all the neighborhood children feel very special.

Island Boy

Author: Barbara Cooney
Publisher: Viking
Length: 26 **Age:** 3–8 **Date:** 1988
Main Character: white male
Other Topics: N/A
Overview: This story tells of four generations of a New England family who settled on Tibbett's Island.

Journey from Peppermint Street

Author: Meindert DeJong
Publisher: Harper and Row
Length: 242 **Age:** 8–12 **Date:** 1968
Main Character: white male
Other Topics: N/A
Overview: This is the story of a warm and loving relationship between Siebren and his grandfather.

Kevin's Grandma

Author: Barbara Williams
Publisher: Dutton
Length: 26 **Age:** 3–8 **Date:** 1975
Main Character: white female

Kevin's Grandma (cont.)

Other Topics: N/A
Overview: Two grandmothers are depicted—one is traditional and one is not so traditional.

Loop the Loop

Author: Barbara Dugan
Publisher: Greenwillow
Length: 28 **Age:** 3–8 **Date:** 1992
Main Character: white female
Other Topics: N/A
Overview: A bored young girl and a feisty old woman develop a friendship.

Miss Maggie

Author: Cynthia Rylant
Publisher: Dutton
Length: 26 **Age:** 6–9 **Date:** 1983
Main Character: white female
Other Topics: Fear
Overview: Young Nat is afraid of old Miss Maggie and her rotting old house until his heart conquers his fears.

Miss Rumphius

Author: Barbara Cooney
Publisher: Viking
Length: 26 **Age:** 6–8 **Date:** 1982
Main Character: white female
Other Topics: N/A
Overview: This intergenerational book describes the love between Miss Rumphius and her grandfather. He inspired her to make the world more beautiful. As the years passed, she planted lupine all over her little seacoast village.

Mr. Silver and Mrs. Gold

Author: Dale B. Fink
Publisher: Human Sciences Press
Length: 29 **Age:** 4–8 **Date:** 1980

Intergenerational

(cont.)

Mr. Silver and Mrs. Gold (cont.)

Main Character: white male and female
Other Topics: Friendship
Overview: Two elderly people become friends and share time and activities together.

Music, Music for Everyone

Author: Vera B. Williams
Publisher: Greenwillow
Length: 32 **Age:** 5–8 **Date:** 1984
Main Character: African American female
Other Topics: poverty
Overview: Rosa organizes a band to help pay for expenses caused by her grandmother's illness.

My Grammy

Author: Marsha Kibbey
Publisher: Carolrhoda Books
Length: 38 **Age:** 6–9 **Date:** 1988
Main Character: white female
Other Topics: N/A
Overview: Amy becomes confused and resentful when her grandmother's personality changes.

My Grandma's in a Nursing Home

Author: Judy Delton and Dorothy Tucker
Publisher: Albert Whitman
Length: 27 **Age:** 6–8 **Date:** 1986
Main Character: white male
Other Topics: N/A
Overview: At first Jason hates to visit his grandmother in the nursing home until he discovers what it means to her and other residents.

My Grandson Lew

Author: Charlotte Zolotow
Publisher: Harper and Row
Length: 32 **Age:** 3–7 **Date:** 1974
Main Character: white male
Other Topics: Death of a Grandparent
Overview: Mother and son remember grandfather and call forth happy times.

My Great-Aunt Arizona

Author: Gloria Houston
Publisher: Harper Collins
Length: 32 **Age:** 6–9 **Date:** 1992
Main Character: white female
Other Topics: N/A
Overview: Arizona was born in a cabin in the Blue Ridge Mountains. She never travels but stays at home to become a special teacher. She dies on her 93rd birthday.

My Great Grandpa

Author: Martin Waddell
Publisher: Putnam
Length: 24 **Age:** 5–8 **Date:** 1990
Main Character: white female
Other Topics: Wheelchair
Overview: A little girl loves to spend time with her great-grandfather. She wheels him around in his wheelchair and enjoys their talks.

My Poppa Loves Old Movies

Author: Libby Handy
Publisher: Ashton Scholastics
Length: 27 **Age:** 5–8 **Date:** 1986
Main Character: African American male
Other Topics: N/A
Overview: A young boy learns not to interrupt his grandfather's movie watching.

Night Noises

Author: Mem Fox
Publisher: Harcourt
Length: 32 **Age:** 3–8 **Date:** 1989
Main Character: white female
Other Topics: N/A
Overview: Ninety-year-old Lily Laceby drifts off to sleep. Strange noises disturb Butch Aggie, her dog, but Lily dreams on. Finally the noises grow louder and Lily awakens to find her family coming to wish her happy birthday.

Old Henry

Author: Joan Blos
Publisher: Morrow
Length: 30 **Age:** 4–8 **Date:** 1987
Main Character: white male
Other Topics: People Who Are Different
Overview: Old Henry rents a dilapidated house in town, but fails to clean it up. The neighbors' complaints drive him away, but they begin to miss him. Old Henry misses his house and neighborhood, too. He writes to the mayor, saying he will mend his ways, but he still wants to let the grass grow.

Oliver, Amanda, and Grandmother Pig

Author: Jean Van Leeuwen
Publisher: Dial
Length: 56 **Age:** 4–8 **Date:** 1987
Main Character: animal
Other Topics: N/A
Overview: When Grandmother pig comes to visit Oliver and Amanda, they discover that she is not too old to do many things.

Oma and Bobo

Author: Amy Schwartz
Publisher: Bradbury Press
Length: 32 **Age:** 4–7 **Date:** 1987

Oma and Bobo (cont.)

Main Character: white female
Other Topics: N/A
Overview: Alice's grandmother, Oma, is critical of Amy's dog, Bobo, until she is slowly won over.

Poem for Grandmothers

Author: Myra Cohn Livingston
Publisher: Holiday House
Length: 32 **Age:** 4–18 **Date:** 1990
Main Character: multicultural females
Other Topics: N/A
Overview: This illustrated collection of poems celebrates grandmothers.

Song and Dance Man

Author: Karen Ackerman
Publisher: Knopf
Length: 29 **Age:** 6–8 **Date:** 1988
Main Character: white male
Other Topics: N/A
Overview: Grandfather shares his vaudeville years with his three grandchildren.

Stina

Author: Lena Anderson
Publisher: Greenwillow
Length: 32 **Age:** 4–8 **Date:** 1988
Main Character: white female
Other Topics: Fear
Overview: Stina visits her grandfather's house by the sea and is frightened by a storm until her grandfather watches it with her.

Storm in the Night

Author: Mary Stolz
Publisher: Harper
Length: 29 **Age:** 6–8 **Date:** 1988

Intergenerational

(cont.)

Storm in the Night (cont.)

Main Character: African American males
Other Topics: Fear
Overview: Since a storm has cut off the electricity, a grandfather and his grandson sit together in the dark and enjoy the smell and sound of the rain. The grandfather tells a story about a storm during his childhood and how he overcame his fear of the dark.

The Crack-of-Dawn Walkers

Author: Amy Hest
Publisher: Macmillan
Length: 32 **Age:** 3–8 **Date:** 1984
Main Character: white female and male
Other Topics: N/A
Overview: Sunday mornings find Sadie and her grandfather sharing a walk.

The Downtown Day

Author: Linda Strauss Edwards
Publisher: Pantheon
Length: 36 **Age:** 4–8 **Date:** 1983
Main Character: white female
Other Topics: Going to School
Overview: Linda's two elderly aunts take her shopping downtown to shop for school clothes, but the only thing Linda wants is a red sweater.

The Get-Away Car

Author: Eleanor Clymer
Publisher: Dutton
Length: 149 **Age:** 9–11 **Date:** 1978
Main Character: white female
Other Topics: N/A

The Get-Away Car (cont.)

Overview: Maggie and her grandmother prove that grandmother is not ready for a senior citizen's home.

The Helping Place

Author: Marsha Kibbey
Publisher: Carolrhoda Books
Length: 38 **Age:** 6–9 **Date:** 1991
Main Character: white female
Other Topics: N/A
Overview: A nursing home is depicted as a friendly place where the elderly and disabled reside.

The House of Wings

Author: Betsy Byars
Publisher: Viking
Length: 142 **Age:** 8–12 **Date:** 1972
Main Character: white male
Other Topics: N/A
Overview: When Sammy's parents try to find a place to live in Detroit, they leave Sammy with his elderly grandfather in an old run-down house. Together they care for an injured crane.

The Hundred Penny Box

Author: Sharon Bell Mathis
Publisher: Viking
Length: 48 **Age:** 8–11 **Date:** 1975
Main Character: African American female and male
Other Topics: N/A
Overview: Michael has a special relationship with his 100-year-old Aunt Dew, who keeps a box full of pennies, one for each year of her life. Michael listens to her stories as Aunt Dew counts her pennies.

The Keeping Quilt

Author: Patricia Polacco
Publisher: Simon and Schuster

The Keeping Quilt (cont.)

Length: 30 **Age:** 4–8 **Date:** 1988
Main Character: Asian female
Other Topics: N/A
Overview: To help the family always remember their homeland, Great Gramma Ann, a Russian Jew, made a quilt. It follows four generations of the family.

The Midnight Eaters

Author: Amy Hest
Publisher: Macmillan
Length: 28 **Age:** 5–8 **Date:** 1989
Main Character: white female
Other Topics: N/A
Overview: Samantha and her grandmother enjoy midnight raids on the kitchen where they eat ice-cream sundaes and look at old photographs.

The Patchwork Quilt

Author: Valerie Flourney
Publisher: Dial
Length: 30 **Age:** 5–8 **Date:** 1985
Main Character: African American female
Other Topics: N/A
Overview: When grandma becomes too ill to work on the quilt of family memories, Tonya and her family continue to piece together the quilt squares. The book shows the love of a family and the importance of shared memories.

The Rocking Chair Rebellion

Author: Eth Clifford
Publisher: Houghton Mifflin
Length: 147 **Age:** 10–12 **Date:** 1978
Main Character: white female
Other Topics: Growing Up
Overview: Fourteen-year-old Opie volunteers at the Maple Ridge Home for the

The Rocking Chair Rebellion (cont.)

Aged when her neighbor moves there. She helps several of the residents leave to set up their own group home.

The War with Grandpa

Author: Robert K. Smith
Publisher: Delacorte
Length: 140 **Age:** 9–12 **Date:** 1984
Main Character: white male
Other Topics: N/A
Overview: Peter is excited to learn his grandfather is coming to live with them until his grandfather takes Peter's room.

Things I Like about Grandma

Author: Francine Haskins
Publisher: Children's Press
Length: 32 **Age:** 4–8 **Date:** 1992
Main Character: African American male
Other Topics: N/A
Overview: A young African American girl shares everyday activities with her grandmother in an urban, African American neighborhood.

Thunder Cake

Author: Patricia Polacco
Publisher: Philomel
Length: 30 **Age:** 5–8 **Date:** 1990
Main Character: Russian females
Other Topics: Fear
Overview: A little girl is afraid of thunderstorms until her grandmother teaches her to make a special Thundercake.

Trouble River

Author: Betsy Byars
Publisher: Viking
Length: 158 **Age:** 7–12 **Date:** 1969
Main Character: white male
Other Topics: Racism, Prejudice

Intergenerational

(cont.)

Trouble River (cont.)

Overview: Dewey and his grandmother are alone in their cabin one night when a Native American attacks.

We're Very Good Friends, My Grandpa and I

Author: P. K. Halliman
Publisher: Children's Press
Length: 29   **Age:**   5–8   **Date:**   1989
Main Character: white male
Other Topics: N/A
Overview: A young boy and his grandpa are good friends. Even though they are very different, they can share something that will last a lifetime.

When Grandpa Kissed His Elbow

Author: Cynthia De Felice
Publisher: Macmillan
Length: 29   **Age:**   6–8   **Date:**   1992
Main Character: white female
Other Topics: N/A
Overview: When Grandpa kissed his elbow, the world became a magical place.

When I Was Young in the Mountains

Author: Cynthia Rylant
Publisher: E. P. Dutton
Length: 26   **Age:**   6–9   **Date:**   1982
Main Character: white female
Other Topics: N/A
Overview: A little girl lives with her grandparents in the mountains.

Wilfrid Gordon McDonald Partridge

Author: Mem Fox
Publisher: Kane J. Miller

Length: 32   **Age:**   5–8   **Date:**   1985
Main Character: white male
Other Topics: N/A
Overview: A young boy's friendship with an elderly woman from the nursing home next door is a lesson in the joy of giving. Miss Nancy is losing her memory and Wilfrid helps her remember some of her life experiences.

Window Washing

Author: Jeannette Caines
Publisher: Harper Collins
Length: 20   **Age:**   5–7   **Date:**   1980
Main Character: African American male
Other Topics: N/A
Overview: A sister and brother spend a vacation with their fun and unconventional grandmother.

Won't Know Till I Get There

Author: Walter Dean Myers
Publisher: Viking
Length: 176   **Age:**   10–13   **Date:**   1982
Main Character: African American male
Other Topics: Foster Home
Overview: Fourteen-year-old Steve Perry's family takes in a foster child— streetwise thirteen-year-old Earl Goins. When Steve and Earl are charged with defacing public property, they are sentenced to volunteer work at an inner-city home for the elderly.

Invisible Playmates

Crocodarling

Author: Mary Rayner
Publisher: Bradbury

Crocodarling (cont.)

Length: 32 **Age:** 4–7 **Date:** 1985
Main Character: white male
Other Topics: Going to School
Overview: Four-year-old Sam has made Crocodarling (a puppet) the culprit for everything that goes wrong as he adjusts to nursery school.

Jessica

Author: Kevin Henkes
Publisher: Greenwillow
Length: 30 **Age:** 4–8 **Date:** 1989
Main Character: white female
Other Topics: Going to School
Overview: Ruthie is the only one who can see her playmate, Jessica. What will happen to Jessica when Ruthie starts school? There Ruthie finds a new (real) playmate—and her name is Jessica!

The Horse in Harry's Room

Author: Syd Hoff
Publisher: Harper
Length: 32 **Age:** 4–8 **Date:** 1970
Main Character: white male
Other Topics: N/A
Overview: A kind teacher accepts Harry's imaginary friend—a horse.

The Three Funny Friends

Author: Charlotte Zolotow
Publisher: Harper and Row
Length: 32 **Age:** 4–6 **Date:** 1961
Main Character: white female
Other Topics: Moving
Overview: Guy-Guy, Bickerina, and Mr. Dobie were all friends of the little girl in her new house. But her parents never saw them. When she finds a new friend named Tony, her invisible playmates never return.

Trigwater Did It

Author: Lissa Rovetch
Publisher: Puffin
Length: 32 **Age:** 3–8 **Date:** 1991
Main Character: white male
Other Topics: N/A
Overview: Annie is always the one who is blamed for everything, but the real culprit is Trigwater, a mischievous green friend no one else can see.

Will's Mammoth

Author: Rafe Martin
Publisher: Putnam
Length: 30 **Age:** 4–8 **Date:** 1989
Main Character: white male
Other Topics: N/A
Overview: Will dreams about having a wonderful adventure riding on the back of his own mammoth.

Jealousy

His Mother's Dog

Author: Liesel M. Skorpen
Publisher: Harper and Row
Length: 46 **Age:** 4–9 **Date:** 1978
Main Character: white male
Other Topics: New Baby
Overview: A young boy is jealous of both a dog and a new baby.

I Wish I Was Sick, Too!

Author: Franz Brandenberg
Publisher: Greenwillow
Length: 28 **Age:** 4–8 **Date:** 1976
Main Character: animal
Other Topics: N/A
Overview: Elizabeth is jealous of her brother's pampered treatment when he gets sick.

Jealousy (cont.)

Peter's Chair

Author: Ezra Jack Keats
Publisher: Harper and Row
Length: 28 **Age:** 3–8 **Date:** 1967
Main Character: African American male
Other Topics: N/A
Overview: Peter overcomes his jealousy when he paints his chair for his new sister.

She Come Bringing Me That Little Baby Girl

Author: Eloise Greenfield
Publisher: Lippincott
Length: 27 **Age:** 3–7 **Date:** 1974
Main Character: African American male
Other Topics: Sibling Rivalry
Overview: Kevin dislikes all the attention given to his new sister.

Stevie

Author: John Steptoe
Publisher: Harper
Length: 20 **Age:** 5–7 **Date:** 1969
Main Character: African American male
Other Topics: Anger, Moving
Overview: Robert remembers how he felt when his mother babysat Stevie. He felt jealous of the attention Stevie got and angry when Stevie played with his toys. After Stevie moved away, Robert's jealousy turned to love.

Sugar Blue

Author: Vera and Bill Cleaver
Publisher: Lothrop
Length: 155 **Age:** 9–11 **Date:** 1984
Main Character: white female
Other Topics: N/A

Sugar Blue (cont.)

Overview: Eleven-year-old Amy Blue must share her closed world with her four-year-old niece, Ella.

Latchkey Children

All Alone after School

Author: Muriel Stanek
Publisher: Albert Whitman
Length: 32 **Age:** 6–10 **Date:** 1985
Main Character: white male
Other Topics: N/A
Overview: In simple story form, this book discusses the problems of latchkey children.

Jerry on the Line

Author: Brenda Seabrooke
Publisher: Puffin
Length: 128 **Age:** 8–12 **Date:** 1992
Main Character: white male
Other Topics: N/A
Overview: There are two things most important to Jerry Johnson—playing soccer and his latchkey.

Latch Key Kid

Author: Irene Cumming Kleeberg
Publisher: Franklin Watts
Length: 97 **Age:** 8–12 **Date:** 1985
Main Character: cartoon characters
Other Topics: N/A
Overview: This informational text gives advice to children who are alone at home after school.

The Latchkey Kids

Author: Susan Terris
Publisher: Farrar
Length: 167 **Age:** 9–11 **Date:** 1986
Main Character: white female
Other Topics: Depression, Working Mother
Overview: At age eleven, Callie resents being responsible as the oldest in a family of latchkey children. Their father is suffering from severe depression.

Loneliness

Best Friends for Frances

Author: Russell Hoban
Publisher: Harper and Row
Length: 31 **Age:** 4–8 **Date:** 1969
Main Character: animal
Other Topics: N/A
Overview: Frances discovers that her little sister can be a lot of fun and a friend when she is lonely.

Blackboard Bear

Author: Martha Alexander
Publisher: Dial
Length: 25 **Age:** 4–8 **Date:** 1969
Main Character: white male
Other Topics: N/A
Overview: Feeling lonely, a young boy dreams up a new playmate.

Crow Boy

Author: Taro Yashima
Publisher: Viking
Length: 37 **Age:** 5–8 **Date:** 1955
Main Character: Japanese male
Other Topics: Fear

Crow Boy (cont.)

Overview: A painfully shy Japanese boy, nicknamed Chibi by his classmates, feels lonely and ostracized at school. Finally, his sixth-grade teacher discovers and appreciates Chibi's special talents. Chibi imitates the voices of crows in the school talent show and earns a new name—Crow Boy.

Fiona's Bee

Author: Beverly Keller
Publisher: Yearling Books
Length: 47 **Age:** 8–12 **Date:** 1975
Main Character: white female
Other Topics: Shyness
Overview: Fiona is very shy and lonely. She befriends a bee, an act that attracts the company of many boys and girls.

Lexie on Her Own

Author: Lisa Eisenberg
Publisher: Viking
Length: 122 **Age:** 9–12 **Date:** 1992
Main Character: white female
Other Topics: Moving
Overview: Fifth grader Lexie Nelson is lonely when her best friend moves away.

Lonesome Boy

Author: Arna Bontemps
Publisher: Beacon Press
Length: 28 **Age:** 8–12 **Date:** 1955
Main Character: African American male
Other Topics: N/A
Overview: Bubber is a lonely river boy with a silver trumpet.

Lonesome Lester

Author: Ida Luttrell
Publisher: Harper and Row
Length: 39 **Age:** 5–8 **Date:** 1984

Loneliness (cont.)

Lonesome Lester (cont.)

Main Character: animals
Other Topics: N/A
Overview: A prairie dog who lives alone discovers the difference between good company, bad company, and being alone.

Lonesome Little Colt

Author: C.W. Anderson
Publisher: Macmillan
Length: 47 **Age:** 6–8 **Date:** 1961
Main Character: animal
Other Topics: Adoption, Death (General)
Overview: Each pony on the farm is paired up with its own little colt—except for one. His mother has died and left him alone and lonely until he is happily adopted by a pony who lost her own colt.

Mandy

Author: Julie Edwards
Publisher: Harper Trophy
Length: 279 **Age:** 9–12 **Date:** 1971
Main Character: white female
Other Topics: Adoption
Overview: Ten-year-old Mandy lives in an old stone orphanage, the only home she has ever known. One day she discovers an abandoned cottage in the woods. Mandy makes this her very own home— but something is still missing.

Oliver Button Is a Sissy

Author: Tomie de Paola
Publisher: Harcourt Brace Jovanovich
Length: 44 **Age:** 5–8 **Date:** 1979
Main Character: white male
Other Topics: Sexism

Oliver Button Is a Sissy (cont.)

Overview: Oliver wants to dance and his classmates call him a sissy until they see Oliver dance in the talent show.

The Boy Who Wasn't Lonely

Author: Richard Parker
Publisher: Bobbs-Merrill
Length: 141 **Age:** 8–12 **Date:** 1965
Main Character: white male
Other Topics: Only Child
Overview: Cricket Morley is an only child who shuns the company of other children until he meets Rain, whose friendship he enjoys.

The Hundred Dresses

Author: Eleanor Estes
Publisher: Harcourt, Brace
Length: 80 **Age:** 5–8 **Date:** 1944
Main Character: Polish female
Other Topics: Moving, Prejudice, Poverty
Overview: Wanda and her Polish American family feel unwelcome in a small town and move to the city. Wanda's classmates tease her until she wins a school contest with her 100 drawings of dresses. It is too late because she's moved again.

The Lonely Skyscraper

Author: Jenny Hawkesworth
Publisher: Doubleday and Co.
Length: 26 **Age:** 5–8 **Date:** 1980
Main Character: object
Other Topics: N/A
Overview: A big, city skyscraper is lonely when the workers go home at night, but it finds a new and happy life in the country as a home for forest animals.

The Loner

Author: Bianca Bradbury
Publisher: Houghton Mifflin
Length: 140 **Age:** 8–12 **Date:** 1970
Main Character: white male
Other Topics: Sibling Rivalry
Overview: Jay is very lonely and feels like a loser until he gets a summer job at a marina.

The Scarebird

Author: Sid Fleischman
Publisher: Greenwillow
Length: 29 **Age:** 7–10 **Date:** 1988
Main Character: white male
Other Topics: Orphan, Friendship
Overview: Lonesome John befriends Sam, an orphan boy.

Looking Different

Arthur's Nose

Author: Marc Brown
Publisher: Little, Brown, and Co.
Length: 29 **Age:** 4–7 **Date:** 1976
Main Character: animal
Other Topics: N/A
Overview: Since Arthur is unhappy with the way his nose looks, he visits a doctor to have it changed.

Donkey-donkey

Author: Roger Duvoisin
Publisher: Parents' Magazine Press
Length: 40 **Age:** 4–8 **Date:** 1940
Main Character: animal
Other Topics: N/A

Donkey-donkey (cont.)

Overview: Donkey-donkey is unhappy about his ears. They are very long and stand straight up. He soon learns that that is the way donkeys should look.

Elihu the Elephant

Author: Gale Brennan
Publisher: Children's Press
Length: 15 **Age:** 4–6 **Date:** 1980
Main Character: animal
Other Topics: N/A
Overview: All of the animals in the jungle make fun of Elihu, the elephant, because of his long, long nose. Their opinion changes when he saves the life of a monkey.

Freckle Juice

Author: Judy Blume
Publisher: Four Winds
Length: 40 **Age:** 7–9 **Date:** 1971
Main Character: white male
Other Topics: N/A
Overview: Andrew wants freckles so badly that he buys Sharon's freckle recipe for fifty cents.

Hector: The Accordion-Nosed Dog

Author: John Stadler
Publisher: Reading Rainbow Library
Length: 64 **Age:** 6–8 **Date:** 1986
Main Character: animal
Other Topics: N/A
Overview: When Hector is in an accident, his nose becomes shaped like an accordion.

I've Got Your Nose

Author: Nancy Bentley
Publisher: Doubleday
Length: 32 **Age:** 5–7 **Date:** 1991

Looking Different (cont.)

I've Got Your Nose (cont.)

Main Character: cartoon character
Other Topics: N/A
Overview: A witch tries to cast a spell to change her nose since it is too long, pointy, and covered with warts.

Kim/Kimi

Author: Hadley Irwin
Publisher: Margaret K. McElderry Books
Length: 200 **Age:** 10–18 **Date:** 1987
Main Character: Japanese American female
Other Topics: Stepfamilies
Overview: Sixteen-year-old Kim/Kimi looks different from her friends. She wants to know more about her Japanese American father, who died before she was born.

Leo the Lop

Author: Steven Cosgrove
Publisher: Serendipity
Length: 26 **Age:** 5–8 **Date:** 1977
Main Character: animal
Other Topics: N/A
Overview: Leo looks slightly different from the other rabbits.

Magic Growing Powder

Author: Janet Quin-Harkin
Publisher: Parents' Magazine Press
Length: 36 **Age:** 4–8 **Date:** 1980
Main Character: white male
Other Topics: N/A

Magic Growing Powder (cont.)

Overview: King Max does not like being short, so he promises half his kingdom and his daughter's hand in marriage for some magic growing powder.

Rat Teeth

Author: Patricia Reilly Giff
Publisher: Delacorte
Length: 144 **Age:** 9–12 **Date:** 1984
Main Character: white male
Other Topics: Divorce
Overview: Cliffie has divorced parents, two front teeth that stick out, and he even loses a baseball game to fourth graders. Perhaps he should run away.

Reserved for Mark Anthony Crowder

Author: Alison Smith
Publisher: E. P. Dutton
Length: 123 **Age:** 10–12 **Date:** 1978
Main Character: white male
Other Topics: Clumsiness
Overview: Sixth grader Mark Anthony Crowder thinks he is too tall, too nearsighted, and too clumsy.

So What?

Author: Miriam Cohen
Publisher: Doubleday
Length: 29 **Age:** 5–8 **Date:** 1982
Main Character: multicultural males and females
Other Topics: N/A
Overview: Jim is the shortest boy in the class. A new girl from Chicago helps him learn to accept himself.

The Biggest Nose

Author: Kathy Caple
Publisher: Houghton Mifflin
Length: 32 **Age:** 4–7 **Date:** 1985

The Biggest Nose (cont.)

Main Character: animal
Other Topics: N/A
Overview: Eleanor the elephant is self-conscious about her large nose.

The Ugly Duckling

Author: Hans Christian Andersen
Publisher: Macmillan
Length: 32 **Age:** 6–8 **Date:** 1955
Main Character: animal
Other Topics: Loneliness
Overview: An ugly duckling turns into a beautiful swan.

Loose Tooth

Airmail to the Moon

Author: Tom Birdseye
Publisher: Holiday House
Length: 32 **Age:** 5–8 **Date:** 1989
Main Character: white female
Other Topics: Anger
Overview: Ora Mae is very angry when she discovers someone stole her tooth and she can't put it under her pillow for the tooth fairy.

Albert's Toothache

Author: Barbara Williams
Publisher: Dutton
Length: 26 **Age:** 4–6 **Date:** 1974
Main Character: animal
Other Topics: N/A
Overview: No one believes Albert when he complains of a toothache.

Alligator's Toothache

Author: Diane DeGroat
Publisher: Crown

Alligator's Toothache (cont.)

Length: 30 **Age:** 2–6 **Date:** 1977
Main Character: animal
Other Topics: Hospitalization, Doctor's Office
Overview: This wordless picture book depicts the serious problem of an alligator's toothache and his fear of dentists.

Arthur's Loose Tooth

Author: Lilian Hoban
Publisher: Harper and Row, Publishers
Length: 64 **Age:** 5–8 **Date:** 1985
Main Character: animal
Other Topics: N/A
Overview: Arthur is a little afraid of losing his tooth until his sitter shows him the real meaning of bravery.

Arthur's Tooth

Author: Marc Brown
Publisher: Atlantic Monthly Press
Length: 32 **Age:** 5–8 **Date:** 1985
Main Character: animal
Other Topics: N/A
Overview: Arthur is the only one in his class who still has all his baby teeth. He waits patiently for a loose tooth.

How Many Teeth?

Author: Paul Showers
Publisher: Crowell
Length: 32 **Age:** 5–8 **Date:** 1962
Main Character: cartoon characters
Other Topics: N/A
Overview: An easy-to-read informative book about teeth, tooth care, and losing teeth.

Little Rabbit's Loose Tooth

Author: Lucy Bate
Publisher: Crown

Loose Tooth (cont.)

Little Rabbit's Loose Tooth (cont.)

Length: 32 **Age:** 4–8 **Date:** 1975
Main Character: animal
Other Topics: N/A
Overview: Little Rabbit is about to lose his first baby tooth. He is both excited and frightened.

Lizzie and the Tooth Fairy

Author: Judith Wolman
Publisher: Dandelion Books
Length: 32 **Age:** 4–7 **Date:** 1979
Main Character: white female
Other Topics: N/A
Overview: Lizzie has been looking forward to having a loose tooth since she was four years old. She was very excited when she not only lost a tooth, but also met the Tooth Fairy.

Loose Tooth

Author: Steven Kroll
Publisher: Holiday House
Length: 32 **Age:** 5–8 **Date:** 1984
Main Character: animal
Other Topics: N/A
Overview: A bat is ignored until he gets a loose tooth.

My Tooth Is Loose!

Author: Martin Silverman
Publisher: Viking
Length: 32 **Age:** 4–8 **Date:** 1991
Main Character: white male
Other Topics: N/A
Overview: A young boy has a loose tooth.

One Morning in Maine

Author: Robert McCloskey
Publisher: Viking
Length: 64 **Age:** 6–7 **Date:** 1952
Main Character: white female
Other Topics: N/A
Overview: Young Sal wakes one morning to discover a loose tooth. She tells everyone she sees. When Sal loses the tooth on the beach, she substitutes a gull's feather to put under her pillow.

Our Tooth Story

Author: Ethel and Leonard Kessler
Publisher: Dodd, Mead and Co.
Length: 40 **Age:** 4–6 **Date:** 1972
Main Character: cartoon characters
Other Topics: N/A
Overview: Various children describe what happened when they lost a tooth.

The Bear's Toothache

Author: David McPhail
Publisher: Puffin Books
Length: 26 **Age:** 4–8 **Date:** 1972
Main Character: white male
Other Topics: N/A
Overview: A little boy awakens one night to hear a bear with a toothache howling outside his window.

The Mango Tooth

Author: Charlotte Pomerantz
Publisher: Greenwillow
Length: 26 **Age:** 5–8 **Date:** 1977
Main Character: white female
Other Topics: N/A
Overview: Posy loses four teeth.

Losing Things

Anna in Charge

Author: Yoriko Tsutsui
Publisher: Puffin
Length: 32 **Age:** 3–8 **Date:** 1991
Main Character: Asian female
Other Topics: N/A
Overview: What could be worse than losing your little sister when you are left in charge?

Losing Things at Mr. Mudd's

Author: Carolyn Coman
Publisher: Farrar, Straus and Giroux
Length: 26 **Age:** 6–8 **Date:** 1992
Main Character: white female
Other Topics: N/A
Overview: Six-year-old Lucy visits a distant relative whose name is Bernard Mudd. He gives her a valuable ring but insists that she not wear it. When she sneaks the ring to wear, Lucy loses it.

Lost in the Storm

Author: Carol Corrick
Publisher: Clarion
Length: 29 **Age:** 6–10 **Date:** 1974
Main Character: white male
Other Topics: Friendship
Overview: Christopher must wait out a long fretful night before searching for his lost dog.

Molly's Moe

Author: Kay Chorao
Publisher: Seabury Press
Length: 31 **Age:** 5–8 **Date:** 1976
Main Character: white female
Other Topics: N/A
Overview: Molly has a tendency to lose things. When she begins to search for her

Molly's Moe (cont.)

lost stuffed dinosaur, Moe, she also finds lots of other lost items.

The Day of the Rainbow

Author: Ruth Craft
Publisher: Puffin
Length: 32 **Age:** 3–8 **Date:** 1991
Main Character: African Americans
Other Topics: N/A
Overview: On a summer day in the city, three people lose something.

Theodore Turtle

Author: Ellen MacGregor
Publisher: McGraw Hill
Length: 32 **Age:** 5–7 **Date:** 1955
Main Character: animal
Other Topics: N/A
Overview: Theodore Turtle has a difficult time keeping up with his raincoats.

Where's My Monkey?

Author: Dieter Schubert
Publisher: Puffin
Length: 32 **Age:** 3–7 **Date:** 1992
Main Character: white male
Other Topics: N/A
Overview: A little boy and his monkey are best friends. During a storm, a strong wind whips the monkey away. The boy searches everywhere, wondering when he will see his friend again.

Manners

Animal Manners

Author: Barbara S. Hazen
Publisher: Western Publishing Co.
Length: 38 **Age:** 4–8 **Date:** 1974

Manners (cont.)

Animal Manners (cont.)

Main Character: animal
Other Topics: N/A
Overview: This book of rhyming verse describes multiple types of appropriate behavior.

Circus Baby

Author: Maud and Miska Petersham
Publisher: Macmillan
Length: 32 **Age:** 4–6 **Date:** 1950
Main Character: animal
Other Topics: N/A
Overview: A mother elephant tries to teach table manners to her baby.

Clifford's Manners

Author: Norman Bridwell
Publisher: Scholastic
Length: 32 **Age:** 5–8 **Date:** 1987
Main Character: animal
Other Topics: N/A
Overview: Manners are taught in this easy-to-read book.

Dinner at Alberta's

Author: Russell Hoban
Publisher: Thomas Crowell
Length: 36 **Age:** 5–8 **Date:** 1975
Main Character: animal
Other Topics: N/A
Overview: Arthur Crocodile has a difficult time learning table manners until his sister brings her girlfriend to visit.

Every Kid's Guide to Good Manners

Author: Joy Berry
Publisher: Living Skills Press
Length: 48 **Age:** 5–8 **Date:** 1987

Every Kid's Guide to Good Manners (cont.)

Main Character: cartoon characters
Other Topics: N/A
Overview: Different social situations are addressed.

Excuse Me, Certainly

Author: Louis Slobodkin
Publisher: Vanguard Press
Length: 25 **Age:** 4–6 **Date:** 1959
Main Character: white male
Other Topics: N/A
Overview: Willie White was not very polite. He did not even say, "Excuse me."

Hello Gnu, How Do You Do? A Beginning Guide to Positively Polite Behavior

Author: Barbara Shook Hazen
Publisher: Doubleday
Length: 64 **Age:** 5–9 **Date:** 1990
Main Character: animal
Other Topics: N/A
Overview: Animal characters are used to teach proper behavior.

"I'm Sorry"

Author: Janet Riehecky
Publisher: Children's Press
Length: 32 **Age:** 3–6 **Date:** 1989
Main Character: white male
Other Topics: N/A
Overview: Various situations are described in which "I'm sorry" is an appropriate response.

Let's Find out about Manners

Author: Valerie Pitt
Publisher: Franklin Watts
Length: 32 **Age:** 5–8 **Date:** 1972
Main Character: multicultural males and females

Let's Find out about Manners (cont.)

Other Topics: N/A
Overview: A friendly guide to good manners.

Magic Monsters Learn about Manners

Author: Jane B. Moncure
Publisher: Children's Press
Length: 32 **Age:** 3–7 **Date:** 1980
Main Character: monsters
Other Topics: N/A
Overview: Magic Monsters demonstrate good manners in social situations.

Manners

Author: Aliki
Publisher: Greenwillow
Length: 29 **Age:** 5–8 **Date:** 1990
Main Character: cartoon characters
Other Topics: N/A
Overview: Discusses manners and gives examples of good manners and bad manners.

Manners Can Be Fun

Author: Munro Leaf
Publisher: Lippincott
Length: 48 **Age:** 4–8 **Date:** 1958
Main Character: cartoon characters
Other Topics: N/A
Overview: Cartoon characters explain good manners.

Mind Your Manners

Author: Peggy Parrish
Publisher: Greenwillow
Length: 55 **Age:** 5–8 **Date:** 1978
Main Character: cartoon characters
Other Topics: N/A
Overview: An introduction to proper manners for meeting new people, receiving gifts, using the telephone, dining out, and other social situations.

Muppet Manners (or the Night Gonzo Gave a Party)

Author: Pat Relf
Publisher: Random House
Length: 28 **Age:** 4–8 **Date:** 1981
Main Character: objects
Other Topics: N/A
Overview: A party-giver's guide.

Please Pass the P's and Q's

Author: Barbara Hazen
Publisher: World Publishing Co.
Length: 128 **Age:** 6–9 **Date:** 1967
Main Character: cartoon characters
Other Topics: N/A
Overview: A guide to good manners.

Soup Should Be Seen, Not Heard: The Kid's Etiquette Book

Author: Beth Brainard and Shelia Behr
Publisher: Dell
Length: 160 **Age:** 4–12 **Date:** 1988
Main Character: cartoon characters
Other Topics: N/A
Overview: Guidelines for etiquette are offered in an amusing way.

"Thank You"

Author: Janet Riehecky
Publisher: Children's Press
Length: 32 **Age:** 3–6 **Date:** 1989
Main Character: African American female
Other Topics: N/A
Overview: Various situations are described in which "thank you" is an appropriate response.

The Berenstain Bears Forget Their Manners

Author: Stan and Jan Berenstain
Publisher: Random House
Length: 29 **Age:** 4–8 **Date:** 1985

Manners (cont.)

The Berenstain Bears Forget Their Manners (cont.)

Main Character: animal
Other Topics: N/A
Overview: When the Berenstain bears forget their manners, Mama Bear comes up with a plan to help them remember.

The Manners Book

Author: June Behrens
Publisher: Children's Press
Length: 31 **Age:** 4–6 **Date:** 1980
Main Character: white male
Other Topics: N/A
Overview: Photographs show Chris and his stuffed bear, Ned, answering questions about proper social behavior.

What to Do When Your Mom or Dad Says . . . Don't Slurp Your Soup

Author: Joy Wilt Berry
Publisher: Living Skills Press
Length: 48 **Age:** 6–8 **Date:** 1984
Main Character: multicultural males and females
Other Topics: N/A
Overview: Children in various situations describe appropriate dining manners.

You Know Better Than That

Author: Norah Smaridge
Publisher: Abingdon Press
Length: 29 **Age:** 5–7 **Date:** 1973
Main Character: multicultural males and females
Other Topics: N/A
Overview: Fourteen humorous verses advise on correct conduct.

Mental Illness

My Sister, Then and Now: A Book about Mental Illness

Author: Virginia L. Kroll
Publisher: Carolrhoda
Length: 40 **Age:** 5–8 **Date:** 1992
Main Character: white female
Other Topics: N/A
Overview: Ten-year-old Rachael explains that her older sister, Karen, is mentally ill. She has been diagnosed as schizophrenic.

Notes for Another Life

Author: Sue Ellen Bridgers
Publisher: Alfred A. Knopf
Length: 250 **Age:** 10–12 **Date:** 1981
Main Character: white female
Other Topics: Intergenerational
Overview: Thirteen-year-old Wren lives with an older brother, a father with an incurable mental illness, and a mother who is unable to cope. Her grandparents offer help.

Rabble Starkey

Author: Lois Lowry
Publisher: Houghton Mifflin
Length: 192 **Age:** 10–18 **Date:** 1987
Main Character: white female
Other Topics: Growing Up
Overview: When Mrs. Bigelow is hospitalized because of mental illness, Rabble Starkey and her mother move into the Bigelows' home to care for Veronica, her best friend, Gunther, and Mr. Bigelow.

The Boy with a Problem

Author: Joan Fassler
Publisher: Behavioral Publishing
Length: 28 **Age:** 7–10 **Date:** 1971

The Boy with a Problem (cont.)

Main Character: white male
Other Topics: N/A
Overview: Johnny is a boy with a problem—he is so depressed that he doesn't feel like eating, doing school work, or playing. His friend Peter takes the time to listen to Johnny and Johnny begins to feel better.

The Facts about Mental and Emotional Disabilities

Author: Jean Dick
Publisher: Crestwood House
Length: 48 **Age:** 8–12 **Date:** 1988
Main Character: multicultural
Other Topics: N/A
Overview: This comprehensive book discusses autism, depression, mental retardation, and other disabilities.

The Keeper

Author: Phyllis Reynolds Naylor
Publisher: Atheneum
Length: 228 **Age:** 12–15 **Date:** 1986
Main Character: white male
Other Topics: N/A
Overview: Nick knows he must seek help for his father's paranoia.

The Moves Make the Man

Author: Bruce Brooks
Publisher: Harper
Length: 252 **Age:** 10–18 **Date:** 1984
Main Character: African American male, white male
Other Topics: Friendship
Overview: The mental breakdown of a young boy's mother almost causes his own breakdown.

Mentally Handicapped

A Look at Mental Retardation

Author: Rebecca Anders
Publisher: Lerner Publications Co.
Length: 31 **Age:** 8–12 **Date:** 1976
Main Character: multicultural males and females
Other Topics: N/A
Overview: Text and photographs are used to describe problems encountered by people who are mentally handicapped.

Don't Take Teddy

Author: Babbis Friis-Baastad
Publisher: Scribner
Length: 218 **Age:** 10–18 **Date:** 1967
Main Character: white male
Other Topics: N/A
Overview: A young boy protects his older retarded brother.

Every Living Thing

Author: Cynthia Rylant
Publisher: Bradbury
Length: 81 **Age:** 8–10 **Date:** 1985
Main Character: white male
Other Topics: N/A
Overview: Leo hates attending his special education class since he is separated from the rest of his class. "Slower than the Rest" is one of twelve short stories in which Rylant explores the times when people's lives change and they see things in a different way.

M.E. and Morton

Author: Sylvia Cassedy
Publisher: Crowell

Mentally Handicapped (cont.)

M.E. and Morton (cont.)

Length: 312 **Age:** 10–13 **Date:** 1987
Main Character: white male, white female
Other Topics: Friendship
Overview: An eleven-year-old girl has ambivalent feelings about her brother, who is retarded.

My Brother Steven Is Retarded

Author: Harriett Langsam Sobol
Publisher: Macmillan
Length: 26 **Age:** 7–11 **Date:** 1977
Main Character: white male
Other Topics: N/A
Overview: This first-person narrative and use of photographs explain the range of emotions of a normal sibling. Beth is eleven with an older brother who is mentally handicapped. Sometimes she is embarrassed, sometimes angry.

My Father, the Nutcase

Author: Judith Caseley
Publisher: Alfred A. Knopf
Length: 185 **Age:** 10–14 **Date:** 1992
Main Character: white female
Other Topics: N/A
Overview: Fifteen-year-old Zoe worries that her father's clinical depression will overwhelm the entire family.

My Friend Jacob

Author: Lucille Clifton
Publisher: Dutton
Length: 24 **Age:** 5–7 **Date:** 1980
Main Character: African American male, white male

My Friend Jacob (cont.)

Other Topics: Friendship
Overview: A tender story of the friendship between a small African American boy and a retarded white teenager.

My Sister

Author: Karen Hirsch
Publisher: Carolrhoda Books, Inc.
Length: 28 **Age:** 5–8 **Date:** 1977
Main Character: white female
Other Topics: N/A
Overview: A sister discusses her little sister's mental retardation.

One Little Girl

Author: Joan Fassler
Publisher: Behavioral Publications
Length: 19 **Age:** 5–8 **Date:** 1969
Main Character: white female
Other Topics: N/A
Overview: Because Laurie is somewhat retarded, grownups call her a "slow" child. Laurie learns that she is not slow at everything.

Risk 'n Roses

Author: Jan Slepian
Publisher: Philomel
Length: 175 **Age:** 8–12 **Date:** 1990
Main Character: white female
Other Topics: Moving, Loneliness, Racism, Prejudice
Overview: Skip feels responsible for her older and mentally handicapped sister, Angela. The family moves to a new neighborhood so that Angela can be closer to a special school. Skip is lonely for a friend and makes a dangerous choice.

Somebody Called Me a Retard Today … and My Heart Felt Sad

Author: Ellen O'Shaughnessy
Publisher: Walker
Length: 24 **Age:** 4–8 **Date:** 1992
Main Character: cartoon
Other Topics: N/A
Overview: After she is called a retard, the girl's father extols her strengths.

Stay Away from Simon

Author: Carol Carrick
Publisher: Clarion
Length: 63 **Age:** 7–10 **Date:** 1985
Main Character: white male
Other Topics: N/A
Overview: A mentally retarded boy shows two other children that he is much like them.

The Reason for Janey

Author: Nancy Hope Wilson
Publisher: Macmillan
Length: 160 **Age:** 10–12 **Date:** 1994
Main Character: white female
Other Topics: Divorce
Overview: When Philly's parents divorce, her mother takes in Janey, a mentally handicapped adult.

The Summer of the Swans

Author: Betsy Byars
Publisher: Viking
Length: 144 **Age:** 11–13 **Date:** 1970
Main Character: white female
Other Topics: N/A
Overview: Story of a young teenage girl whose life changed one day while rescuing her handicapped younger brother.

We Laugh, We Love, We Cry: Children Living with Mental Retardation

Author: Thomas Bergman
Publisher: Gareth Stevens
Length: 48 **Age:** 5–10 **Date:** 1989
Main Character: white females
Other Topics: N/A
Overview: This photo-essay describes the life, physiotherapy, and schooling of two mentally retarded sisters.

Welcome Home, Jellybean

Author: Marlene Fanta Shyer
Publisher: Macmillan
Length: 152 **Age:** 9–13 **Date:** 1978
Main Character: white female
Other Topics: N/A
Overview: Neil's older sister is coming home to live after spending most of her life in an institution for mentally handicapped children.

What about Me?

Author: Colby Rodowsky
Publisher: Sunburst
Length: 144 **Age:** 10–14 **Date:** 1989
Main Character: white female
Other Topics: Sibling Rivalry
Overview: Dorrie finds herself resenting her eleven-year-old brother, who is mentally handicapped and very demanding of her time.

Messiness

A Christmas Card for Mr. McFizz

Author: Obren Bokich
Publisher: Green Tiger Press
Length: 30 **Age:** 4–8 **Date:** 1987
Main Character: animal
Other Topics: Friendship

Messiness (cont.)

A Christmas Card for Mr. McFizz (cont.)

Overview: Mr. McFizz and Mr. Grizwold were neighbors. Mr. McFizz was very neat and clean and Mr. Grizwold was very messy.

Messy Bessy

Author: Patricia and Fredrick McKissack
Publisher: Children's Press
Length: 30 **Age:** 4–6 **Date:** 1987
Main Character: African American female
Other Topics: N/A
Overview: Bessy finally cleans up her messy room.

The Very Messy Room

Author: Elizabeth and Henry Stanton
Publisher: Albert Whitman and Co.
Length: 30 **Age:** 4–8 **Date:** 1978
Main Character: white female
Other Topics: N/A
Overview: A young girl and her parents compromise over the condition of her messy room.

When I'm Alone

Author: Carol P. Ochs
Publisher: Carolrhoda Books, Inc.
Length: 30 **Age:** 4–6 **Date:** 1993
Main Character: African American female
Other Topics: N/A
Overview: A little girl blames her messiness on an assortment of animals.

Moving

A New House

Author: Deborah Manley
Publisher: Raintree Children's Press
Length: 32 **Age:** 5–8 **Date:** 1979
Main Character: multicultural males and females
Other Topics: N/A
Overview: The experiences of moving and building a new house are described.

Annie Bananie

Author: Leah Komaiko
Publisher: Harper and Row
Length: 29 **Age:** 3–6 **Date:** 1987
Main Character: white female
Other Topics: N/A
Overview: A little girl is sad because her best friend, Annie Bananie, is moving away.

Dragonwings

Author: Lawrence Yep
Publisher: Harper
Length: 248 **Age:** 5–6 **Date:** 1975
Main Character: Chinese male
Other Topics: N/A
Overview: Eight-year-old Moon Shadow must move from his home in China to join his father in San Francisco's Chinatown. Finally, father and son move again to pursue father's dream of flying as the Wright Brothers had.

Elaine, Mary Lewis, and the Frogs

Author: Heidi Chang
Publisher: Crown
Length: 64 **Age:** 8–10 **Date:** 1988
Main Character: Chinese female
Other Topics: Loneliness, Intergenerational

Elaine, Mary Lewis, and the Frogs (cont.)

Overview: When Elaine Chow, a young Chinese American girl, moves from San Francisco to Iowa, she feels lonely in her new school until she begins work on a science project with Mary.

Go Away Monsters, Lickety Split

Author: Nancy Evans Cooney
Publisher: Putnam
Length: 32   **Age:** 4–7   **Date:** 1990
Main Character: white male
Other Topics: Fear
Overview: Jeffrey must move to a new house and a new neighborhood with a new kitten, Lickety, who helps him transcend the need for a flashlight or nightlight.

Goodbye House

Author: Frank Asch
Publisher: Prentice Hall, Inc.
Length: 28   **Age:** 3–6   **Date:** 1986
Main Character: animal
Other Topics: N/A
Overview: Little Bear says goodbye to his surroundings before he moves away with his family.

Homesick: My Own Story

Author: Jean Fritz
Publisher: Putnam
Length: 163   **Age:** 10–12   **Date:** 1982
Main Character: Chinese female
Other Topics: N/A
Overview: The autobiography of Jean Fritz. This story tells of her childhood in China.

I Don't Live Here

Author: Pam Conrad
Publisher: Dutton

I Don't Live Here (cont.)

Length: 60   **Age:** 8–10   **Date:** 1984
Main Character: white female
Other Topics: N/A
Overview: Eight-year-old Nicki believes she will never be happy in the large old house her family has moved to even if it does have a gazebo in the yard.

In the Year of the Boar and Jackie Robinson

Author: Bette Bao Lord
Publisher: Harper
Length: 169   **Age:** 8–12   **Date:** 1984
Main Character: Chinese American female
Other Topics: Loneliness
Overview: Shirley Temple Wong, a Chinese girl, moves from Chung-King, China, to Brooklyn, New York. She feels lonely at school until she becomes friends with a classsmate who introduces Shirley to baseball and Jackie Robinson.

Ira Says Goodbye

Author: Bernard Waber
Publisher: Houghton Mifflin
Length: 38   **Age:** 4–7   **Date:** 1988
Main Character: white male
Other Topics: N/A
Overview: Ira learns that his best friend, Reggie, is moving.

Julie's New Home

Author: Jennie Davis
Publisher: Children's Press
Length: 30   **Age:** 4–8   **Date:** 1982
Main Character: white female
Other Topics: Loneliness, Friendship
Overview: Julie is lonely in her new home until she discovers that it is necessary to be friendly in order to make friends.

Moving (cont.)

Kevin Corbett Eats Flies

Author: Patricia Hermes
Publisher: Harcourt, Brace, and Jovanovich
Length: 160 **Age:** 8–11 **Date:** 1986
Main Character: white male
Other Topics: Death of a Parent
Overview: Kevin tries to get his father to fall in love so they won't have to move again.

Maggie Doesn't Want to Move

Author: Elizabeth Lee O'Donnell
Publisher: Four Winds Press
Length: 32 **Age:** 5–8 **Date:** 1987
Main Character: white female and male
Other Topics: N/A
Overview: Simon is reluctant to move but claims that it is really Maggie, his little sister, who doesn't want to move.

Moving Day

Author: Tobi Tobias
Publisher: Alfred Knopf
Length: 26 **Age:** 4–6 **Date:** 1976
Main Character: white female
Other Topics: N/A
Overview: A little girl has mixed feelings about moving.

Next-Door Neighbors

Author: Sara Ellis
Publisher: Macmillan
Length: 154 **Age:** 10–12 **Date:** 1990
Main Character: white female
Other Topics: Shyness
Overview: A girl moves and has difficulty making friends her own age.

Santiago

Author: Pura Belpré
Publisher: Frederick Warne and Co.
Length: 26 **Age:** 7–10 **Date:** 1969
Main Character: Hispanic male
Other Topics: Friendship, Multiculturalism
Overview: Santiago and his family moved to New York from Puerto Rico. He was lonely until he met Ernie and gained a new friend.

The Berenstain Bears' Moving Day

Author: Stan and Jan Berenstain
Publisher: Random House
Length: 30 **Age:** 4–6 **Date:** 1981
Main Character: animal
Other Topics: N/A
Overview: The Berenstain Bears move to a better place, a tree house.

The Kid in the Red Jacket

Author: Barbara Park
Publisher: Knopf
Length: 113 **Age:** 10–12 **Date:** 1987
Main Character: white male
Other Topics: New School, Friendship
Overview: A boy must adjust to a new home, a new school, and the adoration of a little first-grade girl, determined to be his friend.

The Leaving Morning

Author: Angela Johnson
Publisher: Orchard Books
Length: 32 **Age:** 5–9 **Date:** 1992
Main Character: African Americans
Other Topics: N/A
Overview: Two children must say goodbye to their home and friends.

The Move

Author: Elizabeth Billington
Publisher: Frederick Warne and Co.
Length: 124 **Age:** 7–10 **Date:** 1984
Main Character: white male
Other Topics: N/A
Overview: When twelve-year-old Tim's mother is mugged in New York, this African American family moves to the suburbs where Tim is afraid they will never be a happy family again.

The Rabbi's Girls

Author: Johanna Hurwitz
Publisher: William Morrow and Co.
Length: 158 **Age:** 8–12 **Date:** 1982
Main Character: white females
Other Topics: N/A
Overview: Carrie is the rabbi's daughter. When they move to a new town, she must face a new school and a new neighborhood.

The Trip

Author: Ezra Jack Keats
Publisher: Greenwillow
Length: 32 **Age:** 3–8 **Date:** 1978
Main Character: African American male
Other Topics: Loneliness
Overview: Young Louie feels lonely in the new neighborhood.

Time to Go

Author: Beverly and David Fiday
Publisher: Harcourt Brace Jovanovich
Length: 29 **Age:** 6–10 **Date:** 1990
Main Character: white male
Other Topics: N/A
Overview: As he and his family prepare to move, a child takes one last look at their farm home.

We Are Best Friends

Author: Aliki
Publisher: Greenwillow
Length: 28 **Age:** 4–6 **Date:** 1982
Main Character: white males
Other Topics: Loneliness
Overview: Two best friends must make new friends when one moves away.

Mute

A Certain Small Shepherd

Author: Rebecca Caudill
Publisher: Holt
Length: 48 **Age:** 7–9 **Date:** 1965
Main Character: white male
Other Topics: N/A
Overview: This contemporary version of the Christmas story involves a supposedly mute Appalachian boy and a newborn African American baby.

Blind Outlaw

Author: Glen Rounds
Publisher: Holiday House
Length: 96 **Age:** 9–12 **Date:** 1980
Main Character: white male
Other Topics: N/A
Overview: A mute boy tames a wild horse through trust.

Burnish Me Bright

Author: Julia Cunningham
Publisher: Pantheon
Length: 80 **Age:** 8–12 **Date:** 1970
Main Character: white male
Other Topics: N/A
Overview: A retired actor teaches a young mute boy to pantomime.

Mute (cont.)

Cat's Got Your Tongue? A Story for Children Afraid to Speak

Author: Charles E. Shaefer
Publisher: Magination
Length: 32 **Age:** 4–8 **Date:** 1992
Main Character: white female
Other Topics: Going to School
Overview: Anna is afraid of strangers and so becomes an elective mute when she enters kindergarten. With the help of a doctor and her family, she becomes confident enough to speak and make friends.

Silent Lotus

Author: Jeanne M. Lee
Publisher: Farrar, Straus and Giroux
Length: 32 **Age:** 5–8 **Date:** 1991
Main Character: Cambodian female
Other Topics: N/A
Overview: Lotus cannot speak or hear but learns to perform the complex story dances of the Cambodian court ballet.

The Silent Voice

Author: Julia Cunningham
Publisher: Dutton
Length: 145 **Age:** 10–12 **Date:** 1981
Main Character: white male
Other Topics: Orphan
Overview: Parisian performers help a mute boy.

Only Child

Confessions of an Only Child

Author: Norma Klein
Publisher: Pantheon
Length: 93 **Age:** 9–11 **Date:** 1974

Confessions of an Only Child (cont.)

Main Character: white female
Other Topics: Death of a Sibling
Overview: Eight-year-old Tonia expresses her feelings about the death of a premature baby brother, and her acceptance of a brother born a year later.

Physical Disabilities

A Look at Physical Handicaps

Author: Margaret S. Punsell
Publisher: Lerner
Length: 31 **Age:** 8–10 **Date:** 1976
Main Character: white males and females
Other Topics: N/A
Overview: Text and photographs describe problems faced by people with physical handicaps.

About Handicaps: An Open Family Book for Parents and Children Together

Author: Sara B. Stein
Publisher: Walker
Length: 47 **Age:** 3–18 **Date:** 1974
Main Character: white males
Other Topics: N/A
Overview: This dual textbook can be used by children and adults. The relationship between two children is explored. One is handicapped, the other is not. Photographs help tell their story.

Crutches

Author: Peter Hartling
Publisher: Lothrop, Lee and Shepard
Length: 160 **Age:** 9–12 **Date:** 1988
Main Character: white male

Crutches (cont.)

Other Topics: Friendship
Overview: Twelve-year-old Thomas befriends a man with one leg, whom everyone calls Crutches.

Don't Feel Sorry for Paul

Author: Bernard Wolf
Publisher: Harper and Row
Length: 96 **Age:** 8–12 **Date:** 1974
Main Character: white male
Other Topics: N/A
Overview: This real life account of Paul Jackimo shows the challenges he faces each day with his orthopedic handicap.

Harry and Willy and Carrothead

Author: Judith Caseley
Publisher: Greenwillow
Length: 24 **Age:** 4–8 **Date:** 1991
Main Character: white males
Other Topics: Teasing
Overview: Harry was born with no left hand. This real-life story depicts Harry as an athletic young boy.

Helping Hands: How Monkeys Assist People Who Are Disabled

Author: Suzanne Haldane
Publisher: Dutton
Length: 48 **Age:** 8–12 **Date:** 1991
Main Character: white male
Other Topics: N/A
Overview: Greg is a teenager with quadriplegia. His helper is a monkey named Willie.

It's Okay to Look at Jamie

Author: Patricia D. Frevert
Publisher: Creative Education, Inc.
Length: 48 **Age:** 6–10 **Date:** 1988
Main Character: white female
Other Topics: N/A

It's Okay to Look at Jamie (cont.)

Overview: Eleven-year-old Jamie was born with spina bifida and must wear leg braces.

Let the Balloon Go

Author: Ivan Southhall
Publisher: Bradbury
Length: 144 **Age:** 11–13 **Date:** 1968
Main Character: Australian male
Other Topics: N/A
Overview: John Sumner is an eleven-year-old boy attending regular school in Australia. He has occasional and unpredictable spasms and stuttering and longs for a friend. His mother is overprotective and John longs to be free.

My Brother, Matthew

Author: Mary Thompson
Publisher: Woodbine
Length: 29 **Age:** 4–8 **Date:** 1992
Main Character: white male
Other Topics: Sibling Rivalry
Overview: David understands his disabled brother better than his parents do. He does experience some frustration and resentment at times, however, as would any sibling.

On Our Own Terms: Children Living with Physical Disablities

Author: Thomas Bergman
Publisher: Gareth Stevens Children Books
Length: 48 **Age:** 8–10 **Date:** 1989
Main Character: white males and females
Other Topics: N/A
Overview: This photographic essay describes the activities at the Caroline Hospital in Stockholm, where children with physical disabilities are treated.

Physical Disabilities (cont.)

P. S. Write Soon

Author: Colby Rodowsky
Publisher: Sunburst
Length: 160 **Age:** 8–12 **Date:** 1987
Main Character: white female
Other Topics: Youngest Child, Smallest Child
Overview: Tanner is unhappy because she must wear a leg brace on her paralyzed leg and because she is the youngest child in her bright, accomplished family.

Someone Special, Just Like You

Author: Tricia Brown
Publisher: Holt
Length: 64 **Age:** 5–9 **Date:** 1984
Main Character: multicultural males and females
Other Topics: N/A
Overview: Young children with various handicaps are photographed, radiating a sense of self-worth.

The Acorn People

Author: Ron Jones
Publisher: Bantam Books
Length: 81 **Age:** 10–18 **Date:** 1976
Main Character: multicultural males and females
Other Topics: N/A
Overview: Camp Wiggin is a summer camp for special children. Multiple handicaps are described.

The Balancing Girl

Author: Bernice Rabe
Publisher: Dutton
Length: 29 **Age:** 7–9 **Date:** 1981

The Balancing Girl (cont.)

Main Character: white female
Other Topics: Wheelchair
Overview: A young girl who is physically disabled shows how capable she really is.

The Facts about the Physically Disabled

Author: Connie Baron
Publisher: Crestwood House
Length: 48 **Age:** 8–12 **Date:** 1988
Main Character: white males and females
Other Topics: N/A
Overview: This factual text uses photographs to discuss various diseases and conditions that can cause physical disabilities, including cerebral palsy, multiple sclerosis, arthritis, muscular dystrophy, and visual and hearing impairments. A glossary and index are also included.

The Flawed Glass

Author: Ian Strachan
Publisher: Little, Brown
Length: 204 **Age:** 10–12 **Date:** 1989
Main Character: white female
Other Topics: N/A
Overview: Shona's life on a remote Scottish island is made difficult because of a physical handicap. When an American businessman buys the island and Shona learns about computers, new possibilities open up for her.

Poverty

A Little Princess

Author: Frances Hodgson Burnett
Publisher: Lippincott

A Little Princess (cont.)

Length: 232 **Age:** 10–14 **Date:** 1963
Main Character: white female
Other Topics: Death of a Parent
Overview: Sara Crewe's father dies and leaves her penniless. She must leave her elite boarding school and becomes an abused working-class scullery maid.

A Migrant Family

Author: Larry Dane Brimner
Publisher: Lerner
Length: 40 **Age:** 9–12 **Date:** 1992
Main Character: Hispanic male
Other Topics: N/A
Overview: Twelve-year-old Juan and his family are migrant workers from Mexico who live in a camp near San Diego.

Afternoon of the Elves

Author: Janet Taylor Lisle
Publisher: Orchard
Length: 122 **Age:** 8–10 **Date:** 1989
Main Character: white female
Other Topics: Mental Illness, Friendship
Overview: Hillary, age nine, comes from a middle-class background, while Sara-Kate, age eleven, comes from a poor home, is poorly dressed, and malnourished. Their friendship deepens when Hillary discovers Sara-Kate is taking care of her mentally ill mother.

Blue Willow

Author: Doris Gates
Publisher: Viking
Length: 180 **Age:** 8–12 **Date:** 1940
Main Character: white female
Other Topics: Growing Up
Overview: Ten-year-old Janey dreams of stability for her migrant family.

Hey, Al

Author: Arthur Yorinks
Publisher: Farrar, Straus, and Giroux
Length: 27 **Age:** 6–10 **Date:** 1986
Main Character: white male
Other Topics: N/A
Overview: Al and his dog Eddie struggle in poverty and unhappiness until magic transports them to a luxurious paradise. When the two make their way back home, however, they find out home is the best place to be.

Judy's Journey

Author: Lois Lenski
Publisher: Lippincott
Length: 212 **Age:** 8–10 **Date:** 1947
Main Character: white female
Other Topics: N/A
Overview: Judy's family members are migrant workers, following the crops from California to Florida and New Jersey.

My Daddy Don't Go to Work

Author: Madeena Spray Nolan
Publisher: Carolrhoda Books
Length: 28 **Age:** 3–6 **Date:** 1978
Main Character: African American female
Other Topics: Anger, Separation Anxiety
Overview: A young girl is very sad when her father must leave their home in search of work.

Pax and the Mutt

Author: Beverly J. Letchworth
Publisher: Crestwood House
Length: 48 **Age:** 6–10 **Date:** 1981
Main Character: white male
Other Topics: N/A

Poverty (cont.)

Pax and the Mutt (cont.)

Overview: Eleven-year-old Jamie does not receive a birthday present because there is not enough money. He is consoled when he finds a little lost puppy. But there is not enough money to feed him. Pax lends a hand.

Roosevelt Grady

Author: Louisa Shotwell
Publisher: World
Length: 151 **Age:** 9–11 **Date:** 1963
Main Character: African American male
Other Topics: N/A
Overview: A migrant family wishes for stability and educational opportunities.

Stone Fox

Author: John Reynolds Gardiner
Publisher: Crowell
Length: 96 **Age:** 7–11 **Date:** 1980
Main Character: white male
Other Topics: N/A
Overview: A boy tries to save his family farm from foreclosure.

Strawberry Girl

Author: Lois Lenski
Publisher: Lippincott
Length: 194 **Age:** 9–12 **Date:** 1945
Main Character: white female
Other Topics: N/A
Overview: Birdie Boyer and her family move to Florida's backwoods to farm.

Striped Ice Cream

Author: Joan Lexau
Publisher: Lippincott

Striped Ice Cream (cont.)

Length: 95 **Age:** 7–9 **Date:** 1968
Main Character: African American female
Other Topics: Youngest Child
Overview: A young girl from a modest home tires of hand-me-down dresses from her sisters. For her birthday, she is thrilled to receive a new dress and striped ice cream.

The Bear's House

Author: Marilyn Sachs
Publisher: Doubleday
Length: 81 **Age:** 9–12 **Date:** 1971
Main Character: white female
Other Topics: N/A
Overview: Fletcher and Fran Ellen are faced with a broken home and a mother who won't face reality.

The Moffats

Author: Eleanor Estes
Publisher: Harcourt
Length: 290 **Age:** 8–10 **Date:** 1968
Main Character: white female
Other Topics: War
Overview: The Moffat family enjoy life in a small town in Connecticut during World War I—even though they are poor.

The Potato Kid

Author: Barbara Corcoran
Publisher: Atheneum
Length: 172 **Age:** 10–12 **Date:** 1989
Main Character: white female
Other Topics: N/A
Overview: A girl from a poor farming community gets to spend the summer with a rich family.

The Rag Coat

Author: Lauren Mills
Publisher: Little, Brown, and Co.
Length: 28 **Age:** 5–8 **Date:** 1991
Main Character: white female
Other Topics: N/A
Overview: Minna proudly wears her new coat of clothing scraps to school, where the other children laugh at her until she tells them the stories behind the scraps.

Tight Times

Author: Barbara Shook Hazen
Publisher: Viking Press
Length: 28 **Age:** 4–8 **Date:** 1979
Main Character: white male
Other Topics: N/A
Overview: Times are tight when a little boy's father loses his job.

Tough Tiffany

Author: Belinda Hurmence
Publisher: Doubleday
Length: 166 **Age:** 10–12 **Date:** 1980
Main Character: African American female
Other Topics: Intergenerational, Growing Up
Overview: Eleven-year-old Tiffany must cope with poverty, a grouchy grandmother, and a spendthrift mother.

When the Stars Begin to Fall

Author: James L. Collier
Publisher: Delacorte Press
Length: 160 **Age:** 10–14 **Date:** 1986
Main Character: white male
Other Topics: N/A
Overview: Fourteen-year-old Harry resents the fact that his family is considered to be poor trash. He sets out to prove that a factory is polluting their community.

Where the Lillies Bloom

Author: Vera and Bill Cleaver
Publisher: Lippincott
Length: 176 **Age:** 11–15 **Date:** 1969
Main Character: white female
Other Topics: Death of a Parent, Mentally Handicapped
Overview: When her father dies, a fourteen-year-old Appalachian girl struggles to keep her family together.

Racism, Prejudice

A Jar of Dreams

Author: Yoshiko Uchida
Publisher: Atheneum
Length: 131 **Age:** 8–10 **Date:** 1981
Main Character: Japanese American female
Other Topics: N/A
Overview: Rinko is embarrassed over her Japanese heritage in this Depression Era story. Her aunt changes her mind.

A Look at Prejudice and Understanding

Author: Rebecca Anders
Publisher: Lerner Publications
Length: 32 **Age:** 6–8 **Date:** 1976
Main Character: multicultural males and females
Other Topics: N/A
Overview: Text and photographs stress the importance of accepting one another.

A Wonderful, Terrible Time

Author: Mary Stolz
Publisher: Harper
Length: 182 **Age:** 9–11 **Date:** 1967

Racism, Prejudice (cont.)

A Wonderful, Terrible Time (cont.)

Main Character: African American females
Other Topics: N/A
Overview: Two African American girls attend an interracial summer camp. Sue Ellen is skeptical but Mandy is elated.

All It Takes Is Practice

Author: Betty Miles
Publisher: Alfred A. Knopf
Length: 101   **Age:**   8–12   **Date:**   1976
Main Character: white male
Other Topics: Diverse Families
Overview: Racial tensions surround Stuart's new relationship with Peter Baker, who comes from an interracial family.

Amazing Grace

Author: Mary Hoffman
Publisher: Dial
Length: 24   **Age:**   5–8   **Date:**   1991
Main Character: African American male
Other Topics: Sexism
Overview: Grace is a child who loves to listen to and act out stories. When her teacher announces that the class will be doing the play Peter Pan, Grace knows the part she wants. She is told by a classmate that she can't be Peter because she is a girl—and black. Her grandmother convinces her that she can be anything if she puts her mind to it.

Ann Aurelia and Dorothy

Author: Natalie Savage Carlson
Publisher: Harper
Length: 130   **Age:**   8–10   **Date:**   1968

Ann Aurelia and Dorothy (cont.)

Main Character: African American females and white females
Other Topics: Foster Home
Overview: Story of an interracial friendship.

Black, White, Just Right!

Author: Marguerite Davol
Publisher: Albert Whitman and Co.
Length: 32   **Age:**   6–8   **Date:**   1993
Main Character: mixed race female
Other Topics: N/A
Overview: A mixed-race child celebrates the rich inclusiveness of her life with her mother's chestnut brown skin and her father's white skin.

Bright April

Author: Marguerite de Angeli
Publisher: Doubleday
Length: 88   **Age:**   8–11   **Date:**   1946
Main Character: African American female
Other Topics: N/A
Overview: April finds a solution to her problems with prejudice in her Brownie troop.

Checking 'em Out and Sizing 'em Up

Author: Joy Wilt
Publisher: Weekly Reader Books
Length: 128   **Age:**   8–12   **Date:**   1980
Main Character: cartoon characters
Other Topics: N/A
Overview: This chapter book explains opinions and prejudices in a nonjudgmental way.

Circle of Fire

Author: William Hooks
Publisher: Macmillan Publishing Co.

Circle of Fire (cont.)

Length: 147 **Age:** 9–12 **Date:** 1982
Main Character: white male
Other Topics: N/A
Overview: In this story set in the tidewater of North Carolina in 1936, eleven-year-old Harrison overhears the planning of a KKK raid on Irish tinkers.

Every Kid's Guide to Overcoming Prejudice and Discrimination

Author: Joy Berry
Publisher: Children's Press
Length: 48 **Age:** 6–10 **Date:** 1987
Main Character: multicultural males and females
Other Topics: N/A
Overview: This discussion of prejudice and discrimination includes information about what opinions are, where opinions come from, and how to form opinions.

Harriet and the Runaway Book

Author: Johanna Johnston
Publisher: Harper
Length: 80 **Age:** 10–12 **Date:** 1977
Main Character: African American male
Other Topics: N/A
Overview: This is a lively account of the experiences of Harriet Beecher Stowe.

Iggie's House

Author: Judy Blume
Publisher: Dell Publishing
Length: 117 **Age:** 8–12 **Date:** 1970
Main Character: white female
Other Topics: N/A
Overview: When Iggie and her family moved to Tokyo, Winnie was without a friend until the Garber family moved in. The Garbers were African Americans, and Winnie learns that not everyone in the neighborhood welcomed them.

Life and Death of Martin Luther King, Jr.

Author: James Haskins
Publisher: Lothrop
Length: 160 **Age:** 11–14 **Date:** 1977
Main Character: African American male
Other Topics: N/A
Overview: This book examines the stories of both the civil rights leader, Martin Luther King, and his assassin.

Ludie's Song

Author: Dirlie Herlihy
Publisher: Penguin
Length: 212 **Age:** 10–18 **Date:** 1988
Main Character: white female, African American female
Other Topics: Friendship, Mute
Overview: Twelve-year-old Marty befriends Ludie, a young African American woman who cannot speak.

Malcolm X

Author: Arnold Adoff
Publisher: Harper Trophy
Length: 41 **Age:** 7–12 **Date:** 1988
Main Character: African American male
Other Topics: N/A
Overview: A biography of Malcolm X.

Marchers for the Dream

Author: Natalie Savage Carlson
Publisher: Harper and Row
Length: 130 **Age:** 9–11 **Date:** 1969
Main Character: African American female
Other Topics: N/A
Overview: An eleven-year-old girl goes with her grandmother to Washington to participate in the Poor People's March.

Racism, Prejudice (cont.)

Mississippi Bridge

Author: Mildred D. Taylor
Publisher: Penguin
Length: 64 **Age:** 7–11 **Date:** 1990
Main Character: African Americans
Other Topics: N/A
Overview: When a fully loaded bus is about to depart during a heavy rainstorm, the driver demands that the black passengers get out and walk. The bus plunges over a bridge into a river and these same black passengers offer help to the survivors.

Number the Stars

Author: Lois Lowry
Publisher: Houghton Mifflin
Length: 137 **Age:** 10–18 **Date:** 1989
Main Character: Jewish female
Other Topics: War
Overview: This is the story of Danish efforts to save Jewish citizens in World War II.

People

Author: Peter Spier
Publisher: Doubleday
Length: 48 **Age:** 6–9 **Date:** 1980
Main Character: multicultural males and females
Other Topics: N/A
Overview: The pictures and text of this picture book stress the universality of the human experience and make a strong statement about racial tolerance and international cooperation.

Peter and Veronica

Author: Marilyn Sachs
Publisher: Doubleday and Co., Inc.
Length: 174 **Age:** 8–12 **Date:** 1969
Main Character: white male and female
Other Topics: Friendship
Overview: Peter is Jewish and Veronica is not. Their parents are not pleased with their friendship.

Roll of Thunder, Hear My Cry

Author: Mildred Taylor
Publisher: Dial
Length: 276 **Age:** 10–13 **Date:** 1976
Main Character: African American family
Other Topics: Poverty
Overview: Story of a black family's struggle to maintain its dignity during the Depression.

Rosa Parks

Author: Eloise Greenfield
Publisher: Harper
Length: 32 **Age:** 7–9 **Date:** 1973
Main Character: African American male
Other Topics: N/A
Overview: This is the story of Rosa Parks, who refused to give up her seat on the bus, an act which sparked the Montgomery, Alabama, bus boycott.

Sounder

Author: William Armstrong
Publisher: Harper and Row
Length: 128 **Age:** 10–14 **Date:** 1969
Main Character: African American family
Other Topics: Poverty

Sounder (cont.)

Overview: This is a stark tale of an African American sharecropper and his family who face cruelty and injustice with courage and dignity.

Straight Talk about Prejudice

Author: Rachel Kranz
Publisher: Facts on File, Inc.
Length: 124   **Age:**   10–14   **Date:**   1992
Main Character: N/A
Other Topics: N/A
Overview: The causes and effects of prejudice and stereotyping are discussed.

The Eternal Spring of Mr. Ito

Author: Shelia Garrigue
Publisher: Bradbury
Length: 163   **Age:**   9–11   **Date:**   1985
Main Character: Japanese male
Other Topics: N/A
Overview: Sara stays in Canada during World War II and helps change her family's prejudice against their Japanese gardener.

The Journey

Author: Sheila Hamanaka
Publisher: Orchard Books
Length: 40   **Age:**   10–18   **Date:**   1990
Main Character: Japanese American male and female
Other Topics: Incarceration
Overview: The author relives the history of Japanese Americans and her own family, who were imprisoned in U.S. concentration camps.

The Road to Memphis

Author: Mildred D. Taylor
Publisher: Puffin
Length: 304   **Age:**   10–18   **Date:**   1992

The Road to Memphis (cont.)

Main Character: African American female
Other Topics: N/A
Overview: In this, the third book in the saga of the Logan family, Cassie Logan tells of the injustices in the 1940s.

The Star Fisher

Author: Laurence Yep
Publisher: Morrow
Length: 147   **Age:**   10–18   **Date:**   1991
Main Character: Chinese Americans
Other Topics: Moving
Overview: In 1927, the Lee family moves to West Virginia. Not all Clarksburg's residents welcome the Chinese American family.

The Tough Guy: Black in a White World

Author: Jane Clay Pool Miner
Publisher: Crestwood
Length: 64   **Age:**   10–12   **Date:**   1982
Main Character: African American male
Other Topics: Anger, Loneliness
Overview: At first, Larry is uncomfortable when he attends a new high school and discovers that he is only one of six African American students.

The Upstairs Room

Author: Johanna Reiss
Publisher: Crowell
Length: 196   **Age:**   10–13   **Date:**   1972
Main Character: Jewish females
Other Topics: N/A
Overview: Annie and her sister take refuge in an upstairs room of a Dutch farmhouse, hiding from the Nazis.

Racism, Prejudice (cont.)

Vatsana's Lucky New Year

Author: Sara Gogol
Publisher: Lerner
Length: 156 **Age:** 9–12 **Date:** 1992
Main Character: Asian American female
Other Topics: Bullies
Overview: Vatsana is a twelve-year-old Laotian American who is bullied by a racist classmate. Her pride helps her overcome prejudice.

Whose Town?

Author: Lorenz Graham
Publisher: Crowell
Length: 246 **Age:** 11–14 **Date:** 1969
Main Character: African American family
Other Topics: Moving
Overview: The Williams family tries to get away from discrimination by moving from the South to the North. They find prejudice there as well.

Words By Heart

Author: Ouida Sebestyen
Publisher: Little
Length: 162 **Age:** 11–13 **Date:** 1971
Main Character: African American male
Other Topics: N/A
Overview: Ben Sills is an African American who has moved his family to an all-white community in the West and hired on to work for rich Mrs. Chism. Ben must endure the hatred of her tenant farmer, Mr. Haney, and his son, Tater.

Retention in School

Erin McEwan, Your Days Are Numbered

Author: Alan Ritchie
Publisher: Alfred A. Knopf
Length: 188 **Age:** 8–12 **Date:** 1990
Main Character: white female
Other Topics: Math Anxiety
Overview: If Erin is not successful in her math class, she will be retained.

First Grade Can Wait

Author: Lorraine Asettine
Publisher: Albert Whitman
Length: 32 **Age:** 4–6 **Date:** 1988
Main Character: N/A
Other Topics: N/A
Overview: This supportive book discusses holding children back rather than starting them in school.

The Beast in Mrs. Rooney's Room

Author: Patricia Reilly Giff
Publisher: Dell
Length: 80 **Age:** 6–9 **Date:** 1985
Main Character: white male
Other Topics: N/A
Overview: It's difficult for Richard "Beast" Best to be the best at school. School and reading give him problems so he is "left back" in second grade. With the extra help from Mrs. Paris, the reading teacher, Beast starts to enjoy reading.

The Flunking of Joshua T. Bates

Author: Susan Shere
Publisher: Knopf
Length: 82 **Age:** 8–10 **Date:** 1984
Main Character: white male
Other Topics: N/A

The Flunking of Joshua T. Bates (cont.)

Overview: Joshua Bates is "held back" because he has not mastered reading. However, with the help of a kind tutor, he is able to rejoin his class by Thanksgiving.

Scoliosis

Even Pretty Girls Cry at Night

Author: Merril Joan Gerber
Publisher: Crosswinds
Length: 156 **Age:** 12–18 **Date:** 1988
Main Character: white female
Other Topics: Death of a Parent, War
Overview: Faye feels overwhelmed: a twisted back, her mother's death, a sad and distant father who relives the Vietnam War.

Self-Centered

Me First

Author: Helen Lester
Publisher: Houghton Mifflin
Length: 32 **Age:** 4–6 **Date:** 1992
Main Character: animal
Other Topics: N/A
Overview: Pushy Pinkerton is an overly aggressive pig. He learns that first is not always best on a day trip to the beach.

Rachel Parker, Kindergarten Show-Off

Author: Ann Martin
Publisher: Holiday House
Length: 32 **Age:** 4–6 **Date:** 1992
Main Character: white female
Other Topics: N/A

Rachel Parker, Kindergarten Show-Off (cont.)

Overview: Olivia has a new neighbor and classmate who is very competitive.

Rackety, That Very Special Rabbit

Author: Margaret Frishey
Publisher: Children's Press
Length: 29 **Age:** 4–6 **Date:** 1975
Main Character: animal
Other Topics: N/A
Overview: Rackety Rabbit thinks he is special until he realizes that every animal in the forest is special in his own way.

Separation Anxiety

Amifika

Author: Lucille Clifton
Publisher: Dutton
Length: 24 **Age:** 4–7 **Date:** 1977
Main Character: African American male
Other Topics: N/A
Overview: Little Amifika is afraid his father won't remember him after being away in the army.

Fletcher and the Great Big Dog

Author: Jane Kopper Hilleary
Publisher: Houghton Mifflin Co.
Length: 32 **Age:** 4–8 **Date:** 1988
Main Character: white male
Other Topics: N/A
Overview: When Fletcher tries to escape on his Big Wheel from a big dog, he gets lost.

Separation Anxiety (cont.)

Into the Great Forest: A Story for Children away from Parents for the First Time

Author: Irene Wineman Marcus and Paul Marcus
Publisher: Magination
Length: 32 **Age:** 4–8 **Date:** 1992
Main Character: white male
Other Topics: Going to School
Overview: A dream within a story helps a young boy overcome his fears about the first day of school.

Ira Sleeps Over

Author: Bernard Waber
Publisher: Houghton Mifflin
Length: 48 **Age:** 4–6 **Date:** 1972
Main Character: white male
Other Topics: Sibling Rivalry
Overview: Ira has a problem—he has never spent the night away from home or a night without his teddy bear.

Lost

Author: Sonia O. Lisker
Publisher: Harcourt Brace Jovanovich
Length: 43 **Age:** 4–7 **Date:** 1975
Main Character: white male
Other Topics: Fear
Overview: This wordless picture book shows how a little boy gets separated from his family at the zoo.

Princess Bee and the Royal Good-Night Story

Author: Sandy Asher
Publisher: Albert Whitman
Length: 32 **Age:** 4–6 **Date:** 1990
Main Character: white female

Princess Bee and the Royal Good-Night Story (cont.)

Other Topics: N/A
Overview: Even a princess in the Royal Palace likes her own mother to tell her a good-night story.

The Good-Bye Book

Author: Judith Viorst
Publisher: Atheneum
Length: 28 **Age:** 4–7 **Date:** 1988
Main Character: white male
Other Topics: N/A
Overview: A little boy fights to keep his parents from going out to dinner—until he meets his baby sitter.

Where's Our Mama?

Author: Diane Goode
Publisher: Dutton
Length: 32 **Age:** 3–7 **Date:** 1991
Main Character: white male and female
Other Topics: N/A
Overview: Two children become separated from their mother at the train station in Paris.

Sexism

A Girl from Yamhill: A Memoir

Author: Beverly Cleary
Publisher: Morrow
Length: 279 **Age:** 10–18 **Date:** 1989
Main Character: white female
Other Topics: N/A
Overview: This book is Beverly Cleary's memoir.

Girls are Equal Too: The Woman's Movement for Teenagers

Author: Dale B. Carlson
Publisher: Atheneum
Length: 146 **Age:** 10–18 **Date:** 1973
Main Character: females
Other Topics: N/A
Overview: A discussion of the causes of and solutions to sexism.

Hey, Didi Darling

Author: S. A. Kennedy
Publisher: Bantam Books
Length: 150 **Age:** 10–12 **Date:** 1983
Main Character: white female
Other Topics: N/A
Overview: Tammy and her friends decide that a girls' rock band could succeed just as well as a boys' band.

Justin and the Best Biscuits in the World

Author: Mildred Pitts Walter
Publisher: Lothrop
Length: 122 **Age:** 8–10 **Date:** 1986
Main Character: African American male
Other Topics: N/A
Overview: Justin, age ten, visits Grandpa's ranch and enjoys a break from his mother and two sisters. He learns that "women's work" isn't that bad if you know how to do it.

Like Jake and Me

Author: Mavis Jukes
Publisher: Knopf
Length: 32 **Age:** 7–8 **Date:** 1984
Main Character: white male
Other Topics: Intergenerational, Stepfamilies
Overview: Alan questions his decision to study ballet as he struggles to win the approval of his very macho stepfather.

Max

Author: Rachel Isadora
Publisher: Macmillan
Length: 26 **Age:** 6–8 **Date:** 1976
Main Character: white male
Other Topics: N/A
Overview: Max decides to join his sister's ballet class to warm up for baseball.

Rupert Piper and the Boy Who Could Knit

Author: Ethelyn M. Parkinson
Publisher: Abingdon
Length: 159 **Age:** 8–12 **Date:** 1979
Main Character: white male
Other Topics: Growing Up
Overview: Shirley Vincent is a boy who likes knitting, cooking, and girls and who keeps a diary.

The Berenstain Bears: No Girls Allowed

Author: Stan and Jan Berenstain
Publisher: Random House
Length: 29 **Age:** 4–8 **Date:** 1986
Main Character: animal
Other Topics: Sibling Rivalry
Overview: Brother Bear and his friends exclude Sister Bear from their club.

The Great Male Conspiracy

Author: Betty Bates
Publisher: Holiday House
Length: 176 **Age:** 9–12 **Date:** 1986
Main Character: white female
Other Topics: N/A
Overview: Maggie believes that there is a great male conspiracy against all girls.

The Real Me

Author: Betty Miles
Publisher: Knopf
Length: 122 **Age:** 9–11 **Date:** 1974
Main Character: white female

Sexism (cont.)

The Real Me (cont.)

Other Topics: N/A
Overview: Barbara takes over her brother's paper route, which is against company policy.

The Rooftop Mystery

Author: Joan Lexau
Publisher: Harper
Length: 64 **Age:** 4–7 **Date:** 1968
Main Character: African American male
Other Topics: Friendship
Overview: Two boys are embarrassed when they are caught carrying dolls on moving day.

Tough Eddie

Author: Elizabeth Winthrop
Publisher: Dutton
Length: 30 **Age:** 3–8 **Date:** 1985
Main Character: white male
Other Topics: Friendship
Overview: All Eddie's friends think he is tough. Then they discover his doll-house.

William's Doll

Author: Charlotte Zolotow
Publisher: Harper
Length: 32 **Age:** 5–8 **Date:** 1972
Main Character: white male
Other Topics: Intergenerational
Overview: Grandmother understands William's need for a doll when no one else seems to.

Sharing

A Chair for My Mother

Author: Vera B. Williams
Publisher: Morrow
Length: 32 **Age:** 5–7 **Date:** 1988
Main Character: Hispanic female
Other Topics: Intergenerational
Overview: A fire destroys everthing Rosa's family owns. Relatives and neighbors help Rosa, her mother, and grandmother start over. To buy an easy chair, they save coins in a glass jar.

Come a Tide

Author: George Ella Lyon
Publisher: Orchard
Length: 30 **Age:** 5–8 **Date:** 1990
Main Character: white female
Other Topics: N/A
Overview: A family and a community band together to help each other during a spring flood. The Rescue Wagon provides food.

It's Mine!

Author: Leo Lionni
Publisher: Alfred A. Knopf
Length: 28 **Age:** 5–7 **Date:** 1985
Main Character: animal
Other Topics: Selfishness
Overview: Three frogs are very selfish and argue over who owns the pond. A sudden storm teaches them the value of sharing.

It's Mine—A Greedy Book

Author: Crosby Bonsall
Publisher: Harper and Row
Length: 32 **Age:** 5–8 **Date:** 1964
Main Character: white male and female
Other Topics: Friendship

It's Mine—A Greedy Book (cont.)

Overview: Best friends quarrel over sharing toys.

Janet's Thingamajigs

Author: Beverly Cleary
Publisher: Morrow
Length: 30 **Age:** 4–8 **Date:** 1987
Main Character: white female
Other Topics: Twins, Growing Up
Overview: Jimmy is envious of his twin Janet's treasures, which she hides in her crib.

Let's Talk about Being Greedy

Author: Joy Berry
Publisher: Children's Press
Length: 32 **Age:** 4–6 **Date:** 1984
Main Character: white male and female
Other Topics: N/A
Overview: This cartoon-style picture book discusses being greedy and how important it is to share.

Mine, Yours, Ours

Author: Barton Albert
Publisher: Albert Whitman
Length: 32 **Age:** 4–6 **Date:** 1977
Main Character: multicultural males and females
Other Topics: N/A
Overview: This picture book teaches concepts of owning and sharing with pictures and three words: mine, yours, ours.

Ming Ling

Author: Stephen Cosgrove
Publisher: Price, Stern, Sloan
Length: 27 **Age:** 5–8 **Date:** 1983
Main Character: animal
Other Topics: Bad Day

Ming Ling (cont.)

Overview: Ming Ling must learn to share the forest.

Say Cheese

Author: Betty Bates
Publisher: Holiday House
Length: 100 **Age:** 9–12 **Date:** 1984
Main Character: white female
Other Topics: N/A
Overview: Christy wins $100 in a contest and must choose between buying Christmas presents for others or a dress for herself.

That's Mine

Author: Elizabeth Winthrop
Publisher: Holiday House
Length: 29 **Age:** 4–6 **Date:** 1977
Main Character: white male and female
Other Topics: Friendship
Overview: A young boy and girl fight over building blocks until they discover that sharing the blocks allows them to build a castle.

That's Mine, That's Yours

Author: Chris Sage
Publisher: Viking
Length: 32 **Age:** 2–6 **Date:** 1991
Main Character: white males and females
Other Topics: N/A
Overview: Siblings work at learning to share.

The Old Man and the Bear

Author: Janosch
Publisher: Bradbury Press
Length: 32 **Age:** 4–8 **Date:** 1987
Main Character: white male
Other Topics: N/A

Sharing (cont.)

The Old Man and the Bear (cont.)

Overview: Gregory buys caged birds, only to set them free. This fable teaches the importance of sharing.

We All Share

Author: Dorothy Corey
Publisher: Albert Whitman and Company
Length: 30 **Age:** 4–6 **Date:** 1980
Main Character: multicultural males and females
Other Topics: N/A
Overview: Very brief text and simple pictures describe situations in life in which sharing is necessary.

What Mary Jo Shared

Author: Janice May Udry
Publisher: Albert Whitman
Length: 40 **Age:** 5–8 **Date:** 1966
Main Character: African American female
Other Topics: Shyness
Overview: In this classic story about a black family, shy Mary Jo shares her father at Show and Tell.

Shyness

All I See

Author: Cynthia Rylant
Publisher: Orchard
Length: 28 **Age:** 6–8 **Date:** 1988
Main Character: white male
Other Topics: Friendship
Overview: Charlie is a shy and quiet boy who befriends an artist named Gregory.

Isabelle and the Library Cat

Author: Lillian Bason
Publisher: Lothrop, Lee and Shepard
Length: 21 **Age:** 4–6 **Date:** 1966
Main Character: white female
Other Topics: N/A
Overview: Isabelle was very shy. She befriends a cat she meets in the library and finds it necessary to overcome her shyness in order to rescue the cat.

Say Hello, Vanessa

Author: Marjorie W. Sharmat
Publisher: Holiday House
Length: 32 **Age:** 5–8 **Date:** 1979
Main Character: animal
Other Topics: N/A
Overview: Vanessa Mouse is very shy until she meets a friend.

Shy Charles

Author: Rosemary Wells
Publisher: Dial
Length: 32 **Age:** 5–8 **Date:** 1988
Main Character: animal
Other Topics: N/A
Overview: Charles is a shy mouse who doesn't want to take ballet lessons or play football. All he wants is to stay home and play by himself. In an emergency, however, he pulls through.

Shy Girl

Author: Miriam Gilbert
Publisher: Doubleday and Company
Length: 144 **Age:** 10–12 **Date:** 1965
Main Character: white female
Other Topics: N/A
Overview: This is the biography of Eleanor Roosevelt, an ugly duckling story of one of the world's most loved women.

Stop That Garbage Truck

Author: Linda Glaser
Publisher: Albert Whitman and Co.
Length: 32 **Age:** 3–7 **Date:** 1993
Main Character: African American males
Other Topics: N/A
Overview: When Daddy forgets to take the garbage cans to the curb on garbage collection day, can shy Henry save the day?

Superduper Teddy

Author: Johanna Hurwitz
Publisher: Puffin
Length: 80 **Age:** 7–10 **Date:** 1991
Main Character: white male
Other Topics: N/A
Overview: Teddy is not like his sister Nora. He is shy.

Tell Them My Name Is Amanda

Author: JoAnne Wold
Publisher: Albert Whitman and Co.
Length: 26 **Age:** 5–8 **Date:** 1977
Main Character: white female
Other Topics: N/A
Overview: Shy Amanda gets frustrated when everyone mispronounces her name.

The Bashful Bear

Author: Earle Goodenow
Publisher: Follett Pub. Co.
Length: 28 **Age:** 4–8 **Date:** 1963
Main Character: animal
Other Topics: Youngest Child, Smallest Child
Overview: This story tells of a bashful bear who is also the smallest bear in the valley. He discovers that sometimes being the smallest has its advantages.

Tommy the Timid Fool

Author: Esta de Fossard
Publisher: Gareth Stevens Publishing
Length: 32 **Age:** 4–6 **Date:** 1985
Main Character: animal
Other Topics: N/A
Overview: Tommy is so shy that he has a difficult time making friends.

Toto, the Timid Turtle

Author: Howard Goldsmith
Publisher: Human Sciences Press
Length: 27 **Age:** 4–8 **Date:** 1980
Main Character: animal
Other Topics: N/A
Overview: A timid turtle learns it is just as much fun outside of his shell as it is inside.

What to Say to Clara

Author: Barney Saltzberg
Publisher: Altheneum
Length: 28 **Age:** 4–7 **Date:** 1984
Main Character: white female
Other Topics: Friendship
Overview: Eric is too shy to speak to Clara, the new girl at school.

Willa and Old Miss Annie

Author: Berlie Doherty
Publisher: Candlewick Press
Length: 96 **Age:** 8–12 **Date:** 1994
Main Character: white female
Other Topics: Intergenerational, Moving
Overview: Willa is a shy little girl who has difficulty adjusting to her family's move until she befriends Old Miss Annie.

Sibling Rivalry

A Baby Sister for Frances

Author: Russell Hoban
Publisher: Harper
Length: 32 **Age:** 5–8 **Date:** 1964
Main Character: animal
Other Topics: N/A
Overview: Frances (a badger) decides that her baby sister, Gloria, is receiving too much attention, so she packs up her knapsack and runs away—under the dining room table.

Amy and Laura

Author: Marilyn Sachs
Publisher: Doubleday
Length: 176 **Age:** 8–12 **Date:** 1966
Main Character: white female
Other Topics: N/A
Overview: Amy and Laura are sisters who are close until, as hall monitor, Laura reports Amy for bad behavior.

Arthur's Baby

Author: Marc Brown
Publisher: Little, Brown
Length: 30 **Age:** 3–6 **Date:** 1987
Main Character: cartoon characters
Other Topics: N/A
Overview: Arthur must adjust to the new baby in the family.

Baby Brother Blues

Author: Maria Polushkin
Publisher: Bradbury Press
Length: 32 **Age:** 4–7 **Date:** 1987
Main Character: white male and female
Other Topics: N/A
Overview: Big sister feels like an outsider when baby brother arrives—until he needs her to hold him when he cries.

Billy and Belle

Author: Sarah Garland
Publisher: Viking
Length: 32 **Age:** 3–8 **Date:** 1992
Main Character: African American male and female
Other Topics: N/A
Overview: Billy and Belle anxiously await the arrival of their new baby.

Billy and Our New Baby

Author: Helene S. Arnstein
Publisher: Behavioral Publications
Length: 30 **Age:** 4–6 **Date:** 1973
Main Character: white male
Other Topics: Growing Up
Overview: Billy feels jealous of his new baby brother, so he begins to act like a baby too. He eventually discovers that it's more fun to be a big boy.

Dynamite Dinah

Author: Claudia Mills
Publisher: Macmillan
Length: 120 **Age:** 8–12 **Date:** 1990
Main Character: white female
Other Topics: Jealousy, Loneliness
Overview: Dinah is the performing artist of the fifth grade. She is upstaged by the arrival of her baby brother, however, and faces jealousy and loneliness.

Go and Hush the Baby

Author: Betsy Byars
Publisher: Viking Press
Length: 26 **Age:** 3–6 **Date:** 1971
Main Character: white male
Other Topics: N/A
Overview: Will tries to help his mother calm his baby brother.

I Hate My Brother Harry

Author: Crescent Dragon Wagon
Publisher: Harper and Row
Length: 32 **Age:** 5–8 **Date:** 1983
Main Character: white male and female
Other Topics: N/A
Overview: Nobody believes Harry's little sister hates him. Then mother explains that it's something brothers and sisters go through.

If It Weren't for Benjamin

Author: Barbara S. Hazen
Publisher: Human Sciences Press
Length: 28 **Age:** 4–8 **Date:** 1979
Main Character: white male
Other Topics: N/A
Overview: A young boy describes some of the frustrations and advantages of being a younger brother.

John Brown, Rose and the Midnight Cat

Author: Jenny Wagner
Publisher: Bradbury
Length: 33 **Age:** 4–8 **Date:** 1978
Main Character: white female
Other Topics: Jealousy
Overview: Rose lives alone with her sheepdog, John Brown. One night she discovers a cat in the garden. When she takes the cat in, John Brown is jealous.

Junie B. Jones and a Little Monkey Business

Author: Barbara Park
Publisher: Random House
Length: 68 **Age:** 6–9 **Date:** 1993
Main Character: white female
Other Topics: N/A
Overview: Junie B. believes her grandmother when she says the new baby is the "cutest little monkey" she ever saw. Maybe she can bring him to school on Pet Day.

Kiki's New Sister

Author: Jennifer Barrett
Publisher: Bantam
Length: 32 **Age:** 3–7 **Date:** 1992
Main Character: animal
Other Topics: N/A
Overview: Kiki's not sure her new baby sister is so great, until she is asked to take care of the baby.

Let Me Tell You about My Baby

Author: Roslyn Banish
Publisher: Harper and Row
Length: 61 **Age:** 4–8 **Date:** 1982
Main Character: white male
Other Topics: N/A
Overview: A young boy explains his mother's pregnancy, the birth and care of the baby, and his feelings about his new brother.

Little Sister for Sale

Author: Morse Hamilton
Publisher: Cobblehill
Length: 32 **Age:** 4–8 **Date:** 1992
Main Character: white females
Other Topics: N/A
Overview: Kate discovers that being a big sister isn't so bad after all.

My Name Is Emily

Author: Morse and Emily Hamilton
Publisher: Greenwillow Books
Length: 25 **Age:** 5–8 **Date:** 1979
Main Character: white female
Other Topics: Running Away
Overview: Emily runs away from home after a new baby arrives at her house. She and her father play a game to make things right again.

Sibling Rivalry (cont.)

New Baby

Author: Emily A. McCully
Publisher: Harper and Row
Length: 28 **Age:** 4–6 **Date:** 1988
Main Character: animal
Other Topics: N/A
Overview: This wordless picture book depicts the youngest mouse in a large family experiencing both frustration and excitement when a new baby arrives.

No More Cornflakes

Author: Polly Horvath
Publisher: Sunburst
Length: 144 **Age:** 8–12 **Date:** 1990
Main Character: white female
Other Topics: N/A
Overview: Ten-year-old Hortense Hemple is overwhelmed with the thought of a baby sibling. She also feels very left out.

Nobody Asked Me If I Wanted a Baby Sister

Author: Martha Alexander
Publisher: Dial
Length: 28 **Age:** 5–8 **Date:** 1971
Main Character: white male
Other Topics: N/A
Overview: In this sequel to *When the New Baby Comes, I'm Moving Out*, Oliver is angry about all the attention his new baby sister receives, so he puts her in his red wagon and tries to give her away.

On Mother's Lap

Author: Ann Herbert Scott
Publisher: McGraw-Hill
Length: 34 **Age:** 4–7 **Date:** 1972

On Mother's Lap (cont.)

Main Character: Eskimo male
Other Topics: Sharing
Overview: Michael is a small Eskimo boy who loves to sit on his mother's lap and rock. He is afraid there will not be enough room for him when his baby sister is born. They discover there is always room on Mother's lap.

Poor Carl

Author: Nancy Carlson
Publisher: Puffin
Length: 32 **Age:** 4–8 **Date:** 1991
Main Character: animal
Other Topics: Jealousy
Overview: Carl's older brother pities his little brother when he has to eat strained prunes instead of pancakes. But sometimes he wishes he were Carl.

Rachel and Obadiah

Author: Brinton Turkle
Publisher: E. P. Dutton
Length: 28 **Age:** 3–8 **Date:** 1978
Main Character: white male and female
Other Topics: N/A
Overview: Obadiah and his sister Rachel fight. They both want to earn money and compete.

Russell and Elisa

Author: Johanna Hurwitz
Publisher: Morrow
Length: 88 **Age:** 7–10 **Date:** 1989
Main Character: white male and female
Other Topics: N/A
Overview: Seven-year-old Russell and his three-year-old sister, Elisa, have adventures with friends and family in their apartment. Sometimes Elisa is a real embarrassment to Russell.

Silly Billy!

Author: Pat Hutchins
Publisher: Greenwillow
Length: 32 **Age:** 4–8 **Date:** 1992
Main Character: animal
Other Topics: N/A
Overview: When Hazel's parents and grandparents ask her to include her little brother Billy in her games, he ruins each one—until she teaches him a new game called "sleep-in-the-toy-box."

Superfudge

Author: Judy Blume
Publisher: Dutton
Length: 166 **Age:** 7–10 **Date:** 1980
Main Character: white male
Other Topics: Moving, Going to School
Overview: Peter has complications in his life—a new baby sister, a new school, and new friends—when his family moves to New Jersey. Also, his brother Fudge begins kindergarten.

Surviving Fights with Your Brothers and Sisters

Author: Joy Wilt
Publisher: Educational Products Division
Length: 128 **Age:** 6–9 **Date:** 1978
Main Character: white males and females
Other Topics: N/A
Overview: This book about sibling rivalry discusses all aspects of having a brother or sister.

Tales of a Fourth Grade Nothing

Author: Judy Blume
Publisher: Dutton
Length: 120 **Age:** 8–9 **Date:** 1972
Main Character: white male
Other Topics: N/A

Tales of a Fourth Grade Nothing (cont.)

Overview: Peter Hatcher faces many problems with his brother, Fudge, age two.

That New Baby

Author: Peggy Mann
Publisher: Coward-McCann
Length: 26 **Age:** 4–8 **Date:** 1967
Main Character: white female
Other Topics: N/A
Overview: Jenny learns to accept the arrival of a new baby in the family.

That New Baby

Author: Patricia Relf
Publisher: Golden Press
Length: 20 **Age:** 4–6 **Date:** 1980
Main Character: white female
Other Topics: Jealousy
Overview: When Elizabeth receives a new baby brother, she doesn't understand why there is such a big fuss.

The Baby

Author: John Burningham
Publisher: Thomas Y. Crowell
Length: 17 **Age:** 3–6 **Date:** 1974
Main Character: white male
Other Topics: N/A
Overview: A brother tells about his new baby.

The Berenstain Bears' New Baby

Author: Stan and Jan Berenstain
Publisher: Random House
Length: 29 **Age:** 4–8 **Date:** 1974
Main Character: animal
Other Topics: Growing Up
Overview: Small Bear must welcome a new baby in the family.

Sibling Rivalry (cont.)

The Day I Had to Play with My Sister

Author: Crosby Bonsall
Publisher: Harper and Row
Length: 32 **Age:** 4–7 **Date:** 1972
Main Character: white male
Other Topics: Sharing
Overview: In this easy-to-read book, a boy teaches his sister to play hide-and-seek.

The Knee-Baby

Author: Symeon Shimin
Publisher: Sunburst
Length: 32 **Age:** 5–8 **Date:** 1988
Main Character: white male
Other Topics: N/A
Overview: Three-year-old Alan has to be the "knee-baby" since his new baby sister is the "lap baby." He delights in possessing a skill that she does not have—he can talk!

The New Baby at Your House

Author: Joanne Cole
Publisher: William Morrow and Co., Inc.
Length: 48 **Age:** 3–6 **Date:** 1985
Main Character: multicultural males and females
Other Topics: Jealousy
Overview: Fifty photographs and easy text offer reassurance for siblings expecting a new baby.

The Pain and the Great One

Author: Judy Blume
Publisher: Dell
Length: 26 **Age:** 5–8 **Date:** 1974

The Pain and the Great One (cont.)

Main Character: white male and white female
Other Topics: N/A
Overview: A sister and her little brother express, in no uncertain terms, how they feel about each other.

The Very Worst Monster

Author: Pat Hutchins
Publisher: Greenwillow
Length: 27 **Age:** 4–7 **Date:** 1985
Main Character: animal
Other Topics: N/A
Overview: Hazel is jealous of her new "monster" brother, Billy.

Waiting for Baby

Author: Tom Birdseye
Publisher: Holiday House
Length: 32 **Age:** 3–8 **Date:** 1991
Main Character: white male
Other Topics: Relationships
Overview: A little boy imagines what it will be like when the new baby comes.

Western Wind

Author: Paula Fox
Publisher: Orchard Books
Length: 201 **Age:** 10–12 **Date:** 1993
Main Character: white female
Other Topics: Intergenerational, Jealousy
Overview: Twelve-year-old Elizabeth resents having to stay on a small Maine island with her grandmother when a new brother arrives. She soon sees things differently.

Stepfamilies

All about Families the Second Time Around

Author: Helen Coale Lewis
Publisher: Peachtree Publishers, Ltd.
Length: 125 **Age:** 8–12 **Date:** 1980
Main Character: multicultural males and females
Other Topics: N/A
Overview: This book is designed for boys and girls, their parents and stepparents. It is a guide for forming new relationships.

Daddy

Author: Jeannette Caines
Publisher: Harper
Length: 32 **Age:** 4–7 **Date:** 1977
Main Character: African American female
Other Topics: Fear
Overview: An African American girl visits her father and new stepmother, Paula. They enjoy coloring, reading, and playing dress-up. However, she worries until he comes for her again.

Everything You Need to Know about Stepfamilies

Author: Bruce Glassman
Publisher: Rosen Publishing Group
Length: 64 **Age:** 8–10 **Date:** 1988
Main Character: multicultural males and females
Other Topics: Death of a Parent, Divorce
Overview: Adjustments must be made when a parent remarries and a new stepfamily is formed.

I and Sproggy

Author: Constance Greene
Publisher: Dell

I and Sproggy (cont.)

Length: 155 **Age:** 7–12 **Date:** 1978
Main Character: white male and female
Other Topics: N/A
Overview: A ten-year-old boy must accept his new English stepsister.

My Mother Got Married (and Other Disasters)

Author: Barbara Park
Publisher: Knopf
Length: 138 **Age:** 8–12 **Date:** 1989
Main Character: white male
Other Topics: Sharing
Overview: Eleven-year-old Charlie Hickle is just beginning to adjust to his parents' divorce when disaster strikes again. His mother remarries and his new stepfather moves in with his two children.

My Other-Mother, My Other-Father

Author: Harriet Langsam Sobol
Publisher: Macmillan
Length: 48 **Age:** 8–12 **Date:** 1979
Main Character: white female
Other Topics: Divorce
Overview: Twelve-year-old Andrea discusses her life when her parents remarry.

No Scarlet Ribbons

Author: Susan Terris
Publisher: Farrar-Straus-Giroux
Length: 154 **Age:** 10–12 **Date:** 1981
Main Character: white female
Other Topics: Death of a Parent
Overview: Rachel soon realizes that her mother's new marriage and her new stepfamily may not be all she had hoped for.

Stepfamilies (cont.)

Sam Is My Half Brother

Author: Lizzi Boyd
Publisher: Puffin
Length: 32 **Age:** 3–8 **Date:** 1992
Main Character: white male and female
Other Topics: N/A
Overview: An older sibling has a new half-sibling.

Sarah, Plain and Tall

Author: Patricia MacLachlan
Publisher: Harper
Length: 58 **Age:** 8–12 **Date:** 1985
Main Character: white male and female
Other Topics: N/A
Overview: Set during pioneer times, this is the story of Sarah, a mail-order bride whose two stepchildren love her instantly.

She's Not My Real Mother

Author: Judith Vigna
Publisher: Albert Whitman
Length: 32 **Age:** 6–10 **Date:** 1980
Main Character: white male
Other Topics: N/A
Overview: A small child realizes that a stepmother can be a caregiver too.

Stepfamilies: New Patterns of Harmony

Author: Linda Craven
Publisher: Simon and Schuster, Inc.
Length: 186 **Age:** 10–14 **Date:** 1982
Main Character: N/A
Other Topics: N/A
Overview: A very positive approach to conflicts that arise when families merge.

Talking About Stepfamilies

Author: Maxine Rosenberg
Publisher: Bradbury
Length: 145 **Age:** 10–14 **Date:** 1990
Main Character: white male and females
Other Topics: N/A
Overview: Children and adults who are part of stepfamilies describe their experiences in coping with stepfamilies.

The Original Freddie Ackerman

Author: Hadley Irwin
Publisher: McElderry
Length: 183 **Age:** 9–12 **Date:** 1992
Main Character: white male
Other Topics: Intergenerational
Overview: Twelve-year-old Trevor Ackerman spends the summer with two great aunts, a nice alternative from being with his parents, stepparents, stepsisters, and stepbrothers.

When Christmas Comes

Author: Elizabeth Starr Hill
Publisher: Puffin
Length: 208 **Age:** 8–12 **Date:** 1991
Main Character: white female
Other Topics: N/A
Overview: Callie's father remarries and moves her to a trailer park. Callie must adjust to the divorce, the move, and her new stepmother.

Stuttering

The Shiniest Rock of All

Author: Nancy Ruth Patterson
Publisher: Farrar, Straus, and Giroux
Length: 80 **Age:** 8–12 **Date:** 1991
Main Character: white male

The Shiniest Rock of All (cont.)

Other Topics: N/A
Overview: Robert Reynolds is a fourth grader who learns that nobody is perfect as he tries to overcome his speech impediment.

Success, Failure

Heather Hits Her First Home Run

Author: Ted Plantos
Publisher: Black Moss Press
Length: 32 **Age:** 5–8 **Date:** 1989
Main Character: white female
Other Topics: Perseverance, Cooperation
Overview: Although Heather doesn't actually hit a home run, she does win the game for her team with a hit that sends in three runs.

I Never Win!

Author: Judy Delton
Publisher: Dell
Length: 32 **Age:** 5–8 **Date:** 1981
Main Character: white male
Other Topics: N/A
Overview: Charlie is frustrated because he cannot win at anything.

Never Fear, the Dip Is Here

Author: Philip Hanft
Publisher: Dial
Length: 32 **Age:** 4–8 **Date:** 1991
Main Character: white male and African American male
Other Topics: N/A
Overview: Flip wants to play baseball more than anything, but he is just not good at it. Buster, a sculptor and painter who once played minor-league ball, offers to coach Flip.

Perfect or Not, Here I Come

Author: Kristi D. Holl
Publisher: Troll Associates
Length: 146 **Age:** 9–12 **Date:** 1986
Main Character: white female
Other Topics: Racism, Prejudice
Overview: Sixth-grader Tara's play is chosen for drama night and she is proud of her success. But when budget cuts mean that her teacher is to be fired, the play doesn't seem as important as saving Miss Dalton's job.

Queenie Peavy

Author: Robert Burch
Publisher: Penguin
Length: 160 **Age:** 9–12 **Date:** 1966
Main Character: white female
Other Topics: Incarceration
Overview: Thirteen-year-old Queenie Peavy accepts her father's undependability and allows herself to be successful.

S.O.R. Losers

Author: Avi
Publisher: Bradbury
Length: 112 **Age:** 10–18 **Date:** 1984
Main Character: white male
Other Topics: N/A
Overview: A boys' soccer team seems to be the worst team in history.

The Glory Girl

Author: Betsy Byars
Publisher: Viking Press
Length: 122 **Age:** 10–14 **Date:** 1983
Main Character: white female
Other Topics: Growing Up
Overview: A young girl grows up amid the struggles of a performing family. As the only nonsinging member of this gospel-singing family, she feels left out until the family bus is involved in an accident.

Success, Failure (cont.)

The Little Gymnast

Author: Sheila Haigh
Publisher: Scholastic
Length: 134 **Age:** 9–12 **Date:** 1982
Main Character: white female
Other Topics: Poverty
Overview: Anda works hard to become the best gymnast in her class. Money is not plentiful in her family, however, so she must win a scholarship to continue her work.

The One in the Middle Is the Green Kangaroo

Author: Judy Blume
Publisher: Bradbury
Length: 39 **Age:** 6–9 **Date:** 1981
Main Character: white male
Other Topics: Self-Esteem
Overview: A middle child feels better about himself when he gets a part in the school play.

Thomas Tuttle, Just in Time

Author: Becky T. Lindberg
Publisher: Albert Whitman and Co.
Length: 144 **Age:** 7–9 **Date:** 1994
Main Character: white male
Other Topics: N/A
Overview: Thomas Tuttle wants success to come easily but soon learns that is not possible.

Winning and Losing

Author: Lowell Dickmeyer and Martha Humphreys
Publisher: Franklin Watts
Length: 47 **Age:** 8–10 **Date:** 1984

Winning and Losing (cont.)

Main Character: N/A
Other Topics: N/A
Overview: This easy-to-read sports book examines the concepts of winning and losing. It also discusses what it means to be a team member and how to cope with losing.

Talkative

Boris the Boring Bear

Author: Ellen Jackson
Publisher: Macmillan
Length: 32 **Age:** 4–8 **Date:** 1992
Main Character: animal
Other Topics: N/A
Overview: Boris talks too much, but this comes in handy when a wolf captures him for dinner. Boris initiates a conversation that draws on the wolf's interests and learns a lesson about talking.

Gabby

Author: Stephen Cosgrove
Publisher: Price, Stern, Sloan
Length: 27 **Age:** 5–8 **Date:** 1983
Main Character: animal
Other Topics: N/A
Overview: Gabby is a brown-eyed Furry who has a tendency to talk too much. She must learn that there is a time for talk and a time for silence.

Tardiness

Hurry Up, Franklin

Author: Paulette Bourgeois
Publisher: Scholastic

Hurry Up, Franklin (cont.)

Length: 29 **Age:** 4–8 **Date:** 1989
Main Character: animal
Other Topics: N/A
Overview: Franklin is very slow, even for a turtle.

The Easter Bunny That Overslept

Author: Priscilla Friedrick
Publisher: Lothrop, Lee, Shepard Co., Inc.
Length: 32 **Age:** 5–7 **Date:** 1957
Main Character: animal
Other Topics: N/A
Overview: A funny story about how the Easter Bunny slept through Easter.

Toilet Training

Dry Days, Wet Nights

Author: Maribeth Boelts
Publisher: Albert Whitman and Co.
Length: 32 **Age:** 4–6 **Date:** 1994
Main Character: animal
Other Topics: N/A
Overview: Little Bunny stays dry all day so he doesn't want to wear a diaper at night. This story is appropriate for potty-trained children who still have nighttime accidents.

Twins, Triplets

How Do I Feel?

Author: Norma Simon
Publisher: Whitman
Length: 34 **Age:** 5–8 **Date:** 1970
Main Character: white males

How Do I Feel? (cont.)

Other Topics: Sibling Rivalry
Overview: A boy has a difficult time dealing with both a twin and an older brother.

Jacob Have I Loved

Author: Katherine Paterson
Publisher: Thomas Y. Crowell
Length: 175 **Age:** 11–14 **Date:** 1980
Main Character: white female
Other Topics: Sibling Rivalry
Overview: A girl who grows up in the shadow of her twin sister discovers that what she had become was beyond her sister's reach.

Me and the Terrible Two

Author: Ellen Conford
Publisher: Little
Length: 128 **Age:** 9–11 **Date:** 1974
Main Character: white male and female
Other Topics: Friendship
Overview: Dorrie is upset when Marlene moves away, but she is even more exasperated when identical twin boys move in, full of tricks and pranks.

Mysterious Doubles: The Story of Twins

Author: Liz Bowden
Publisher: Contemporary Perspectives, Inc.
Length: 48 **Age:** 8–12 **Date:** 1979
Main Character: white males and females
Other Topics: N/A
Overview: This chapter book focuses on the different types of twins: identical, fraternal, mirror-image, and conjoined twins.

Twins, Triplets (cont.)

The Twins, Two by Two

Author: Catherine and Laurence Anholt
Publisher: Candlewick Press
Length: 32 **Age:** 3–6 **Date:** 1992
Main Character: white male and female
Other Topics: N/A
Overview: Minnie and Max are twins with vivid imaginations.

Triplets

Author: Felix Pirani
Publisher: Viking
Length: 32 **Age:** 3–8 **Date:** 1991
Main Character: white females
Other Topics: N/A
Overview: Rosie, Susie, and Tracy are triplets. Since they are identical, people mix them up.

Twin and Super-Twin

Author: Gillian Cross
Publisher: Holiday House
Length: 169 **Age:** 8–10 **Date:** 1990
Main Character: white males
Other Topics: N/A
Overview: A fantasy story of the interaction between two gangs when David, one of a set of twins, finds his arm transforming into a snake, sausages, and other bizarre objects.

Two Dog Biscuits

Author: Beverly Cleary
Publisher: William Morrow and Co.
Length: 30 **Age:** 4–7 **Date:** 1961
Main Character: white male and female
Other Topics: N/A

Two Dog Biscuits (cont.)

Overview: Jimmy and Janet are four-year-old twins in search of a dog to eat their two dog biscuits.

Value of Work

Impossible, Possum

Author: Ellen Conford
Publisher: Little, Brown and Co.
Length: 32 **Age:** 5–8 **Date:** 1971
Main Character: animal
Other Topics: N/A
Overview: Randolph is a young possum who cannot hang by his tail. He finally convinces himself that he can, with a little help from his sister.

Mike Mulligan and His Steam Shovel

Author: Virginia Lee Burton
Publisher: Houghton Mifflin
Length: 42 **Age:** 4–8 **Date:** 1939
Main Character: white male
Other Topics: Friendship
Overview: Mike Mulligan and his steam shovel, Mary Ann, prove that she can dig more in one day than 100 men can dig in a week.

The Little Engine That Could

Author: Watty Piper
Publisher: Putnam
Length: 40 **Age:** 4–8 **Date:** 1929
Main Character: object
Other Topics: N/A
Overview: The little engine must get the toys over the mountain to the children.

The Very Busy Spider

Author: Eric Carle
Publisher: Philomel

The Very Busy Spider (cont.)

Length: 22 **Age:** 2–6 **Date:** 1984
Main Character: animal
Other Topics: N/A
Overview: A spider busily spins a web and ignores the invitations of various farm animals.

Working Kids on Working

Author: Sheila Cole
Publisher: Lothrop, Lee and Shepard
Length: 219 **Age:** 10–14 **Date:** 1980
Main Character: multicultural males and females
Other Topics: N/A
Overview: Children who work are interviewed, some as young as nine.

War

A Wall of Names: The Story of the Vietnam Veterans Memorial

Author: Judy Donnelly
Publisher: Random House
Length: 48 **Age:** 5–8 **Date:** 1991
Main Character: multicultural males
Other Topics: N/A
Overview: This easy-to-read book tells the story of the Vietnam Veterans Memorial.

Journey Home

Author: Yoshiko Uchida
Publisher: Atheneum
Length: 131 **Age:** 10–12 **Date:** 1978
Main Character: Japanese American female
Other Topics: Moving, Incarceration
Overview: This sequel to *Journey to Topaz: A Story of the Japanese-American*

Journey Home (cont.)

Evacuation continues the story of Yuki and her family after their release from Topaz, an internment camp.

Journey to Topaz: A Story of the Japanese American Evacuation

Author: Yoshiko Uchida
Publisher: Creative Arts
Length: 149 **Age:** 10–15 **Date:** 1985
Main Character: Japanese American female
Other Topics: Moving
Overview: After the Japanese bombing of Pearl Harbor, eleven-year-old Yuki and her family are among 110,000 Japanese Americans evacuated from the West Coast.

Kiss the Dust

Author: Elizabeth Laird
Publisher: Dutton
Length: 279 **Age:** 11–14 **Date:** 1991
Main Character: female Kurd
Other Topics: N/A
Overview: Tara is a thirteen-year-old Kurd living with her wealthy family in Iraq. Her life changes when the Iraqi police arrest her father. The family flees first to the mountains of Kurdistan, then to Iran. The family finally finds refuge in London.

My Daddy Was a Soldier: A World War II Story

Author: Deborah K. Ray
Publisher: Holiday House
Length: 37 **Age:** 6–9 **Date:** 1990
Main Character: white female
Other Topics: Loneliness
Overview: While Jeannie waits for her father to return home from the war, she plants a garden, collects scraps, and sends letters to her father.

War (cont.)

My Hiroshima

Author: Junko Morimoto
Publisher: Viking
Length: 30 **Age:** 6–8 **Date:** 1987
Main Character: Japanese female
Other Topics: N/A
Overview: Junko is the youngest in a family of four children. This story depicts her life before the war and immediately after the atomic bomb fell.

Nobody Wants a Nuclear War

Author: Judith Vigna
Publisher: Albert Whitman
Length: 40 **Age:** 4–8 **Date:** 1986
Main Character: white male and female
Other Topics: N/A
Overview: This book is designed for young children and addresses the issue of nuclear war.

Stepping on the Cracks

Author: Mary Downing Hahn
Publisher: Avon Camelot
Length: 216 **Age:** 9–12 **Date:** 1991
Main Character: white female
Other Topics: Alcoholism, Child Abuse, Bullies
Overview: Margaret and Elizabeth are best friends during World War II. They are involved in growing up with the shadow of Hitler clouding their lives and those of their families. They are also tormented by the sixth-grade bully and his friends.

The Sky Is Falling

Author: Kit Pearson
Publisher: Viking Kestrel
Length: 248 **Age:** 8–12 **Date:** 1989

The Sky Is Falling (cont.)

Main Character: white female
Other Topics: Homesickness
Overview: During the summer of 1940, Noah and her brother are sent to Canada to escape the conflicts of war.

The Wall

Author: Eve Bunting
Publisher: Clarion
Length: 28 **Age:** 6–8 **Date:** 1990
Main Character: white male
Other Topics: N/A
Overview: A little boy and his father visit the Vietnam Memorial in Washington, D.C., and find the name of his grandfather on the wall.

Year of the Impossible Goodbyes

Author: Sook Nyul Choi
Publisher: Houghton Mifflin
Length: 169 **Age:** 10–18 **Date:** 1991
Main Character: Korean female
Other Topics: N/A
Overview: Sookan and her brothers are taken to Japanese labor camps during World War II. Since her father is hiding in Manchuria, her family is forced to work for the war effort. They dream of freedom and peace.

Weight Problems

Blubber

Author: Judy Blume
Publisher: Bradbury
Length: 153 **Age:** 9–11 **Date:** 1974
Main Character: white female
Other Topics: N/A
Overview: An overweight girl becomes the victim in peer conflicts.

Eating Disorders: A Question and Answer Book about Anorexia Nervosa and Bulimia Nervosa

Author: Ellen Erlanger
Publisher: Lerner Publications
Length: 60 **Age:** 10–18 **Date:** 1988
Main Character: N/A
Other Topics: N/A
Overview: Advice is given to young people in the form of questions and answers.

Eating Habits and Disorders

Author: Rachel Epstein
Publisher: Chelsea House Publishers
Length: 109 **Age:** 12–14 **Date:** 1990
Main Character: N/A
Other Topics: N/A
Overview: This nonfiction book describes the various types of eating disorders and describes their possible causes, effects, and treatments.

Fattypuffs and Thinifers

Author: Andre Maurois
Publisher: Alfred A. Knopf
Length: 88 **Age:** 8–12 **Date:** 1989
Main Character: cartoon characters
Other Topics: N/A
Overview: This comic fantasy pits Fattypuffs against Thinifers.

Last Was Lloyd

Author: Doris B. Smith
Publisher: Viking
Length: 124 **Age:** 7–12 **Date:** 1981
Main Character: white male
Other Topics: Single Parent
Overview: Lloyd is overweight and clumsy. He doesn't like school because his classmates ridicule him.

Nothing's Fair in Fifth Grade

Author: Berthe DeClements
Publisher: Viking
Length: 140 **Age:** 9–11 **Date:** 1981
Main Character: white female
Other Topics: Friendship
Overview: Elsie is fat but she has special abilities in math. When she offers to tutor Jenny, a friendship evolves.

100 Hamburgers, The Getting Thin Book

Author: Mary Lynn Solot
Publisher: Lothrop, Lee and Shepard
Length: 28 **Age:** 6–8 **Date:** 1972
Main Character: white male
Other Topics: N/A
Overview: A young boy begins to diet so that he won't be so fat. Excellent suggestions are offered by his doctor.

Skinnybones

Author: Barbara Park
Publisher: Alfred A. Knopf
Length: 112 **Age:** 8–12 **Date:** 1982
Main Character: white male
Other Topics: Smallest Child
Overview: Alex's sense of humor helps him survive the school show-off, being the smallest kid on the team, and his lack of athletic skill.

The Cat Ate My Gymsuit

Author: Paula Danziger
Publisher: Delacorte
Length: 128 **Age:** 11–13 **Date:** 1974
Main Character: white female
Other Topics: Self-Concept
Overview: An exceptional teacher means a great deal to self-hating Marcy. When the teacher is fired, Marcy and her friends protest.

Weight Problems (cont.)

The Facts about Anorexia and Bulimia

Author: Dayna Wolhart
Publisher: Crestwood House
Length: 48 **Age:** 8–12 **Date:** 1988
Main Character: white female
Other Topics: N/A
Overview: This book defines anorexia and bulimia and explains the causes, side effects, and treatment of these eating disorders.

The Fat Girl

Author: Marilyn Sachs
Publisher: Dutton
Length: 168 **Age:** 12–14 **Date:** 1983
Main Character: white male and white female
Other Topics: Friendship
Overview: Jeff tries to "make over" fat Ellen in this Pygmalion story.

Too Fat? Too Thin? Do You Have a Choice?

Author: Caroline Arnold
Publisher: William Morrow and Co.
Length: 100 **Age:** 12–14 **Date:** 1984
Main Character: N/A
Other Topics: N/A
Overview: Studies and theories on weight control are discussed. Also included is a chart listing daily nutritional needs.

Wheelchair

A School for Tommy

Author: Elizabeth Pieper
Publisher: Children's Press

A School for Tommy (cont.)

Length: 32 **Age:** 6–8 **Date:** 1979
Main Character: white male
Other Topics: N/A
Overview: Tommy goes in his wheelchair to public school.

Arnie and the New Kid

Author: Nancy Carlson
Publisher: Viking
Length: 32 **Age:** 4–8 **Date:** 1990
Main Character: animal
Other Topics: Teasing
Overview: The new kid gets about in a wheelchair. Arnie teases him until he has an accident, breaks his leg, and ends up in a wheelchair himself.

Colt

Author: Nancy Springer
Publisher: Dial
Length: 128 **Age:** 10–18 **Date:** 1991
Main Character: white male
Other Topics: N/A
Overview: Colt Vittorio hates being confined to a wheelchair. When his therapist introduces him to horses he is hesitant. Eventually, he learns to ride and loves it.

Janet at School

Author: Paul White
Publisher: Crowell
Length: 23 **Age:** 6–9 **Date:** 1978
Main Character: white female
Other Topics: N/A
Overview: Five-year-old Janet has spina bifida and must use a wheelchair. She and her family learn to cope with her physical disability.

Mama Zooms

Author: Jane Cowen-Fletcher
Publisher: Scholastic
Length: 32 **Age:** 3–7 **Date:** 1993
Main Character: white female
Other Topics: N/A
Overview: A little boy likes to "zoom" with his mother in her wheelchair.

Margaret's Moves

Author: Berniece Robe
Publisher: Dutton
Length: 112 **Age:** 8–12 **Date:** 1986
Main Character: white female
Other Topics: N/A
Overview: Margaret has always been in a wheelchair. She decides she needs the new sports model wheelchair.

Move Over, Wheelchairs Coming Through

Author: Ron Roy
Publisher: Clarion
Length: 83 **Age:** 8–13 **Date:** 1985
Main Character: white males and females
Other Topics: N/A
Overview: Photographs illustrate seven children coping with severe handicaps. They all love sports, friends, television, and movies.

Nick Joins In

Author: Joe Lasker
Publisher: Albert Whitman
Length: 29 **Age:** 7–8 **Date:** 1980
Main Character: white male
Other Topics: Going to School
Overview: Nick is afraid to go to school because he is in a wheelchair.

Our Teacher's in a Wheelchair

Author: Mary Ellen Powers
Publisher: Whitman

Our Teacher's in a Wheelchair (cont.)

Length: 32 **Age:** 5–8 **Date:** 1986
Main Character: white male
Other Topics: N/A
Overview: The message in this story is that disability does not mean inability. Text and photographs illustrate the activities of Brian Hanson, a nursery school teacher.

Princess Pooh

Author: Kathleen M. Muldoon
Publisher: Albert Whitman
Length: 32 **Age:** 7–10 **Date:** 1989
Main Character: white female
Other Topics: Sibling Rivalry
Overview: Patty Jean nicknames her sister Princess Pooh because she sits on her "throne on wheels" and orders everyone.

Working Mothers

Ask Me What My Mother Does

Author: Katherine Leiner
Publisher: Franklin Watts
Length: 47 **Age:** 6–10 **Date:** 1978
Main Character: multicultural females
Other Topics: Deafness
Overview: Seventeen working mothers are introduced in photographs.

Both My Parents Work

Author: Katherine Leiner
Publisher: Franklin Watts
Length: 48 **Age:** 5–8 **Date:** 1986
Main Character: multicultural males and females
Other Topics: N/A

Working Mothers (cont.)

Both My Parents Work (cont.)

Overview: Ten children whose parents work describe the complex routines involved in running the family.

Butcher, Baker, Cabinetmaker: Photographs of Women at Work

Author: Wendy Saul
Publisher: Thomas Y. Crowell
Length: 44 **Age:** 6–10 **Date:** 1978
Main Character: African American females and white females
Other Topics: N/A
Overview: Women employed in jobs typically reserved for men are introduced in photographs.

Daddy and Ben Together

Author: Miriam Stecher and Alice Kandell
Publisher: Lothrop, Lee and Shepard
Length: 23 **Age:** 3–6 **Date:** 1981
Main Character: white male
Other Topics: Separation Anxiety
Overview: When Mommy has to go on a business trip, Ben and Daddy are on their own.

Mommies at Work

Author: Eve Merriam
Publisher: Knopf
Length: 32 **Age:** 4–7 **Date:** 1961
Main Character: white female
Other Topics: N/A
Overview: This revision of a 1955 book presents mothers in their various jobs.

My Mom Travels a Lot

Author: Caroline Feller Bauer
Publisher: Frederick Warne
Length: 32 **Age:** 4–8 **Date:** 1981
Main Character: white female
Other Topics: N/A
Overview: There are good and bad things about a working mother who must travel on business.

The Terrible Thing That Happened at Our House

Author: Marge Blaine
Publisher: Scholastic
Length: 32 **Age:** 6–9 **Date:** 1975
Main Character: white female
Other Topics: N/A
Overview: A young girl must adjust to her mother's going back to work.

Where are the Mothers?

Author: Dorothy Marino
Publisher: Lippincott
Length: 30 **Age:** 4–6 **Date:** 1959
Main Character: white female
Other Topics: N/A
Overview: Mothers are described at their various work sites.

Youngest Child, Smallest Child

Dance, Tanya

Author: Patricia L. Gauch
Publisher: Scholastic
Length: 25 **Age:** 4–6 **Date:** 1989
Main Character: white female
Other Topics: N/A
Overview: Tanya longs to equal her older sister Elise at ballet.

Dinnie Abbie Sister-r-r!

Author: Riki Levinson
Publisher: Bradbury Press
Length: 90 **Age:** 6–8 **Date:** 1987
Main Character: white female
Other Topics: Illness
Overview: Five-year-old Jennie feels "left behind" her older brothers.

Fidelia

Author: Ruth Adams
Publisher: Lothrop, Lee, and Shepard
Length: 29 **Age:** 8–10 **Date:** 1970
Main Character: white female
Other Topics: N/A
Overview: Fidelia wanted to learn to play the violin but everyone in her musical family said she was too young.

Friska, The Sheep That Was Too Small

Author: Rob Lewis
Publisher: Starburst
Length: 32 **Age:** 5–8 **Date:** 1989
Main Character: animal
Other Topics: Smallest Child
Overview: Friska is a very small sheep who doesn't grow. When the wolf attacks, however, her size works to her advantage.

Henry's Wild Morning

Author: Margaret Greaves
Publisher: Dial
Length: 40 **Age:** 4–8 **Date:** 1991
Main Character: animal
Other Topics: N/A
Overview: Henry is not only the smallest kitten in the litter but also the only one with stripes.

I Need a Lunch Box

Author: Jeanette Caines
Publisher: Harper and Row

I Need a Lunch Box (cont.)

Length: 30 **Age:** 4–6 **Date:** 1988
Main Character: African American male
Other Topics: Sibling Rivalry
Overview: A little boy wants a lunch box like his big sister's, even though he doesn't go to school yet.

Joel Is the Youngest

Author: Judith Ish-Kishor
Publisher: Washington Square Press
Length: 196 **Age:** 8–12 **Date:** 1967
Main Character: Jewish male
Other Topics: Growing Up
Overview: Joel is eight, the youngest in a Jewish family, where his siblings still treat him as a baby.

Julius, the Baby of the World

Author: Kevin Henkes
Publisher: Greenwillow
Length: 28 **Age:** 4–8 **Date:** 1990
Main Character: animal
Other Topics: Sibling Rivalry
Overview: Lilly thinks that the arrival of her new baby brother is the worst thing that could happen in their house—until her cousin Garland comes to visit!

Katie Couldn't

Author: Becky Bring McDaniel
Publisher: Children's Press
Length: 30 **Age:** 4–6 **Date:** 1985
Main Character: Asian male and females
Other Topics: N/A
Overview: Katie is the youngest in the family. She cannot do everything her brother and sister can do.

Youngest Child, Smallest Child (cont.)

Keep Running, Allen!

Author: Clyde Robert Bulla
Publisher: Thomas Y. Crowell Co.
Length: 26 **Age:** 4–7 **Date:** 1978
Main Character: white male and female
Other Topics: N/A
Overview: Allen is the youngest in the family and has a difficult time keeping up with his siblings.

Least of All

Author: Carol Purdy
Publisher: Macmillan
Length: 25 **Age:** 5–8 **Date:** 1987
Main Character: white female
Other Topics: Illiteracy
Overview: The youngest child in the family learns to read.

Little Penguin

Author: Patrick Benson
Publisher: Philomel
Length: 24 **Age:** 3–6 **Date:** 1990
Main Character: animal
Other Topics: N/A
Overview: Pip, the Penguin, feels unhappy about her small size.

Minikin

Author: Stephen Cosgrove
Publisher: Price, Stern, Sloan
Length: 26 **Age:** 5–8 **Date:** 1984
Main Character: animal
Other Topics: Loneliness

Minikin (cont.)

Overview: Minikin is the smallest lamb in the herd. The other lambs like to tease him and call him names. Minikin learns to accept himself.

Oh, Little Jack

Author: Inga Moore
Publisher: Candlewick Press
Length: 32 **Age:** 3–6 **Date:** 1992
Main Character: animal
Other Topics: N/A
Overview: Little Jack is the youngest in the family and too little to do anything. Grandpa finds a new red tricycle that is just perfect for Jack.

Ollie Knows Everything

Author: Abby Levine
Publisher: Albert Whitman and Co.
Length: 32 **Age:** 4–7 **Date:** 1994
Main Character: animal
Other Topics: Lost Child
Overview: Herbert is the younger brother. He is tired of Ollie knowing everything and wishes he could be the oldest.

Quick Chick

Author: Julia Hoban
Publisher: E. P. Dutton
Length: 40 **Age:** 4–8 **Date:** 1989
Main Character: animal
Other Topics: Smallest Child
Overview: Jenny Hen's youngest chick earns his name—Quick Chick.

Revenge of the Small Small

Author: Jean Little
Publisher: Viking
Length: 32 **Age:** 6–8 **Date:** 1992
Main Character: cartoon character

Revenge of the Small Small (cont.)

Other Topics: Sibling Rivalry
Overview: The smallest of the Small family seeks revenge to teach her older siblings a lesson.

Rosa-Too-Little

Author: Sue Felt
Publisher: Doubleday and Co.
Length: 26 **Age:** 4–8 **Date:** 1950
Main Character: Hispanic female
Other Topics: N/A
Overview: Rosa seems to be too little to do anything she wants to do. She can't wait until she is big enough to have her own library card.

Sam

Author: Ann Herbert Scott
Publisher: McGraw-Hill
Length: 32 **Age:** 3–6 **Date:** 1992
Main Character: African American male
Other Topics: Fast-Track Families
Overview: Sam feels rejected when the other family members are so busy with their own activities that they push him away.

Secrets of a Small Brother

Author: Richard J. Margolis
Publisher: Macmillan
Length: 40 **Age:** 6–9 **Date:** 1984
Main Character: white male
Other Topics: N/A
Overview: A book of poetry about being a younger brother.

Someone I Know

Author: Carol M. Adorjan
Publisher: Random House
Length: 28 **Age:** 4–6 **Date:** 1968
Main Character: white female

Someone I Know (cont.)

Other Topics: Growing Up
Overview: A young girl describes things her older siblings can do that she cannot do.

The Evil Spell

Author: Emily Arnold McCully
Publisher: Harper Collins
Length: 32 **Age:** 5–8 **Date:** 1990
Main Character: animal
Other Topics: Fear
Overview: Edwin is the youngest child in a family of theatrical bears. He experiences stage fright on opening night. His family helps him overcome his fears.

The Smallest Stegosaurus

Author: Lynn Sweat and Louis Phillops
Publisher: Viking
Length: 32 **Age:** 4–8 **Date:** 1993
Main Character: animal
Other Topics: Sibling Rivalry
Overview: One day in the life of a dinosaur family shows how the smallest dinosaur feels.

Titch

Author: Pat Hutchins
Publisher: Macmillan
Length: 32 **Age:** 4–6 **Date:** 1971
Main Character: white male
Other Topics: N/A
Overview: Titch is the youngest and too small to ride a two-wheeler, fly a kite, or use a hammer. He is, however, able to plant a seed and watch it grow.

When I Get Bigger

Author: Mercer Mayer
Publisher: Golden Book
Length: 24 **Age:** 3–6 **Date:** 1983

Youngest Child, Smallest Child (cont.)

When I Get Bigger (cont.)

Main Character: cartoon character
Other Topics: N/A
Overview: A little critter describes all the things he will be able to do when he gets bigger.

Yang and the Youngest and His Terrible Ear

Author: Lensey Namioka
Publisher: Joy Street/Little, Brown
Length: 134 **Age:** 8–10 **Date:** 1992
Main Character: Asian male
Other Topics: Moving
Overview: The musical Yang family moves from China to Seattle. Nine-year-old Yingtao is tone-deaf, however, and plays baseball better than the violin.

Licensing Agreement

You should carefully read the following terms and conditions before opening this disk package. Opening this disk package indicates your acceptance of these terms and conditions. If you do not agree with them, you should promptly return the package unopened.

Allyn and Bacon provides this Program and License its use. You assume responsibility for the selection of the Program to achieve your intended results, and for the installation, use, and results obtained from the Program. This License extends only to use of the Program in the United States or countries in which the Program is marketed by duly authorized distributors.

License Grant

You hereby accept a nonexclusive, nontransferable, permanent License to install and use the Program on a single computer at any given time. You may copy the Program solely for backup or archival purposes in support of your use of the Program on the single computer. You may **not** modify, translate, disassemble, decompile, or reverse engineer the Program, in whole or in part.

Term

This License is effective until terminated. Allyn and Bacon reserves the right to terminate this License automatically if any provision of the License is violated. You may terminate the License at any time. To terminate this License, you must return the Program, including documentation, along with a written warranty stating that all copies of the Program in your possession have been returned or destroyed.

Limited Warranty

The Program is provided "As Is" without warranty of any kind, either express or implied, including, but **not** limited to, the implied warranties or merchantability and fitness for a particular purpose. The entire risk as to the quality and performance of the Program is with you. Should the Program prove defective, you (and **not** Allyn and Bacon or any authorized distributor) assume the entire cost of all necessary servicing, repair, or correction. No oral or written information or advice given by Allyn and Bacon, its dealers, distributors, or agents shall create a warranty or increase the scope of its warranty.

Some states do **not** allow the exclusion of implied warranty, so the above exclusion may **not** apply to you. This warranty gives you specific legal

199

rights and you may also have other rights that vary from state to state.

Allyn and Bacon does **not** warrant that the functions contained in the Program will meet your requirements or that the operation of the Program will be uninterrupted or error free.

However, Allyn and Bacon warrants the disk(s) on which the Program is furnished to be free from defects in material and workmanship under normal use for a period of ninety (90) days from the date of delivery to you as evidenced by a copy of your receipt.

The Program should **not** be relied on as the sole basis to solve a problem whose incorrect solution could result in injury to a person or property. If the Program is employed in such a manner, its is at the user's own risk and Allyn and Bacon explicitly disclaims all liability for such misuse.

Limitation of Remedies

Allyn and Bacon's entire liability and your exclusive remedy shall be:

1. The replacement of any disk **not** meeting Allyn and Bacon's "Limited Warranty" and that is returned to Allyn and Bacon or
2. If Allyn and Bacon is unable to deliver a replacement disk or cassette that is free of defect in materials or workmanship, you may terminate this Agreement by returning the Program.

In no event will Allyn and Bacon be liable to you for any damages, including any lost profits, lost savings, or other incidental or consequential damages arising out of the users inability to use such Program even if Allyn and Bacon or any authorized distributor has been advised of the possibility of such damages of for any claim by any other party.

Some states do **not** allow the limitation or exclusion of liability for incidental or consequential damages, so the a above limitation or exclusion may **not** apply to you.

General

You may **not** sublicense, assign, or transfer the License of the Program. Any attempt to sublicense, assign, or transfer any of the rights, duties, or obligations hereunder is void.

This Agreement will be governed by the laws of the State of Massachusetts.

Should you have any questions concerning this Agreement or any questions concerning technical support, you may contact Allyn and Bacon by writing to:

> Allyn and Bacon
> Simon and Schuster Education Group
> 160 Gould Street
> Needham Heights, MA 02194

You acknowledge that you have read this Agreement, understand it, and agree to be bound by its terms and conditions. You further agree that it is the complete and exclusive statement of the Agreement between us that supersedes any proposal or prior Agreement, oral or written, and any other communications between us relating to the subject matter of this Agreement.

Notice To Government End Users

The Program is provided with restricted rights. Use, duplication, or disclosure by the Government is subject to restrictions set forth in subdivision (b)(3)(iii) of The Rights Technical Data and Computer Software Clause 252.227-701.